SUPREME COURT WATCH 2003

Highlights of the 2001–2003 Terms
Preview of the 2003–2004 Term

DAVID M. O'BRIEN
UNIVERSITY OF VIRGINIA

W • W • **NORTON & COMPANY** • NEW YORK • LONDON

W. W. Norton & Company has been independent since its founding in 1923, when William Warder Norton and Mary D. Herter Norton first published lectures delivered at the People's Institute, the adult education division of New York City's Cooper Union. The Nortons soon expanded their program beyond the Institute, publishing books by celebrated academics from America and abroad. By mid-century, the two major pillars of Norton's publishing program—trade books and college texts—were firmly established. In the 1950s, the Norton family transferred control of the company to its employees, and today—with a staff of four hundred and a comparable number of trade, college, and professional titles published each year—W. W. Norton & Company stands as the largest and oldest publishing house owned wholly by its employees.

ISBN 0-393-92520-X (pbk.)

W. W. Norton & Company, Inc., 500 Fifth Avenue, New York, NY 10110
www.wwnorton.com
W. W. Norton & Company Ltd., Castle House, 75/76 Wells Street,
London W1T 3QT

1 2 3 4 5 6 7 8 9 0

CONTENTS

VOLUME TWO

Preface

Supreme Court Watch 2003 examines the changes and decisions made during the Supreme Court's 2001 and 2002 terms. In addition to highlighting the major constitutional rulings in excerpts from leading cases, I discuss in section-by-section introductions other important decisions and analyze recent developments in various areas of constitutional law. I also preview here the important cases that the Court has granted review and will decide in its 2003–2004 term. To offer even more information in an efficient format, special boxes titled "The Development of Law" and "Inside the Court" are also included.

The favorable reception of previous editions of the *Watch* has been gratifying, and I hope that this 2003 edition will further contribute to students' understanding of constitutional law, politics, and history, as well as to their appreciation for how the politics of constitutional interpretation turns on differing interpretations of constitutional politics and the role of the Supreme Court. I am most grateful to Ann Marcy for doing a terrific and expeditious job of producing this edition.

D.M.O.
June 28, 2003

SUPREME COURT WATCH 2003

VOLUME ONE

2

LAW AND POLITICS IN THE SUPREME COURT: JURISDICTION AND DECISION-MAKING PROCESS

B | *The Court's Docket and Screening Cases*

The Supreme Court continued its practice of deciding fewer than 1 percent of the cases on its docket; it granted and decided only 84 cases in its 2001–2002 term from a docket that reached 9,176 cases, including 2,210 paid cases and 6,958 unpaid cases. In its 2002–2003 term, the Court heard oral arguments in 84 cases from a total docket of 9,406 cases. As is the Court's practice, it also reversed more of the lower courts' decisions in cases it granted than it affirmed.

The Court's Disposition of Appeals in the 2002 Term

	AFFIRMED	REVERSED OR VACATED
First Circuit	1	1
Second Circuit	1	3
Third Circuist		
Fourth Circuit	1	2
Fifth Circuit		2
Sixth Circuit	2	5
Seventh Circuit	1	2
Eighth Circuit		1
Ninth Circuit	4	19
Tenth Circuit		1
Eleventh Circuit	2	2
Federal Circuit	1	1
District of Columbia Circuit	2	
Other Federal Courts	1	5
State Courts and Other	4	16
Totals:*	20	60

*Excludes cases decided on original jurisdiction or dismissed for lack of jurisdiction and remanded. In one case, *Dow Chemical Co. v. Stephenson*, 123 S.Ct. 485 (2003), an equally divided court reversed and affirmed the lower court, and it is counted here twice.

■ INSIDE THE COURT

The Business of the Supreme Court in the 2002–2003 Term

SUBJECT OF COURT OPINIONS*	SUMMARY	PLENARY
Admiralty		
Antitrust		
Bankruptcy		1
Bill of Rights (other than rights of accused) and Equal Protection		9
Commerce Clause		
1. Constitutionality and construction of federal regulation		4
2. Constitutionality of state regulation		6
Common Law		
Miscellaneous Statutory Construction		12
Due process		
1. Economic interests		1
2. Procedure and rights of accused		12
3. Substantive due process (noneconomic)		3
Impairment of Contract and Just Compensation		1
International Law, War, and Peace		
Jurisdiction, Procedure, and Practice	3	11
Land Legislation		
Native Americans		3
Patents, Copyright, and Trademarks		2
Other Suits against the Government	1	5
Suits by States		3
Taxation (federal and state)		2
Totals	4	75

*Note: The classification of cases is that of the author and necessarily invites differences of opinion as to the dominant issue in some cases. The table includes opinions in cases whether decided summarily or given plenary consideration, but not cases summarily disposed of by simple orders, opinions dissenting from the denial of review, and those dismissing cases as improvidently granted.

H | *Opinion Days and Communicating Decisions*

■ INSIDE THE COURT

*Opinion Writing during the 2002–2003 Term**

OPINIONS	MAJORITY	CONCURRING	DISSENTING	SEPARATE	TOTALS
Per Curiam	8				8
Rehnquist	8		4		12
Stevens	9	8	7	2	26
O'Connor	9	6		2	17
Scalia	8	6	8	2	24
Kennedy	7	5	4	2	18
Souter	9	5	4	2	20
Thomas	7	7	11	2	27
Ginsburg	7	3	6	1	17
Breyer	8	3	2	3	16
Totals	80	43	46	16	185

*Note that Court opinions disposing of two or more companion cases are counted only once here. Note also that in *Chavez v. Martinez*, 123 S.Ct. 1994 (2003), Justices Souter and Thomas delivered opinons for the judgment of the Court and each is credited with delivering the opinion of the Court. In addition, this table includes opinions in cases disposed of either summarily or upon plenary consideration, but does not include cases summarily disposed of by simple orders or concurring or dissenting opinions from the denial of *certiorari*.

■ Inside the Court

Voting Alignments in the Rehnquist Court, 1986–2001 Terms

	REHNQUIST	WHITE	BLACKMUN	STEVENS	O'CONNOR	SCALIA	KENNEDY	SOUTER	THOMAS	BRENNAN	MARSHALL	GINSBURG	BREYER
Rehnquist	—	80.8	55.2	51.7	81.4	78.7	82.7	67.7	79.9	47.6	46.4	62.8	61.8
White	80.8	—	62.2	60.4	72.5	69.8	75.7	73.5	67.7	52.9	52.9	68.2	
Blackmun	55.2	62.2	—	72.0	58.4	49.1	57.6	64.8	44.4	77.4	77.0	78.0	77.2
Stevens	51.7	60.4	72.0	—	56.5	46.2	57.3	70.8	44.4	69.9	71.6	66.1	70.7
O'Connor	81.4	72.5	58.4	56.5	—	71.2	78.5	71.4	71.0	49.4	47.9	53.3	51.8
Scalia	78.7	69.8	49.1	46.2	71.2	—	75.8	59.1	87.3	47.5	45.0	66.7	65.6
Kennedy	82.7	75.7	57.6	57.3	78.5	75.8	—	70.1	74.1	53.7	51.2	83.8	82.0
Souter	67.7	73.5	64.8	70.8	71.4	59.1	70.1	—	56.2		54.6	52.3	51.9
Thomas	79.9	67.7	44.4	44.4	71.0	87.3	74.1	56.2	—			52.3	51.9
Brennan	47.6	52.9	77.4	69.9	49.4	47.5	53.7			—	95.0		
Marshall	46.4	52.9	77.0	71.6	47.9	45.0	51.2	54.6		95.0	—		
Ginsburg	62.8	68.2	78.0	66.1	53.3	66.7	83.8	52.3	52.3			—	81.1
Breyer	61.8		77.2	70.7	51.8	65.6	82.0	51.9	51.9			81.1	—

Note: The above are average percentages. The percentages for each term are from Table 1 of the *Harvard Law Review*'s annual review of the Supreme Court's term in volumes 101–116 (1986–2002).

3

PRESIDENTIAL POWER, THE RULE OF LAW, AND FOREIGN AFFAIRS

D | *War-Making and Emergency Powers*

■ CONSTITUTIONAL HISTORY

Terrorists, "Enemy Combatants," and Military Tribunals

Shortly after the terrorist attacks on the World Trade Center and the Pentagon on September 11, 2001, President George W. Bush declared war against Al Qaeda forces in Afghanistan and against international terrorism. He subsequently issued an order, as commander in chief of the armed forces, authorizing the indefinite detention of captured foreign terrorists and directing their trial by special secret military tribunals, without the possibility of appeal.

Bush's order invited controversy because the "detainees" were not to be treated as prisoners of war according to international law. Under the Third Geneva Convention of 1949, prisoners of war are entitled to an independent and impartial trial, the assistance of counsel, and the right of appeal.

Although in *Ex parte Milligan*, 71 U.S. 2 (1866) (excerpted in Vol. 1, Ch. 3), the Supreme Court overruled President Abraham Lincoln's use of military courts to try civilians accused of disloyalty during the Civil War, during World War II it upheld the internment of about 130,000 Japanese Americans

---

in "relocation camps," even though there was no proof that they were disloyal or engaged in sabotage, by a six-to-three vote in *Korematsu v. United States*, 323 U.S. 214 (1944) (excerpted in Vol. 1, Ch. 3). On the same day *Korematsu* was handed down, however, the Court ruled, in *Ex parte Endo*, 323 U.S. 283 (1944), that although the evacuation of Japanese Americans was permissible, the detention of loyal Japanese Americans was unconstitutional.

Notably, in writing for the Court in *Korematsu*, Justice Hugo Black drew a distinction between the rights of citizenship during peacetime and wartime, observing that "hardships are part of war, and war is an aggregation of hardships. All citizens alike, both in and out of uniform, feel the impact of war in greater or lesser measure. Citizenship has its responsibilities as well as its privileges, and in time of war the burden is always heavier."

World War I had also brought a curbing of civil liberties and Charles Evans Hughes, a former justice and future chief justice but at the time New York's governor, captured the view held by many: "The power to wage war is the power to war successfully. . . . That is, there are constantly new applications of unchanged powers. . . . So, also, we have a *fighting* Constitution."★

During World War I, the Senate considered a bill that would have turned the entire country into a military zone. The bill would have made it a crime to publish anything endangering national security, with trials before military tribunals and convictions punishable by death. Instead, President Woodrow Wilson persuaded Congress to enact the less extreme Espionage Act of 1917, making it a crime to interfere with military recruitment and war efforts. Approximately 2,000 individuals were prosecuted under the act for, among other reasons, stating religious objections to the war and advocating draft resistance.

During World War II the Supreme Court also approved President Franklin D. Roosevelt's use of military tribunals to try eight German saboteurs, including one naturalized U.S. Citizen, for sabotaging bridges and utility plants. In the case of the "Nazi Saboteurs," *Ex parte Quirin*, 317 U.S. 1 (1942), the Supreme Court ruled unanimously that the president has the "power . . . to carry into effect . . . all laws defining and punishing offenses against the law of nations, including those which pertain to the conduct of war." Writing for the Court, Chief Justice Stone added that that power includes the authority "to seize and subject to disciplinary measures those enemies who in their attempt to thwart or impede our military effort have violated the law of war." Nor did the chief justice distinguish between U.S. citizens and noncitizens; both were wartime belligerents and treated as such. In his words, "citizenship in the United States of an enemy belligerent does not relieve him from the consequences of a belligerency which is unlawful."

The Court also held, in *Johnson v. Eisentrager*, 339 U.S. 763 (1950), that federal courts have no jurisdiction over *habeas corpus* petitions filed by foreign nationals held overseas by U.S. military forces during World War II.

★Charles Evans Hughes, "War Powers under the Constitution" 62 *American Bar Association Reports* (1917), at 238.

However, in *Reid v. Covert*, 354 U.S. 1 (1957), the Court ruled that U.S. citizens may not be subject to courts–martial or denied the rights guaranteed the accused in the Bill of Rights; the government cannot abridge these rights of U.S. citizenship. For that reason John Walker Lindh, the young American captured fighting with the Taliban in Afghanistan, was accorded counsel and tried in court.

Based on these precedents, after the September 11, 2001, attacks, President Bush issued orders for the detention of U.S. citizens deemed "enemy combatants" because of their cooperation with international terrorists and threat to homeland security. His order authorized their detention in military compounds, without assistance of counsel and a trial in a court of law. The order remains controversial and the detention has been challenged in the courts and will likely be reviewed by the Supreme Court.* The Bush administration initially took the position that courts could not review the basis for detaining "enemy combatants." However, several courts rebuffed that position. In the case of a U.S. citizen declared an "enemy combatant," Yaser Esam Hamdi, the Court of Appeals for the Fourth Circuit rejected the administration's position and sanctioned a limited, highly deferential review of the basis for Hamdi's detention. In doing so, the appellate court underscored that "the nation has fought since its founding for liberty without which security rings hollow and for security without which liberty cannot thrive. . . . Judicial review does not disappear during wartime . . . but the review . . . is a highly deferential one."★★

★See Laurence Tribe, "Citizens, Combatants, and the Constitution" *New York Times*, June 16, 2002, WK 13.

★★*Hamdi v. Rumsfeld*, 316 F.3d 450 (4th Cir., 2003).

■ The Development of Law

*The USA PATRIOT Act of 2001**

Enacted in response to the terrorist attacks of 9/11, the USA PATRIOT Act authorizes sweeping changes in law enforcement, notably lowering the standards for searching and seizing individuals suspected of terrorism, for example, as well as expanding investigatory powers. Among the changes, the law authorizes

- Monitoring of international students.
- Roving wiretaps (wiretaps on any telephone used by a person suspected of terrorism); the use of key-logger devices, which register every stroke made on a computer; and Internet wiretaps.
- Police searches of private property without prior notification of the owners and without a search warrant.
- A lower standard for judicial approval of wiretaps for individuals suspected of terrorist activities.
- The attorney general to designate domestic groups as terrorist organizations and to block the entry into the country of foreigners aligned with them.
- The Central Intelligence Agency to investigate Americans suspected of having connections to terrorism.
- The Department of the Treasury to monitor financial transactions—bank accounts, mutual funds, and brokerage deals—and to obtain medical and other electronic records on individuals.
- The detention and deportation of foreigners suspected of having connections to terrorist organizations.
- Broader searches under the Federal Intelligence Surveillance Act of 1978, which created a special FIS court to approve wiretaps and to ensure that the "sole purpose" of domestic intelligence gathering was obtaining foreign intelligence information. Wiretaps may now be issued if the collection of foreign intelligence has "a significant purpose," and the intelligence community and law enforcement agencies may now share information gathered for both foreign intelligence and routine criminal prosecutions.

*The full title of the law is Uniting and Strengthening America by Providing Appropriate Tools Required to Intercept and Obstruct Terrorism (USA PATRIOT) Act of 2001. For the text and other information go to http://personalinfomediary.com/USAPATRIOTACT_Text.htm

5

CONGRESS: MEMBERSHIP, IMMUNITIES, AND INVESTIGATORY POWERS

A | *Membership and Immunities*

In *Department of Commerce v. U.S. House of Representatives*, 525 U.S. 316 (1999), a bare majority ruled that the use of statistical samplings in the 2000 census would violate the Census Clause's requirement for an actual enumeration. In the 2000 census the Census Bureau nonetheless continued using the statistical technique called "hot-deck imputation," which estimated data on missing households in arriving at the final count. As a result, about 1.2 million people were added—less than one-half of 1 percent—to the final count. On that basis North Carolina received a thirteenth seat in the House of Representatives. Utah sued, claiming it deserved a fourth seat and challenging the constitutionality of the use of the technique of "hot-deck imputation." A bare majority in *Utah v. Evans,* 536 U.S. 452 (2002), upheld the use of that statistical measure, which Congress had approved and which had been used in four previous census counts. Justice Breyer wrote for the Court and was joined by Chief Justice Rehnquist and Justices Stevens, Souter, and Ginsburg. Justices O'Connor, Scalia, Kennedy, and Thomas dissented.

7

THE STATES AND
AMERICAN FEDERALISM

A | States' Power over Commerce and Regulation

■ THE DEVELOPMENT OF LAW

Other Rulings on State Regulatory Powers in Alleged Conflict with Federal Legislation

CASE	RULING
Kentucky Association of Health Plans, Inc. v. Miller, 123 S.Ct. 1471 (2003)	Writing for a unanimous Court, Justice Scalia held that the Employment Retirement Income

Security Act (ERISA) does not preempt Kentucky's Any Willing Provider (AWP) laws because they are regulations of the insurance industry. Health Management Organizations (HMOs) had exclusive networks with health-care providers and sought to have the state's AWP laws invalidated on the ground they were preempted by ERISA's regulation of employee benefit plans. But the Court held that Kentucky's laws regulated insurance programs and thus HMOs in the state could not restrict access to particular health-care providers.

CASE	RULING
Beneficial National Bank v. Anderson, 123 S.Ct. 2058 (2003)	Held that the National Bank Act provides the exclusive basis for usury claims against national

banks and preempts state usury laws.

CASE	RULING
Hillside Dairy, Inc. v. Lyons, 123 S.Ct. 2142 (2003)	Held that California's milk pricing regulations, which favored in-state farmers, was not exempt

from Congress's interstate commerce power and the Federal Agriculture and Reform Act of 1996.

■ The Development of Law

Other Rulings on State Regulation of Commerce in the Absence of Federal Legislation

CASE	VOTE	RULING
Pharmaceutical Research and Manufacturers of America v. Walsh, 123 S.Ct. 1855 (2003)		Held that Maine's Act to Establish Fairer Pricing for Prescription Drugs does not violate the dormant commerce clause. Due to

increasing Medicaid costs for prescription drugs, Congress authorized requiring drug companies to pay rebates to states for their Medicaid purchases. Under Maine's program, the state negotiates rebates with drug companies. If a company does not enter into an agreement, then doctors are required to obtain the state's approval for reimbursement for prescription drugs under Medicaid. Writing for the Court, Justice Stevens held that Maine's law, aimed at promoting discount drugs, did not discriminate against out-of-state drug manufacturers in violation of the commerce clause.

American Insurance Association v. Garamendi, 123 S.Ct. 2374 (2003)		Invalidated California's 1999 Holocaust Victim Insurance Relief Act, which required all insur-

ance companies in the state that sold individual policies in Europe between 1920 and 1945 to disclose the names of policyholders and beneficiaries in order to assist Holocaust survivors in collecting benefits. Writing for the Court, Justice Souter held that the law infringed on the president's foreign policy-making powers, and in particular the German Foundation Agreement, under which the United States and Germany established a fund and a procedure for compensating insurance companies' victims during the Nazi era. Justice Souter also rejected California's assertion that Congress had authorized in the McCarran-Ferguson Act, rather than preempting under its interstate commerce power, state laws of the sort at issue. Justices Ginsburg, Stevens, Scalia, and Thomas dissented.

B | *The Tenth and Eleventh Amendments and the States*

Breaking with a series of rulings on congressional power and states' sovereign immunity from lawsuits under the Eleventh Amendment (see *Kimel v. Florida Board of Regents*, 528 U.S. 62 (2000), and *Seminole Tribe of Florida v. Florida*, 517 U.S. 44 (1996) (excerpted in Vol. I, Ch. 7), and Congress's enforcement power under Section 5 of the Fourteenth Amendment (see *City of Boerne v. Flores*, 521 U.S. 507 (1997) (excerpted in Vol. I, Ch. 6), and *United States v. Morrison*, 529 U.S. 598 (2000) (excerpted in Vol. I, Ch. 6), the Court held that Congress had the power to abrogate states' sovereign immunity in authorizing private lawsuits against states for violations of the Family and Medical Leave Act of 1993 in *Nevada Department of Human Resources v. Hibbs* (excerpted below).

In its 2003–2004 term the Court will also reconsider the scope of the Eleventh Amendment in *Frew v. Hawkins* (No. 02-628). The suit was brought against the administration of the Texas State Medicaid program by parents of indigent children who were denied federally mandated benefits under Texas's Early and Periodic Screening, Diagnostic, and Treatment Services (EPSDT) program. Although the EPSDT program is voluntary for states, once a state elects to participate in the program it must comply with federal mandates set forth in the Medicaid Act. A federal district court certified a class of 1.5 million indigent children who had been denied relief and ordered the parties into settlement negotiations, and they agreed to a consent decree. Subsequently, the state administration failed to comply fully with the consent decree and attorneys filed a motion to force compliance with the decree. State officials, however, claimed immunity under the Eleventh Amendment. The district court concluded that the decree had been violated and was enforceable, but on appeal the Court of Appeals for the Fifth Circuit held that Texas had not waived its Eleventh Amendment immunity and vacated the lower court's decision.

Nevada Department of Human Resources v. Hibbs
123 S.Ct. 1972 (2003)

The Family and Medical Leave Act of 1993 (FMLA) entitles eligible employees to take up to 12 weeks of unpaid leave annually for attending to illnesses within the immediate family. The FMLA also creates a private right of action to seek damages against an employer for violating provisions of the law. Williams Hibbs worked for the Nevada Department of Human Resources and in 1997 sought leave under the FMLA in order to care for his ailing wife. His request was granted but after 12 weeks on leave the agency notified him that he must return to work. When Hibbs failed to do so, his employment was terminated. Subsequently, Hibbs sued Nevada in federal district court for violations of the FMLA. The district court held that Hibbs was barred from filing the FMLA claim against the state on the basis of the Eleventh Amendment. However, on appeal the Court of Appeals for the Ninth Circuit reversed that decision and ruled that states' sovereign immunity under the Eleventh Amendment was overridden by Congress's power under Section 5 of the Fourteenth Amendment to enact laws aimed at enforcing the equal protection of the law and address the persistence of gender discrimination. The state appealed that decision and the Supreme Court granted *certiorari*.

The Supreme Court affirmed by a vote of six to three. Chief Justice Rehnquist delivered the opinion for the Court. Justices Souter and Stevens each filed concurring opinions. Justices Scalia and Kennedy filed dissenting opinions; Justice Thomas joined the latter's dissent.

□ *CHIEF JUSTICE REHNQUIST delivered the opinion of the Court.*

The Family and Medical Leave Act of 1993 (FMLA or Act) entitles eligible employees to take up to 12 work weeks of unpaid leave annually for any of several reasons, including the onset of a "serious health condition" in an employee's spouse, child, or parent. The Act creates a private right of action to seek both equitable relief and money damages "against any employer (including a public agency) in any Federal or State court of competent jurisdiction," Section 2617(a)(2), should that employer "interfere with, restrain, or deny the exercise of" FMLA rights. We hold that employees of the State of Nevada may recover money damages in the event of the State's failure to comply with the family-care provision of the Act. . . .

For over a century now, we have made clear that the Constitution does not provide for federal jurisdiction over suits against nonconsenting States. *Board of Trustees of Univ. of Ala. v. Garrett*, 531 U.S. 356 (2001); *Kimel v. Florida Bd. of Regents*, 528 U.S. 62 (2000); *College Savings Bank v. Florida Prepaid Postsecondary Ed. Expense Bd.*, 527 U.S. 666 (1999); *Seminole Tribe of Fla. v. Florida*, 517 U.S. 44, 54 (1996); *Hans v. Louisiana*, 134 U.S. 1 (1890).

Congress may, however, abrogate such immunity in federal court if it makes its intention to abrogate unmistakably clear in the language of the statute and acts pursuant to a valid exercise of its power under Section 5 of the Fourteenth Amendment. The clarity of Congress's intent here is not fairly debatable. The Act enables employees to seek damages "against any employer (including a public agency) in any Federal or State court of competent jurisdiction," and Congress has defined "public agency" to include both "the government of a State or political subdivision thereof" and "any agency of . . . a State, or a political subdivision of a State." We held in *Kimel* that, by using identical language in the Age Discrimination in Employment Act of 1967 (ADEA),

Congress satisfied the clear statement rule of *Dellmuth* [*v. Muth*, 491 U.S. 223 (1989)]. This case turns, then, on whether Congress acted within its constitutional authority when it sought to abrogate the States' immunity for purposes of the FMLA's family-leave provision.

In enacting the FMLA, Congress relied on two of the powers vested in it by the Constitution: its Article I commerce power and its power under Section 5 of the Fourteenth Amendment to enforce that Amendment's guarantees. Congress may not abrogate the States' sovereign immunity pursuant to its Article I power over commerce. *Seminole Tribe.* Congress may, however, abrogate States' sovereign immunity through a valid exercise of its Section 5 power, for "the Eleventh Amendment, and the principle of state sovereignty which it embodies, are necessarily limited by the enforcement provisions of Section 5 of the Fourteenth Amendment." *Fitzpatrick v. Bitzer*, 427 U.S. 445 (1976). See also *Garrett*; *Kimel*.

Two provisions of the Fourteenth Amendment are relevant here: Section 5 grants Congress the power "to enforce" the substantive guarantees of Section 1—among them, equal protection of the laws—by enacting "appropriate legislation." Congress may, in the exercise of its Section 5 power, do more than simply proscribe conduct that we have held unconstitutional. "'Congress' power to enforce' the Amendment includes the authority both to remedy and to deter violation of rights guaranteed thereunder by prohibiting a somewhat broader swath of conduct, including that which is not itself forbidden by the Amendment's text." *Garrett*; *City of Boerne v. Flores*, 521 U.S. 507 (1997); *Katzenbach v. Morgan*, 384 U.S. 641 (1966). In other words, Congress may enact so-called prophylactic legislation that proscribes facially constitutional conduct, in order to prevent and deter unconstitutional conduct.

City of Boerne also confirmed, however, that it falls to this Court, not Congress, to define the substance of constitutional guarantees. "The ultimate interpretation and determination of the Fourteenth Amendment's substantive meaning remains the province of the Judicial Branch." *Kimel.* Section 5 legislation reaching beyond the scope of Section 1's actual guarantees must be an appropriate remedy for identified constitutional violations, not "an attempt to substantively redefine the States' legal obligations." We distinguish appropriate prophylactic legislation from "substantive redefinition of the Fourteenth Amendment right at issue" by applying the test set forth in *City of Boerne*: Valid Section 5 legislation must exhibit "congruence and proportionality between the injury to be prevented or remedied and the means adopted to that end."

The FMLA aims to protect the right to be free from gender-based discrimination in the workplace. We have held that statutory classifications that distinguish between males and females are subject to heightened scrutiny. See, e.g., *Craig v. Boren*, 429 U.S. 190 (1976). For a gender-based classification to withstand such scrutiny, it must "serv[e] important governmental objectives," and "the discriminatory means employed [must be] substantially related to the achievement of those objectives." *United States v. Virginia*, 518 U.S. 515 (1996). The State's justification for such a classification "must not rely on overbroad generalizations about the different talents, capacities, or preferences of males and females." We now inquire whether Congress had evidence of a pattern of constitutional violations on the part of the States in this area.

The history of the many state laws limiting women's employment opportunities is chronicled in—and, until relatively recently, was sanctioned by—this Court's own opinions. For example, in *Bradwell v. State*, 16 Wall. 130 (1873)

(Illinois), and *Goesaert v. Cleary*, 335 U.S. 464 (1948) (Michigan), the Court upheld state laws prohibiting women from practicing law and tending bar, respectively. State laws frequently subjected women to distinctive restrictions, terms, conditions, and benefits for those jobs they could take. In *Muller v. Oregon*, 208 U.S. 412 (1908), for example, this Court approved a state law limiting the hours that women could work for wages, and observed that 19 States had such laws at the time. Such laws were based on the related beliefs that (1) woman is, and should remain, "the center of home and family life," *Hoyt v. Florida*, 368 U.S. 57 (1961), and (2) "a proper discharge of [a woman's] maternal functions—having in view not merely her own health, but the well-being of the race—justif[ies] legislation to protect her from the greed as well as the passion of man." *Muller*. Until our decision in *Reed v. Reed*, 404 U.S. 71 (1971), "it remained the prevailing doctrine that government, both federal and state, could withhold from women opportunities accorded men so long as any 'basis in reason'"—such as the above beliefs—"could be conceived for the discrimination." *Virginia*.

Congress responded to this history of discrimination by abrogating States' sovereign immunity in Title VII of the Civil Rights Act of 1964, and we sustained this abrogation in *Fitzpatrick*. But state gender discrimination did not cease. "[I]t can hardly be doubted that . . . women still face pervasive, although at times more subtle, discrimination . . . in the job market." *Frontiero v. Richardson*, 411 U.S. 677 (1973). According to evidence that was before Congress when it enacted the FMLA, States continue to rely on invalid gender stereotypes in the employment context, specifically in the administration of leave benefits. Reliance on such stereotypes cannot justify the States' gender discrimination in this area. *Virginia*. The long and extensive history of sex discrimination prompted us to hold that measures that differentiate on the basis of gender warrant heightened scrutiny; here, as in *Fitzpatrick*, the persistence of such unconstitutional discrimination by the States justifies Congress's passage of prophylactic Section 5 legislation.

As the FMLA's legislative record reflects, a 1990 Bureau of Labor Statistics (BLS) survey stated that 37 percent of surveyed private-sector employees were covered by maternity leave policies, while only 18 percent were covered by paternity leave policies. The corresponding numbers from a similar BLS survey the previous year were 33 percent and 16 percent, respectively. While these data show an increase in the percentage of employees eligible for such leave, they also show a widening of the gender gap during the same period. Thus, stereotype-based beliefs about the allocation of family duties remained firmly rooted, and employers' reliance on them in establishing discriminatory leave policies remained widespread.

Congress also heard testimony that "[p]arental leave for fathers . . . is rare. Even . . . [w]here child-care leave policies do exist, men, both in the public and private sectors, receive notoriously discriminatory treatment in their requests for such leave." (Washington Council of Lawyers). Many States offered women extended "maternity" leave that far exceeded the typical 4- to 8-week period of physical disability due to pregnancy and childbirth, but very few States granted men a parallel benefit: Fifteen States provided women up to one year of extended maternity leave, while only four provided men with the same. This and other differential leave policies were not attributable to any differential physical needs of men and women, but rather to the pervasive sex-role stereotype that caring for family members is women's work.

Finally, Congress had evidence that, even where state laws and policies were not facially discriminatory, they were applied in discriminatory ways. . . .

In sum, the States' record of unconstitutional participation in, and fostering of, gender-based discrimination in the administration of leave benefits is weighty enough to justify the enactment of prophylactic Section 5 legislation.

We reached the opposite conclusion in *Garrett* and *Kimel*. In those cases, the Section 5 legislation under review responded to a purported tendency of state officials to make age- or disability-based distinctions. Under our equal protection case law, discrimination on the basis of such characteristics is not judged under a heightened review standard, and passes muster if there is "a rational basis for doing so at a class-based level, even if it 'is probably not true' that those reasons are valid in the majority of cases." *Kimel*. Thus, in order to impugn the constitutionality of state discrimination against the disabled or the elderly, Congress must identify, not just the existence of age- or disability-based state decisions, but a widespread pattern of irrational reliance on such criteria. We found no such showing with respect to the ADEA and Title I of the Americans with Disabilities Act of 1990 (ADA). *Kimel*.

Here, however, Congress directed its attention to state gender discrimination, which triggers a heightened level of scrutiny. Because the standard for demonstrating the constitutionality of a gender-based classification is more difficult to meet than our rational-basis test—it must "serv[e] important governmental objectives" and be "substantially related to the achievement of those objectives," *Virginia*—it was easier for Congress to show a pattern of state constitutional violations. Congress was similarly successful in *South Carolina v. Katzenbach*, 383 U.S. 301 (1966), where we upheld the Voting Rights Act of 1965: Because racial classifications are presumptively invalid, most of the States' acts of race discrimination violated the Fourteenth Amendment. . . .

Unlike the statutes at issue in *City of Boerne, Kimel,* and *Garrett*, which applied broadly to every aspect of state employers' operations, the FMLA is narrowly targeted at the fault line between work and family—precisely where sex-based overgeneralization has been and remains strongest—and affects only one aspect of the employment relationship. . . .

The judgment of the Court of Appeals is therefore Affirmed.

□ *Justice KENNEDY, with whom Justice SCALIA and Justice THOMAS join, dissenting.*

The Family and Medical Leave Act of 1993 makes explicit the congressional intent to invoke Section 5 of the Fourteenth Amendment to abrogate state sovereign immunity and allow suits for money damages in federal courts. The specific question is whether Congress may impose on the States this entitlement program of its own design, with mandated minimums for leave time, and then enforce it by permitting private suits for money damages against the States. This in turn must be answered by asking whether subjecting States and their treasuries to monetary liability at the insistence of private litigants is a congruent and proportional response to a demonstrated pattern of unconstitutional conduct by the States. If we apply the teaching of these and related cases, the family leave provision of the Act, Section 2612(a)(1)(C), in my respectful view, is invalid to the extent it allows for private suits against the unconsenting States.

Congress does not have authority to define the substantive content of the Equal Protection Clause; it may only shape the remedies warranted by the violations of that guarantee. *City of Boerne.* This requirement has special force in the context of the Eleventh Amendment, which protects a State's fiscal integrity from federal intrusion by vesting the States with immunity from private actions for damages pursuant to federal laws. The Commerce Clause likely would permit the National Government to enact an entitlement program such as this one; but when Congress couples the entitlement with the authorization to sue the States for monetary damages, it blurs the line of accountability the State has to its own citizens. These basic concerns underlie cases such as *Garrett* and *Kimel*, and should counsel far more caution than the Court shows in holding Section 2612(a)(1)(C) is somehow a congruent and proportional remedy to an identified pattern of discrimination.

The Court is unable to show that States have engaged in a pattern of unlawful conduct which warrants the remedy of opening state treasuries to private suits. The inability to adduce evidence of alleged discrimination, coupled with the inescapable fact that the federal scheme is not a remedy but a benefit program, demonstrate the lack of the requisite link between any problem Congress has identified and the program it mandated.

In examining whether Congress was addressing a demonstrated "pattern of unconstitutional employment discrimination by the States," the Court gives superficial treatment to the requirement that we "identify with some precision the scope of the constitutional right at issue." *Garrett.* The Court suggests the issue is "the right to be free from gender-based discrimination in the workplace," and then it embarks on a survey of our precedents speaking to "[t]he history of the many state laws limiting women's employment opportunities." All would agree that women historically have been subjected to conditions in which their employment opportunities are more limited than those available to men. As the Court acknowledges, however, Congress responded to this problem by abrogating States' sovereign immunity in Title VII of the Civil Rights Act of 1964. The provision now before us has a different aim than Title VII. It seeks to ensure that eligible employees, irrespective of gender, can take a minimum amount of leave time to care for an ill relative.

The relevant question, as the Court seems to acknowledge, is whether, notwithstanding the passage of Title VII and similar state legislation, the States continued to engage in widespread discrimination on the basis of gender in the provision of family leave benefits. If such a pattern were shown, the Eleventh Amendment would not bar Congress from devising a congruent and proportional remedy. The evidence to substantiate this charge must be far more specific, however, than a simple recitation of a general history of employment discrimination against women. When the federal statute seeks to abrogate state sovereign immunity, the Court should be more careful to insist on adherence to the analytic requirements set forth in its own precedents. Persisting overall effects of gender-based discrimination at the workplace must not be ignored; but simply noting the problem is not a substitute for evidence which identifies some real discrimination the family leave rules are designed to prevent. . . .

Even if there were evidence that individual state employers, in the absence of clear statutory guidelines, discriminated in the administration of leave benefits, this circumstance alone would not support a finding of a state-sponsored pattern of discrimination. The evidence could perhaps support the charge of disparate impact, but not a charge that States have engaged in a pattern of intentional discrimination prohibited by the Fourteenth Amendment. *Garrett*. . . .

The paucity of evidence to support the case the Court tries to make demonstrates that Congress was not responding with a congruent and proportional remedy to a perceived course of unconstitutional conduct. Instead, it enacted a substantive entitlement program of its own. If Congress had been concerned about different treatment of men and women with respect to family leave, a congruent remedy would have sought to ensure the benefits of any leave program enacted by a State are available to men and women on an equal basis. Instead, the Act imposes, across the board, a requirement that States grant a minimum of 12 weeks of leave per year. This requirement may represent Congress's considered judgment as to the optimal balance between the family obligations of workers and the interests of employers, and the States may decide to follow these guidelines in designing their own family leave benefits. It does not follow, however, that if the States choose to enact a different benefit scheme, they should be deemed to engage in unconstitutional conduct and forced to open their treasuries to private suits for damages. . . .

What is at issue is only whether the States can be subjected, without consent, to suits brought by private persons seeking to collect moneys from the state treasury. Their immunity cannot be abrogated without documentation of a pattern of unconstitutional acts by the States, and only then by a congruent and proportional remedy. There has been a complete failure by respondents to carry their burden to establish each of these necessary propositions. I would hold that the Act is not a valid abrogation of state sovereign immunity and dissent with respect from the Court's conclusion to the contrary.

■ THE DEVELOPMENT OF LAW

Other Rulings on the Eleventh Amendment

CASE	VOTE	RULING
Lapides v. Board of Regents of The University System of Georgia, 534 S.Ct. 1052 (2002)	9:0	Writing for a unanimous Court, Justice Breyer held a state's removal of a lawsuit filed against it from a state court to a federal court constitutes a waiver of the

state's Eleventh Amendment immunity.

Verizon Maryland v. Public Service Commission of Maryland, 535 S.Ct. 467 (2002)	8:0	With Justice O'Connor not participating, the Court held unanimously that states are not immune from suits brought over the im- plementation of the Telecom-

munications Act of 1996. Justice Scalia delivered the opinion of the Court and Justices Kennedy and Souter filed concurring opinions.

Federal Maritime Commission v. Carolina State Ports Authority, 535 S.Ct. 743 (2002)	5:4	Writing for the Court, Justice Thomas held that states' sovereign immunity bars the Federal Mari- time Commission (FMC) from adjudicating a private party's com-

plaint against a nonconsenting state in an administrative law proceeding. Justice Thomas reasoned that dual sovereignty is a defining feature of the nation and that an integral component of states' sovereignty is their immunity from private suits. Although the Eleventh Amendment provides that the "judicial Power of the United States" does not "extend to any suit, in law or equity," brought by citizens of one state against another state, that provision does not define states' sovereign immunity but is instead only one exemplification of that immunity. Formalized administrative adjudications were virtually unheard of in the eighteenth and nineteenth centuries, so there is little evidence of the framers' intent. However, because of the presumption that the Constitu- tion was not intended to encourage any proceedings against the state that were "anomalous and unheard of when the Constitution was adopted," *Hans v. Louisiana*, 134 U.S. 1 (1890), the Court should attribute great significance to the fact that the states were not subject to private suits in administrative adjudications at the time of the founding. In deciding whether the *Hans* pre- sumption of immunity applies here, Justice Thomas observed that administra- tive law judges and trial judges play similar roles and that administrative and judicial proceedings share similar features. More specifically, he noted that the FMC adjudications are a proceeding that "walks, talks, and squawks like a lawsuit." In addition, Justice Thomas concluded that it would be strange if Congress were prohibited from exercising its Article I powers to abrogate state sovereign immunity in Article III judicial proceedings but were permitted to create courtlike administrative tribunals to which state sovereign immunity did not apply. Justices Stevens and Breyer each issued dissenting opinions and were joined by Justices Souter and Ginsburg.

8

REPRESENTATIVE
GOVERNMENT,
VOTING RIGHTS, AND
ELECTORAL POLITICS

A | *Representative Government
| and the Franchise*

■ THE DEVELOPMENT OF LAW

Other Rulings Interpreting the Voting Rights Act

CASE	VOTE	RULING
Georgia v. Ashcroft, 123 S.Ct. 2498 (2003)	5:4	The Court held that, under Section 5 of the Voting Rights Act, legislative and congressional dis-

tricts may be redrawn in ways that shrink black voting majorities in order to create more Democratic-leaning districts. Georgia's redistricting reduced black majorities in three districts to just over 50 percent, down from 55 to 62 percent, in order to increase the likelihood of electing Democrats. A federal district court held that this violated the Voting Rights Act, but the Supreme Court reversed in holding that in assessing the racial regressive effect all factors may be considered, including a minority group's voting participation in a coalitional district. Writing for the Court, Justice O'Connor observed: "Various studies suggest that the most effective way to maximize minority voting strength may be to create more influence or coalitional districts. Section 5 allows States to risk having fewer minority representatives in order to achieve greater overall representation of a minority group by increasing the number of representatives sympathetic to the interests of minority voters." Justices Stevens, Souter, Ginsburg, and Breyer dissented and accused the majority of gutting the act's prohibition against redistricting that is retrogressive for minority voting rights.

C | Campaigns and Elections

On an expedited basis, the Court scheduled for September 8, 2003, a special oral argument session for *McConnell v. Federal Election Commission*, appealing the decision of a three-judge panel that struck down major provisions of the Bipartisan Campaign Reform Act, or "McCain-Feingold campaign finance law," as it is known for its sponsors, Arizona's Republican Senator John McCain and New York's Democratic Senator Russell Feingold. In a complicated 1,638-page set of opinions, the federal court invalidated the statute's ban on political parties raising "soft money"—money used for "get-out-the-vote" drives and campaign advertising—from corporations, unions, and individuals. However, the court upheld some of the statute's restrictions on so-called attack ads or issue ads run by political parties and independent interest groups, such as the National Rifle Association. That decision was immediately appealed by one of the law's leading critics, Kentucky's Republican Senator Mitch McConnell, as well as eleven other appeals filed by 80 other individuals and groups. Subsequently the three-judge panel stayed enforcement of its decision, pending the Supreme Court's review. Because of the complexity of the case, the justices scheduled four hours for oral arguments, instead of the usual one hour.

Republican Party of Minnesota v. White
536 U.S. 765, 122 S.CT. 2528 (2002)

The Minnesota Supreme Court adopted a canon of judicial conduct prohibiting candidates for judicial office from announcing their views on disputed legal and political issues. While running for the position of associate justice on that court, Gregory Wersal filed a lawsuit seeking a declaration that this "announce clause" violates the First Amendment. A federal district court disagreed and the Court of Appeals for the Eighth Circuit affirmed, whereupon the Republican Party appealed.

The appellate court's decision was reversed by a five-to-four vote and Justice Scalia delivered an opinion for the Court. Justices Stevens and Ginsburg filed dissenting opinions, which Justices Souter and Breyer joined.

☐ *Justice SCALIA delivered the opinion of the Court.*

The question presented in this case is whether the First Amendment permits the Minnesota Supreme Court to prohibit candidates for judicial election in that State from announcing their views on disputed legal and political issues. . . .

Before considering the constitutionality of the announce clause, we must be clear about its meaning. Its text says that a candidate for judicial office shall not "announce his or her views on disputed legal or political issues."

We know that "announc[ing] . . . views" on an issue covers much more than promising to decide an issue a particular way. The prohibition extends to the candidate's mere statement of his current position, even if he does not bind himself to maintain that position after election. All the parties agree this is the case, because the Minnesota Code contains a so-called "pledges or promises" clause, which separately prohibits judicial candidates from making "pledges or promises of conduct in office other than the faithful and impartial performance of the duties of the office"—a prohibition that is not challenged here and on which we express no view.

There are, however, some limitations that the Minnesota Supreme Court has placed upon the scope of the announce clause that are not (to put it politely) immediately apparent from its text. The statements that formed the basis of the complaint against Wersal in 1996 included criticism of past decisions of the Minnesota Supreme Court. One piece of campaign literature stated that "[t]he Minnesota Supreme Court has issued decisions which are marked by their disregard for the Legislature and a lack of common sense." The Judicial Board issued an opinion stating that judicial candidates may criticize past decisions, and the Lawyers Board refused to discipline Wersal for the foregoing statements because, in part, it thought they did not violate the announce clause. The Eighth Circuit relied on the Judicial Board's opinion in upholding the announce clause, and the Minnesota Supreme Court recently embraced the Eighth Circuit's interpretation.

There are yet further limitations upon the apparent plain meaning of the announce clause: In light of the constitutional concerns, the District Court construed the clause to reach only disputed issues that are likely to come before the candidate if he is elected judge. The Eighth Circuit accepted this limiting interpretation by the District Court, and in addition construed the clause to allow general discussions of case law and judicial philosophy. The Supreme Court of Minnesota adopted these interpretations as well when it ordered enforcement of the announce clause in accordance with the Eighth Circuit's opinion.

It seems to us, however, that—like the text of the announce clause itself—these limitations upon the text of the announce clause are not all that they appear to be. First, respondents acknowledged at oral argument that statements critical of past judicial decisions are not permissible if the candidate also states that he is against *stare decisis*. Thus, candidates must choose between stating their views critical of past decisions and stating their views in opposition to *stare decisis*. Or, to look at it more concretely, they may state their view that prior decisions were erroneous only if they do not assert that they, if elected, have any power to eliminate erroneous decisions. Second, limiting the scope of the clause to issues likely to come before a court is not much of a limitation at all. One would hardly expect the "disputed legal or political issues" raised in the course of a state judicial election to include such matters as whether the Federal Government should end the embargo of Cuba. Quite obviously, they will be those legal or political disputes that are the proper (or by past decisions have been made the improper) business of the state courts. And within that relevant category, "[t]here is almost no legal or political issue that is unlikely to come before a judge of an American court, state or federal, of general jurisdiction." Third, construing the clause to allow "general" discussions of case law and judicial philosophy turns out to be of little help in an election campaign. At oral argument, respondents gave, as an example of this exception, that a candidate is free to assert that he is a "'strict constructionist.'" But that, like most other philosophical generalities, has little meaningful content for the electorate unless it is exemplified by application to a particular issue of construction likely to come before a court—for example, whether a particular statute runs afoul of any provision of the Constitution. Respondents conceded that the announce clause would prohibit the candidate from exemplifying his philosophy in this fashion. Without such application to real-life issues, all candidates can claim to be "strict constructionists" with equal (and unhelpful) plausibility.

In any event, it is clear that the announce clause prohibits a judicial candidate from stating his views on any specific nonfanciful legal question within the province of the court for which he is running, except in the context of discussing past decisions—and in the latter context as well, if he expresses the view that he is not bound by *stare decisis*.

Respondents contend that this still leaves plenty of topics for discussion on the campaign trail. These include a candidate's "character," "education," "work habits," and "how [he] would handle administrative duties if elected." Indeed, the Judicial Board has printed a list of preapproved questions which judicial candidates are allowed to answer. These include how the candidate feels about cameras in the courtroom, how he would go about reducing the caseload, how the costs of judicial administration can be reduced, and how he proposes to ensure that minorities and women are treated more fairly by the court system. Whether this list of preapproved subjects, and other topics not prohibited by the announce clause, adequately fulfill the First Amendment's guarantee of freedom of speech is the question to which we now turn. . . .

We think it plain that the announce clause is not narrowly tailored to serve impartiality (or the appearance of impartiality). . . . Indeed, the clause is barely tailored to serve that interest at all, inasmuch as it does not restrict speech for or against particular parties, but rather speech for or against particular issues. To be sure, when a case arises that turns on a legal issue on which the judge (as a candidate) had taken a particular stand, the party taking the opposite stand is likely to lose. But not because of any bias against that party, or favoritism toward the other party. Any party taking that position is just as likely to lose. The judge is applying the law (as he sees it) evenhandedly.

It is perhaps possible to use the term "impartiality" in the judicial context (though this is certainly not a common usage) to mean lack of preconception in favor of or against a particular legal view. This sort of impartiality would be concerned, not with guaranteeing litigants equal application of the law, but rather with guaranteeing them an equal chance to persuade the court on the legal points in their case. Impartiality in this sense may well be an interest served by the announce clause, but it is not a compelling state interest, as strict scrutiny requires. A judge's lack of predisposition regarding the relevant legal issues in a case has never been thought a necessary component of equal justice, and with good reason. For one thing, it is virtually impossible to find a judge who does not have preconceptions about the law. . . .

A third possible meaning of "impartiality" (again not a common one) might be described as openmindedness. This quality in a judge demands, not that he have no preconceptions on legal issues, but that he be willing to consider views that oppose his preconceptions, and remain open to persuasion, when the issues arise in a pending case. This sort of impartiality seeks to guarantee each litigant, not an equal chance to win the legal points in the case, but at least some chance of doing so. It may well be that impartiality in this sense, and the appearance of it, are desirable in the judiciary, but we need not pursue that inquiry, since we do not believe the Minnesota Supreme Court adopted the announce clause for that purpose.

Respondents argue that the announce clause serves the interest in openmindedness, or at least in the appearance of openmindedness, because it relieves a judge from pressure to rule a certain way in order to maintain consistency with statements the judge has previously made. The problem is, however, that statements in election campaigns are such an infinitesimal portion of the public commitments to legal positions that judges (or judges-to-be) undertake, that this object of the prohibition is implausible. Before they arrive on the bench (whether by election or otherwise) judges have often committed themselves on legal issues that they must later rule upon. . . .

The short of the matter is this: In Minnesota, a candidate for judicial office may not say "I think it is constitutional for the legislature to prohibit same-sex marriages." He may say the very same thing, however, up until the very day before he declares himself a candidate, and may say it repeatedly (until litigation is pending) after he is elected. As a means of pursuing the objective of open-mindedness that respondents now articulate, the announce clause is so woefully underinclusive as to render belief in that purpose a challenge to the credulous. . . .

There is an obvious tension between the article of Minnesota's popularly approved Constitution which provides that judges shall be elected, and the Minnesota Supreme Court's announce clause which places most subjects of interest to the voters off limits. The disparity is perhaps unsurprising, since the ABA, which originated the announce clause, has long been an opponent of judicial elections. That opposition may be well taken (it certainly had the support of the Founders of the Federal Government), but the First Amendment does not permit it to achieve its goal by leaving the principle of elections in place while preventing candidates from discussing what the elections are about.

The Minnesota Supreme Court's canon of judicial conduct prohibiting candidates for judicial election from announcing their views on disputed legal and political issues violates the First Amendment. Accordingly, we reverse the grant of summary judgment to respondents and remand the case for proceedings consistent with this opinion. It is so ordered.

□ *Justice GINSBURG, with whom Justice STEVENS, Justice SOUTER, and Justice BREYER join, dissenting.*

Whether state or federal, elected or appointed, judges perform a function fundamentally different from that of the people's elected representatives. Legislative and executive officials act on behalf of the voters who placed them in office; "judge[s] represen[t] the Law." *Chisom v. Roemer*, 501 U.S. 380 (1991) (SCALIA, J., dissenting). Unlike their counterparts in the political branches, judges are expected to refrain from catering to particular constituencies or committing themselves on controversial issues in advance of adversarial presentation. Their mission is to decide "individual cases and controversies" on individual records, *Plaut v. Spendthrift Farm, Inc.*, 514 U.S. 211 (1995) (STEVENS, J., dissenting), neutrally applying legal principles, and, when necessary, "stand[ing] up to what is generally supreme in a democracy: the popular will," SCALIA, The Rule of Law as a Law of Rules, 56 *U. Chi. L. Rev.* 1175 (1989). . . .

The question this case presents is whether the First Amendment stops Minnesota from furthering its interest in judicial integrity through this precisely targeted speech restriction.

The speech restriction must fail, in the Court's view, because an electoral process is at stake; if Minnesota opts to elect its judges, the Court asserts, the State may not rein in what candidates may say.

I do not agree with this unilocular, "an election is an election," approach. Instead, I would differentiate elections for political offices, in which the First Amendment holds full sway, from elections designed to select those whose office it is to administer justice without respect to persons. Minnesota's choice to elect its judges, I am persuaded, does not preclude the State from installing an election process geared to the judicial office.

Legislative and executive officials serve in representative capacities. . . . Judges, however, are not political actors. They do not sit as representatives of particular persons, communities, or parties; they serve no faction or constituency. "[I]t is the business of judges to be indifferent to popularity." *Chisom*. They must strive to do what is legally right, all the more so when the result is not the one "the home crowd" wants. Even when they develop common law or give concrete meaning to constitutional text, judges act only in the context of individual cases, the outcome of which cannot depend on the will of the public.

Thus, the rationale underlying unconstrained speech in elections for political office—that representative government depends on the public's ability to choose agents who will act at its behest—does not carry over to campaigns for the bench. As to persons aiming to occupy the seat of judgment, the Court's unrelenting reliance on decisions involving contests for legislative and executive posts is manifestly out of place. In view of the magisterial role judges must fill in a system of justice, a role that removes them from the partisan fray, States may limit judicial campaign speech by measures impermissible in elections for political office. . . .

Accordingly, I would affirm the judgment of the Court of Appeals for the Eighth Circuit.

☐ *Justice STEVENS, with whom Justice SOUTER, Justice GINSBURG, and Justice BREYER join, dissenting.*

In her dissenting opinion, Justice GINSBURG has cogently explained why the Court's holding is unsound. I therefore join her opinion without reservation. I add these comments to emphasize the force of her arguments and to explain why I find the Court's reasoning even more troubling than its holding. The limits of the Court's holding are evident: Even if the Minnesota Lawyers Professional Responsibility Board (Board) may not sanction a judicial candidate for announcing his views on issues likely to come before him, it may surely advise the electorate that such announcements demonstrate the speaker's unfitness for judicial office. If the solution to harmful speech must be more speech, so be it. The Court's reasoning, however, will unfortunately endure beyond the next election cycle. By obscuring the fundamental distinction between campaigns for the judiciary and the political branches, and by failing to recognize the difference between statements made in articles or opinions and those made on the campaign trail, the Court defies any sensible notion of the judicial office and the importance of impartiality in that context.

The Court's disposition rests on two seriously flawed premises—an inaccurate appraisal of the importance of judicial independence and impartiality, and an assumption that judicial candidates should have the same freedom " 'to express themselves on matters of current public importance' " as do all other elected officials. Elected judges, no less than appointed judges, occupy an office of trust that is fundamentally different from that occupied by policymaking officials. Although the fact that they must stand for election makes their job more difficult than that of the tenured judge, that fact does not lessen their duty to respect essential attributes of the judicial office that have been embedded in Anglo-American law for centuries. . . .

The disposition of this case on the flawed premise that the criteria for the election to judicial office should mirror the rules applicable to political elections is profoundly misguided. I therefore respectfully dissent.

Federal Election Commission v. Beaumont

123 S.Ct. 2200 (2003)

The Court rejected a First Amendment challenge by the North Carolina Right to Life, Inc. to a federal ban on corporations—even nonprofit advocacy corporations—from directly contributing to candidates for federal office. The facts are further discussed in Justice Souter's opinion for the Court. Justice Thomas filed a dissenting opinion, which Justice Scalia joined.

☐ *Justice SOUTER delivered the opinion of the Court.*

Since 1907, federal law has barred corporations from contributing directly to candidates for federal office. We hold that applying the prohibition to nonprofit advocacy corporations is consistent with the First Amendment.

The current statute makes it "unlawful . . . for any corporation whatever . . . to make a contribution or expenditure in connection with" certain federal elections, Section 441b(a), "contribution or expenditure" each being defined to include "anything of value," Section 441b(b)(2). The prohibition does not, however, forbid "the establishment, administration, and solicitation of contributions to a separate segregated fund to be utilized for political purposes." Such a PAC (so called after the political action committee that runs it) may be wholly controlled by the sponsoring corporation, whose employees and stockholders or members generally may be solicited for contributions. See *Federal Election Comm'n v. National Right to Work Comm.*, 459 U.S. 197 (1982). While federal law requires PACs to register and disclose their activities, the law leaves them free to make contributions as well as other expenditures in connection with federal elections.

Respondents are a corporation known as North Carolina Right to Life, Inc., three of its officers, and a North Carolina voter (here, together, NCRL), who have sued the Federal Election Commission, the independent agency set up to "administer, seek to obtain compliance with, and formulate policy with respect to" the federal electoral laws. NCRL challenges the constitutionality of Section 441b and the FEC's regulations implementing that section, but only so far as they apply to NCRL. The corporation is organized under the laws of North Carolina to provide counseling to pregnant women and to urge alternatives to abortion, and as a nonprofit advocacy corporation it is exempted from federal taxation of the Internal Revenue Code. . . .

Any attack on the federal prohibition of direct corporate political contributions goes against the current of a century of congressional efforts to curb corporations' potentially "deleterious influences on federal elections," which we have canvassed a number of times before. The current law grew out of a "popular feeling" in the late 19th century "that aggregated capital unduly influenced politics, an influence not stopping short of corruption." A demand for congressional action gathered force in the campaign of 1904, which made a national issue of the political leverage exerted through corporate contributions, and after the election and new revelations of corporate political overreaching, President Theodore Roosevelt made banning corporate political contributions a legislative priority. Although some congressional proposals would have "prohibited political contributions by [only] certain classes of corporations," the momentum was "for elections 'free from the power of money,' " and Congress acted on the President's call for an outright ban, not with half measures, but with the Tillman Act. This "first federal campaign finance law" banned "any corporation whatever" from making "a money contribution in connection with" federal elections.

Since 1907, there has been continual congressional attention to corporate political activity, sometimes resulting in refinement of the law, sometimes in overhaul. One feature, however, has stayed intact throughout this "careful legislative adjustment of the federal electoral laws," and much of the periodic amendment was meant to strengthen the original, core prohibition on direct corporate contributions. The Foreign Corrupt Practices Act of 1925, for example, broadened the ban on contributions to include "anything of value," and criminalized the act of receiving a contribution to match the criminality of making one. So, in another instance, the 1947 Labor Management Relations Act drew labor unions permanently within the law's reach and invigorated the earlier prohibition to include "expenditure[s]" as well. . . .

As we explained it in *Austin* [*v. Michigan Chamber of Commerce*, 494 U.S. 652 (1990)],

> State law grants corporations special advantages—such as limited liability, perpetual life, and favorable treatment of the accumulation and distribution of assets—that enhance their ability to attract capital and to deploy their resources in ways that maximize the return on their shareholders' investments. These state-created advantages not only allow corporations to play a dominant role in the Nation's economy, but also permit them to use "resources amassed in the economic marketplace" to obtain "an unfair advantage in the political marketplace."

Hence, the public interest in "restrict[ing] the influence of political war chests funneled through the corporate form."

As these excerpts from recent opinions show, not only has the original ban on direct corporate contributions endured, but so have the original rationales for the law. In barring corporate earnings from conversion into political "war chests," the ban was and is intended to "preven[t] corruption or the appearance of corruption."

Quite aside from war-chest corruption and the interests of contributors and owners, however, another reason for regulating corporate electoral involvement has emerged with restrictions on individual contributions, and recent cases have recognized that restricting contributions by various organizations hedges against their use as conduits for "circumvention of [valid] contribution limits." *Federal Election Comm'n v. Colorado Republican Federal Campaign Comm.*, 533 U.S. 431 (2001). To the degree that a corporation could contribute to political candidates, the individuals "who created it, who own it, or whom it employs," *Cedric Kushner Promotions, Ltd. v. King*, 533 U.S. 158 (2001), could exceed the bounds imposed on their own contributions by diverting money through the corporation.

In sum, our cases on campaign finance regulation represent respect for the "legislative judgment that the special characteristics of the corporate structure require particularly careful regulation." And we have understood that such deference to legislative choice is warranted particularly when Congress regulates campaign contributions, carrying as they do a plain threat to political integrity and a plain warrant to counter the appearance and reality of corruption and the misuse of corporate advantages. See, e.g., *Buckley v. Valeo*, 424 U.S. 1 (1976).

That historical prologue would discourage any broadside attack on corporate campaign finance regulation or regulation of corporate contributions, and NCRL accordingly questions Section 441b only to the extent the law places nonprofit advocacy corporations like itself under the general ban on direct contributions. . . .

It would be hard to read our conclusion in *National Right to Work*, that the PAC solicitation restrictions were constitutional, except on the practical understanding that the corporation's capacity to make contributions was legitimately limited to indirect donations within the scope allowed to PACs. In fact, we specifically rejected the argument made here, that deference to congressional judgments about proper limits on corporate contributions turns on details of corporate form or the affluence of particular corporations. In the same breath, we remarked on the broad applicability of Section 441b to "corporations and labor unions without great financial resources, as well as those more fortunately situated," and made a point of refusing to "second-guess a legislative determination as to the need for prophylactic measures where corruption is the evil feared." . . .

The upshot is that, although we have never squarely held against NCRL's position here, we could not hold for it without recasting our understanding of the risks of harm posed by corporate political contributions, of the expressive significance of contributions, and of the consequent deference owed to legislative judgments on what to do about them. NCRL's efforts, however, fail to unsettle existing law on any of these points. . . .

NCRL cannot prevail, then, simply by arguing that a ban on an advocacy corporation's direct contributions is bad tailoring. NCRL would have to demonstrate that the law violated the First Amendment in allowing contributions to be made only through its PAC and subject to a PAC's administrative burdens. But a unanimous Court in *National Right to Work* did not think the regulatory burdens on PACs, including restrictions on their ability to solicit funds, rendered a PAC unconstitutional as an advocacy corporation's sole avenue for making political contributions. There is no reason to think the burden on advocacy corporations is any greater today, or to reach a different conclusion here.

9

ECONOMIC RIGHTS AND AMERICAN CAPITALISM

C | The "Takings Clause" and Just Compensation

In an important ruling on land-use regulations, in *Tahoe-Sierra Preserva-tion Council, Inc. v. Tahoe Regional Planning Agency* (2002) (excerpted below), the Court rejected a Fifth Amendment Takings Clause challenge to temporary moratoria on construction by a vote of six to three.

Tahoe-Sierra Preservation Council, Inc. v. Tahoe Regional Planning Agency
535 U.S. 302, 122 S.Ct. 1465 (2002)

Lake Tahoe's exceptional clarity is attributed to the absence of algae as a result of the lack of nitrogen and phosphorus in its water. The lake's pristine state, however, has deteriorated during the last 40 years. In the 1960s, when the problems associated with burgeoning development be-gan to receive attention, California and Nevada, five counties, several municipalities, and the U.S. Forest Service shared jurisdiction over the lake. In 1968 the legislatures of both states adopted the Tahoe Regional Planning Compact, which Congress approved in 1969. The compact set goals for the preservation of the lake and created the Tahoe Regional

Planning Agency (TRPA) "to coordinate and regulate development" in the lake's basin and "to conserve its natural resources." In 1980 the compact was redefined and the TRPA was directed to develop regional "standards for air quality, water quality, soil conservation, vegetation preservation and noise." Subsequently, the TRPA ordered two moratoria on construction in the basin in order to maintain the status quo while studying the impact of development on the lake. The first, Ordinance 81-5, was in effect from August 24, 1981, to August 26, 1983, and the second, more restrictive Resolution 83-21 was in effect from August 27, 1983, to April 25, 1984. As a result of those directives, virtually all development on substantial areas of the land within the TRPA's jurisdiction was prohibited for 32 months.

The constitutionality of the moratoria was challenged as a violation of the Fifth Amendment's Takings Clause. A federal district court held that, although the property owners retained some value in the land, the moratoria temporarily deprived them of "all economically viable use of their land" and therefore constituted a "categorical" takings in violation of the Fifth Amendment, based on the rulings in *Lucas v. South Carolina Coastal Council*, 505 U.S. 1003 (1992), and *First English Evangelical Lutheran Church of Glendale v. County of Los Angeles*, 482 U.S. 304 (1987). On appeal, the U.S. Court of Appeals for the Ninth Circuit reversed that decision and held that the moratoria had only a temporary impact on the property owners' economic interests and thus were not categorical takings. That decision was appealed and the Supreme Court granted *certiorari*.

The appellate court's decision was affirmed by a vote of six to three. Justice Stevens delivered the opinion of the Court and Chief Justice Rehnquist filed a dissent, which Justices Scalia and Thomas joined; the latter also issued a separate dissent.

□ *Justice STEVENS delivered the opinion of the Court.*

Petitioners contend that the mere enactment of a temporary regulation that, while in effect, denies a property owner all viable economic use of her property gives rise to an unqualified constitutional obligation to compensate her for the value of its use during that period. . . . For petitioners, it is enough that a regulation imposes a temporary deprivation—no matter how brief—of all economically viable use to trigger a per se rule that a taking has occurred. Petitioners assert that our opinions in *First English* and *Lucas* have already endorsed their view, and that it is a logical application of the principle that the Takings Clause was "designed to bar Government from forcing some people alone to bear burdens which, in all fairness and justice, should be borne by the public as a whole." *Armstrong v. United States*, 364 U.S. 40 (1960).

We shall first explain why our cases do not support their proposed categorical rule—indeed, fairly read, they implicitly reject it. Next, we shall explain why the *Armstrong* principle requires rejection of that rule as well as the less extreme position advanced by petitioners at oral argument. In our view the answer to the abstract question whether a temporary moratorium effects a taking is neither "yes, always" nor "no, never"; the answer depends upon the particular circumstances of the case.

The text of the Fifth Amendment itself provides a basis for drawing a distinction between physical takings and regulatory takings. Its plain language requires the payment of compensation whenever the government acquires private property for a public purpose, whether the acquisition is the result of a condemnation proceeding or a physical appropriation. But the Constitution contains no comparable reference to regulations that prohibit a property owner from making certain uses of her private property. Our jurisprudence involving condemnations and physical takings is as old as the Republic and, for the most part, involves the straightforward application of per se rules. Our regulatory takings jurisprudence, in contrast, is of more recent vintage and is characterized by "essentially ad hoc, factual inquiries," *Penn Central* [*Transportation Co. v. New York City*, 438 U.S. 104 (1978)], designed to allow "careful examination and weighing of all the relevant circumstances."

When the government physically takes possession of an interest in property for some public purpose, it has a categorical duty to compensate the former owner, regardless of whether the interest that is taken constitutes an entire parcel or merely a part thereof. Thus, compensation is mandated when a leasehold is taken and the government occupies the property for its own purposes, even though that use is temporary. But a government regulation that merely prohibits landlords from evicting tenants unwilling to pay a higher rent; that bans certain private uses of a portion of an owner's property; or that forbids the private use of certain airspace, does not constitute a categorical taking. "The first category of cases requires courts to apply a clear rule; the second necessarily entails complex factual assessments of the purposes and economic effects of government actions." *Yee v. Escondido*, 503 U.S. 519 (1992).

This longstanding distinction between acquisitions of property for public use, on the one hand, and regulations prohibiting private uses, on the other, makes it inappropriate to treat cases involving physical takings as controlling precedents for the evaluation of a claim that there has been a "regulatory taking," and vice versa. . . .

Perhaps recognizing this fundamental distinction, petitioners wisely do not place all their emphasis on analogies to physical takings cases. Instead, they rely principally on our decision in *Lucas v. South Carolina Coastal Council*—a regulatory takings case that, nevertheless, applied a categorical rule—to argue that the *Penn Central* framework is inapplicable here. A brief review of some of the cases that led to our decision in *Lucas*, however, will help to explain why the holding in that case does not answer the question presented here.

As we noted in *Lucas*, it was Justice HOLMES' opinion in *Pennsylvania Coal Co. v. Mahon*, 260 U.S. 393 (1922), that gave birth to our regulatory takings jurisprudence. In subsequent opinions we have repeatedly and consistently endorsed HOLMES' observation that "if regulation goes too far it will be recognized as a taking." Justice HOLMES did not provide a standard for determining when a regulation goes "too far," but he did reject the view expressed in Justice BRANDEIS' dissent that there could not be a taking because the property remained in the possession of the owner and had not been appropriated or used by the public. After *Mahon*, neither a physical appropriation nor a public use has ever been a necessary component of a "regulatory taking."

In the decades following that decision, we have "generally eschewed" any set formula for determining how far is too far, choosing instead to engage in "'essentially ad hoc, factual inquiries.'" Indeed, we still resist the temptation to adopt per se rules in our cases involving partial regulatory takings, preferring to examine "a number of factors" rather than a simple "mathematically precise" formula. Justice BRENNAN's opinion for the Court in *Penn Central* did, however, make it clear that even though multiple factors are relevant in the analysis of regulatory takings claims, in such cases we must focus on "the parcel as a whole": "'Taking' jurisprudence does not divide a single parcel into discrete segments and attempt to determine whether rights in a particular segment have been entirely abrogated. In deciding whether a particular governmental action has effected a taking, this Court focuses rather both on the character of the action and on the nature and extent of the interference with rights in the parcel as a whole—here, the city tax block designated as the 'landmark site.'" This requirement that "the aggregate must be viewed in its entirety" explains why, for example, a regulation that prohibited commercial transactions in eagle feathers, but did not bar other uses or impose any physical invasion or restraint upon them, was not a taking. It also clarifies why restrictions on the use of only limited portions of the parcel, such as set-back ordinances, or a requirement that coal pillars be left in place to prevent mine subsidence, were not considered regulatory takings. In each of these cases, we affirmed that "where an owner possesses a full 'bundle' of property rights, the destruction of one 'strand' of the bundle is not a taking."

While the foregoing cases considered whether particular regulations had "gone too far" and were therefore invalid, none of them addressed the separate remedial question of how compensation is measured once a regulatory taking is established. In his dissenting opinion in *San Diego Gas & Elec. Co. v. San Diego*, 450 U.S. 621 (1981), Justice BRENNAN identified that question and explained how he would answer it: "The constitutional rule I propose requires that, once a court finds that a police power regulation has effected a 'taking,' the government entity must pay just compensation for the period commencing on the date the regulation first effected the 'taking,' and ending on the date the government entity chooses to rescind or otherwise amend the regulation." Justice BRENNAN's proposed rule was subsequently endorsed by the Court in *First English*. *First English* was certainly a significant decision, and nothing that we say today qualifies its holding. Nonetheless, it is important to recognize that we did not address in that case the quite different and logically prior question whether the temporary regulation at issue had in fact constituted a taking. . . .

Similarly, our decision in *Lucas* is not dispositive of the question presented. Although *Lucas* endorsed and applied a categorical rule, it was not the one that petitioners propose. . . . The categorical rule that we applied in *Lucas* states that compensation is required when a regulation deprives an owner of "all economically beneficial uses" of his land. But our holding was limited to "the extraordinary circumstance when no productive or economically beneficial use of land is permitted." . . .

Certainly, our holding that the permanent "obliteration of the value" of a fee simple estate constitutes a categorical taking does not answer the question whether a regulation prohibiting any economic use of land for a 32-month period has the same legal effect. Petitioners seek to bring this case under the rule announced in *Lucas* by arguing that we can effectively sever a 32-month segment from the remainder of each landowner's fee simple estate, and then ask whether that segment has been taken in its entirety by the moratoria. Of course, defining the property interest taken in terms of the very regulation being challenged is circular. With property so divided, every delay would become a total ban; the moratorium and the normal permit process alike would constitute categorical takings. . . .

Neither *Lucas*, nor *First English*, nor any of our other regulatory takings cases compels us to accept petitioners' categorical submission. In fact, these cases make clear that the categorical rule in *Lucas* was carved out for the "extraordinary case" in which a regulation permanently deprives property of all value; the default rule remains that, in the regulatory taking context, we require a more fact specific inquiry. . . .

[T]he ultimate constitutional question is whether the concepts of "fairness and justice" that underlie the Takings Clause will be better served by one of these categorical rules or by a *Penn Central* inquiry into all of the relevant circumstances in particular cases. From that perspective, the extreme categorical rule that any deprivation of all economic use, no matter how brief, constitutes a compensable taking surely cannot be sustained. Petitioners' broad submission would apply to numerous "normal delays in obtaining building permits, changes in zoning ordinances, variances, and the like," as well as to orders temporarily prohibiting access to crime scenes, businesses that violate health codes, fire-damaged buildings, or other areas that we cannot now foresee. Such a rule would undoubtedly require changes in numerous practices that have long been considered permissible exercises of the police power. A rule that required compensation for every delay in the use of property would render routine government processes prohibitively expensive or encourage hasty decision-making. Such an important change in the law should be the product of legislative rulemaking rather than adjudication. . . .

The concepts of "fairness and justice" that underlie the Takings Clause, of course, are less than fully determinate. Accordingly, we have eschewed any "set formula" for determining when "justice and fairness" require that economic injuries caused by public action be compensated by the government, rather than remain disproportionately concentrated on a few persons. The outcome instead depends largely "upon the particular circumstances [in that] case." In rejecting petitioners' per se rule, we do not hold that the temporary nature of a land-use restriction precludes finding that it effects a taking; we simply recognize that it should not be given exclusive significance one way or the other.

A narrower rule that excluded the normal delays associated with processing permits, or that covered only delays of more than a year, would certainly have a less severe impact on prevailing practices, but it would still impose serious financial constraints on the planning process. Unlike the "extraordinary circumstance" in which the government deprives a property owner of all economic use, moratoria like Ordinance 81–5 and Resolution 83–21 are used widely among land-use planners to preserve the status quo while formulating a more permanent development strategy. In fact, the consensus in the planning community appears to be that moratoria, or "interim development controls" as they are often called, are an essential tool of successful development. . . .

[T]he interest in protecting the decisional process is even stronger when an agency is developing a regional plan than when it is considering a permit for a single parcel. In the proceedings involving the Lake Tahoe Basin, for example, the moratoria enabled TRPA to obtain the benefit of comments and criticisms from interested parties, such as the petitioners, during its deliberations. Since a categorical rule tied to the length of deliberations would likely create added pressure on decisionmakers to reach a quick resolution of land-use questions, it would only serve to disadvantage those landowners and interest groups who are not as organized or familiar with the planning process. . . .

It may well be true that any moratorium that lasts for more than one year should be viewed with special skepticism. But given the fact that the District Court found that the 32 months required by TRPA to formulate the 1984 Regional Plan was not unreasonable, we could not possibly conclude that every delay of over one year is constitutionally unacceptable. Formulating a general rule of this kind is a suitable task for state legislatures. In our view, the duration of the restriction is one of the important factors that a court must consider in the appraisal of a regulatory takings claim, but with respect to that factor as with respect to other factors, the "temptation to adopt what amount to per se rules in either direction must be resisted." There may be moratoria that last longer than one year which interfere with reasonable investment-backed expectations, but as the District Court's opinion illustrates, petitioners' proposed rule is simply "too blunt an instrument," for identifying those cases. We conclude, therefore, that the interest in "fairness and justice" will be best served by relying on the familiar *Penn Central* approach when deciding cases like this, rather than by attempting to craft a new categorical rule.

☐ *CHIEF JUSTICE REHNQUIST, with whom Justice SCALIA and Justice THOMAS join, dissenting.*

Lucas reaffirmed our "frequently expressed" view that "when the owner of real property has been called upon to sacrifice all economically beneficial uses in the name of the common good, that is, to leave his property economically idle, he has suffered a taking." The Court does not dispute that petitioners were forced to leave their land economically idle during this period. But the Court refuses to apply *Lucas* on the ground that the deprivation was "temporary." Neither the Takings Clause nor our case law supports such a distinction. For one thing, a distinction between "temporary" and "permanent" prohibitions is tenuous. The "temporary" prohibition in this case that the Court finds is not a taking lasted almost six years. The "permanent" prohibition that the Court held to be a taking in *Lucas* lasted less than two years. The "permanent" prohibition in *Lucas* lasted less than two years because the law, as it often does, changed. . . .

[E]ven if a practical distinction between temporary and permanent deprivations were plausible, to treat the two differently in terms of takings law would be at odds with the justification for the *Lucas* rule. The *Lucas* rule is derived from the fact that a "total deprivation of use is, from the landowner's point of view, the equivalent of a physical appropriation." The regulation in *Lucas* was the "practical equivalence" of a long-term physical appropriation, i.e., a condemnation, so the Fifth Amendment required compensation. The "practical equivalence," from the landowner's point of view, of a "temporary" ban on all economic use is a forced leasehold. . . .

When a regulation merely delays a final land-use decision, we have recognized that there are other background principles of state property law that prevent the delay from being deemed a taking. We thus noted in *First English* that our discussion of temporary takings did not apply "in the case of normal delays in obtaining building permits, changes in zoning ordinances, variances, and the like."

But a moratorium prohibiting all economic use for a period of six years is not one of the longstanding, implied limitations of state property law. Moratoria are "interim controls on the use of land that seek to maintain the status quo with respect to land development in an area by either 'freezing' existing land uses or by allowing the issuance of building permits for only certain land uses that would not be inconsistent with a contemplated zoning plan or zoning change." Typical moratoria thus prohibit only certain categories of development, such as fast-food restaurants, or adult businesses, or all commercial development.

Such moratoria do not implicate *Lucas* because they do not deprive landowners of all economically beneficial use of their land. As for moratoria that prohibit all development, these do not have the lineage of permit and zoning requirements and thus it is less certain that property is acquired under the "implied limitation" of a moratorium prohibiting all development. Moreover, unlike a permit system in which it is expected that a project will be approved so long as certain conditions are satisfied, a moratorium that prohibits all uses is by definition contemplating a new land-use plan that would prohibit all uses. . . .

Because the prohibition on development of nearly six years in this case cannot be said to resemble any "implied limitation" of state property law, it is a taking that requires compensation. . . .

☐ *Justice THOMAS, with whom Justice SCALIA joins, dissenting.*

A taking is exactly what occurred in this case. . . . I would hold that regulations prohibiting all productive uses of property are subject to *Lucas'* per se rule, regardless of whether the property so burdened retains theoretical useful life and value if, and when, the "temporary" moratorium is lifted. To my mind, such potential future value bears on the amount of compensation due and has nothing to do with the question whether there was a taking in the first place. It is regrettable that the Court has charted a markedly different path today.

SUPREME COURT WATCH 2003
VOLUME TWO

3

ECONOMIC RIGHTS AND AMERICAN CAPITALISM

C | The "Takings Clause" and Just Compensation

Tahoe-Sierra Preservation Council, Inc. v. Tahoe Regional Planning Agency (2002) is excerpted here in Volume One, Chapter 9 (reprise).

4

THE NATIONALIZATION OF
THE BILL OF RIGHTS

B | *The Rise and Retreat of the "Due Process Revolution"*

In its 2002–2003 term the Court revisited the constitutionality of "Megan's Laws," which all fifty states have enacted and which require convicted sex offenders to register with state and local police, as well as to make available to the public their names, addresses, and photographs. These laws were enacted following the death of Megan Kanka, a New Jersey girl who was raped and murdered in 1994 by a sex offender in her neighborhood whose criminal history was unknown to her parents. Two convicted sex offenders challenged the constitutionality of Connecticut's law that, like those in nineteen other states, requires the public disclosure of personal information and DNA samples as well as the posting of the names, addresses, and photographs of convicted sex offenders on the Internet. A federal district court agreed that the publication and posting on the Web of offenders' personal information without first holding a hearing on their danger to society violated the guarantee of due process. The Court of Appeals for the Second Circuit agreed, but on appeal the Supreme Court reversed and found no due process violation because the registry requirement is based on a criminal conviction, not current dangerousness, in *Connecticut Department of Public Safety v. Doe*, 123 S.Ct. 1160 (2003).

■ THE DEVELOPMENT OF LAW

Rulings on Substantive and Procedural Due Process

CASE	VOTE	RULING
Dusenbery v. United States, 534 U.S. 161 (2002)	5:4	Writing for the Court, Chief Justice Rehnquist upheld the forfeiture of private property of a

prison inmate, who was served notice by certified mail and in the absence of a response to the notice of forfeiture, and held that due process does not require "actual notice," only "an attempt to provide actual notice" of forfeiture. Justices Ginsburg, Stevens, Souter, and Breyer dissented.

| *Kansas v. Crane,* 534 U.S. 407 (2002) | 7:2 | In *Kansas v. Hendricks*, 521 U.S. 346 (1997) (excerpted in Vol. 2, Ch. 4) the Court upheld the state's |

Sexually Violent Predator Act, authorizing the continued civil commitment of convicted sexual offenders who have a "mental abnormality or personality disorder" that renders them dangerous to themselves or others. Subsequently, Kansas sought the continued commitment of Michael Crane, but the state supreme court ruled that due process requires a finding that the defendant "cannot control his dangerous behavior." Writing for the Court, Justice Breyer held that there must be a hearing and finding that a dangerous sexual offender lacks self-control, but also emphasized that under *Hendricks* there is no narrow or technical meaning of "lack of control" and that that must be determined on a case by case basis, depending on the circumstances and psychiatric evaluations. Justices Scalia and Thomas dissented.

| *Connecticut Department of Public Safety v. Doe,* 123 S.Ct. 1160 (2003) | 9:0 | Writing for a unanimous Court, Chief Justice Rehnquist held that due process is not violated by states' requiring convicted sex |

offenders to register personal information, including addresses and photographs, which are then posted on a website, because the registry requirement is based on a prior conviction, not the sex offender's current dangerousness.

| *State Farm Mutual Automobile Insurance v. Campbell,* 123 S.Ct. 1523 (2003) | 6:3 | Writing for the Court, Justice Kennedy held that punitive damages awards must be reasonable and proportionate to the wrong |

committed and that "the wealth of a defendant cannot justify an otherwise unconstitutional punitive damages award." Here, the majority overturned a $145 million jury award against State Farm that was 145 times the amount of the injury as "an irrational and arbitrary deprivation of the property of the defendant." Justices Scalia, Thomas, and Ginsburg dissented.

| *Demore v. Kim,* 123 S.Ct. 1708 (2003) | 5:4 | Writing for the Court, Chief Justice Rehnquist upheld a 1996 federal law authorizing the detention of immigrants, including permanent residents or "green card holders," |

who have committed certain crimes and served their sentences while the government decides whether to deport them. The majority rejected the due process claim that they are entitled to a hearing on whether they would jump bail or posed a danger to society. In the chief justice's words: "Congress may make rules as to aliens that would be unacceptable if applied to citizens." Justice Souter, joined by Justices Stevens and Ginsburg, filed an opinion in part concurring and dissenting that endorsed the substantive and procedural due process claim. In a separate opinion, Justice Breyer concurred and dissented in part.

| *Overton v. Bazzetta,* 123 S.Ct. 2162 (2003) | 9:0 | The Court held that prison regulations limiting inmate visitations do not violate freedom of |

association or substantive due process and are rationally related to penelogical interests.

| *Sell v. United States,* 123 S.Ct. 2174 (2003) | 6:3 | Writing for the Court, Justice Breyer held that antipsychotic drugs may be administered to a |

mentally-ill defendant without his or her consent if the forced medication (1) is necessary to an "important governmental interest," (2) significantly furthers that interest, (3) is medically necessary without a less intrusive alternative, and (4) is medically appropriate.

5

FREEDOM OF EXPRESSION
AND ASSOCIATION

I n *Watchtower Bible & Tract Society of New York, Inc. v. Village of Stratton* (excerpted below) the Court struck down an ordinance requiring a permit for solicitations on private property. The Jehovah's Witnesses challenged the ordinance as a violation of the First Amendment's protection for freedom of speech and religion, and the Court agreed, with only Chief Justice Rehnquist dissenting.

Watchtower Bible & Tract Society of New York, Inc. v. Village of Stratton
536 U.S. 150, 122 S.Ct. 2080 (2002)

The Village of Stratton, Ohio, enacted ordinances prohibiting "canvassers" and others from "going in and upon" private residential property for the purpose of promoting any cause without obtaining a Solicitation Permit from the mayor's office. Once the canvasser had obtained the permit, he or she was authorized to go on the premises listed on the registration form but had to carry the permit and show it if requested to do so by a police officer or resident. The constitutionality of the ordinance was challenged as a violation of the First Amendment's guarantees of freedom of speech and press and of the free exercise of religion by the Watchtower Bible and Tract Society of New York, which coordinates the preaching activities of Jehovah's Witnesses. A federal district court upheld most of the provisions as valid, content-neutral regulations, and the Court of Appeals for the Sixth Circuit affirmed. The latter decision was appealed to the Supreme Court, which granted review.

The lower court's decision was reversed by an eight-to-one vote, and Justice Stevens delivered the opinion of the Court. Justices Breyer and Scalia filed concurring opinions, and Chief Justice Rehnquist issued a dissenting opinion.

□ *Justice STEVENS delivers the opinion of the Court.*

For over 50 years, the Court has invalidated restrictions on door-to-door canvassing and pamphleteering. It is more than historical accident that most of these cases involved First Amendment challenges brought by Jehovah's Witnesses, because door-to-door canvassing is mandated by their religion. As we noted in *Murdock v. Pennsylvania*, 319 U.S. 105 (1943), the Jehovah's Witnesses "claim to follow the example of Paul, teaching 'publicly, and from house to house.' Acts 20:20. They take literally the mandate of the Scriptures, 'Go ye into all the world, and preach the gospel to every creature.' Mark 16:15. In doing so they believe that they are obeying a commandment of God." Moreover, because they lack significant financial resources, the ability of the Witnesses to proselytize is seriously diminished by regulations that burden their efforts to canvass door-to-door.

Although our past cases involving Jehovah's Witnesses, most of which were decided shortly before and during World War II, do not directly control the question we confront today, they provide both a historical and analytical backdrop for consideration of petitioners' First Amendment claim that the breadth of the Village's ordinance offends the First Amendment. Those cases involved petty offenses that raised constitutional questions of the most serious magnitude—questions that implicated the free exercise of religion, the freedom of speech, and the freedom of the press. From these decisions, several themes emerge that guide our consideration of the ordinance at issue here.

First, the cases emphasize the value of the speech involved. For example, in *Murdock v. Pennsylvania*, the Court noted that "hand distribution of religious tracts is an age-old form of missionary evangelism—as old as the history of printing presses. It has been a potent force in various religious movements down through the years. . . . This form of religious activity occupies the same high estate under the First Amendment as do worship in the churches and preaching from the pulpits. It has the same claim to protection as the more orthodox and conventional exercises of religion. It also has the same claim as the others to the guarantees of freedom of speech and freedom of the press."

In addition, the cases discuss extensively the historical importance of door-to-door canvassing and pamphleteering as vehicles for the dissemination of ideas. In *Schneider v. State (Town of Irvington)*, 308 U.S. 147 (1939), the petitioner was a Jehovah's Witness who had been convicted of canvassing without a permit based on evidence that she had gone from house to house offering to leave books or booklets. Writing for the Court, Justice ROBERTS stated that "pamphlets have proved most effective instruments in the dissemination of opinion. And perhaps the most effective way of bringing them to the notice of individuals is their distribution at the homes of the people. On this method of communication the ordinance imposes censorship, abuse of which engendered the struggle in England which eventuated in the establishment of the doctrine of the freedom of the press embodied in our Constitution. To require a censorship through license which makes impossible the free and unhampered distribution of pamphlets strikes at the very heart of the constitutional guarantees."

Despite the emphasis on the important role that door-to-door canvassing and pamphleteering has played in our constitutional tradition of free and open discussion, these early cases also recognized the interests a town may have in some form of regulation, particularly when the solicitation of money is involved. In *Cantwell v. Connecticut*, 310 U.S. 296 (1940), the Court held that an ordinance requiring Jehovah's Witnesses to obtain a license before soliciting door to door was invalid because the issuance of the license depended on the exercise of discretion by a city official. . . .

The Village argues that three interests are served by its ordinance: the prevention of fraud, the prevention of crime, and the protection of residents' privacy. We have no difficulty concluding, in light of our precedent, that these are important interests that the Village may seek to safeguard through some form of regulation of solicitation activity. We must also look, however, to the amount of speech covered by the ordinance and whether there is an appropriate balance between the affected speech and the governmental interests that the ordinance purports to serve.

The text of the Village's ordinance prohibits "canvassers" from going on private property for the purpose of explaining or promoting any "cause," unless they receive a permit and the residents visited have not opted for a "no solicitation" sign. Had this provision been construed to apply only to commercial activities and the solicitation of funds, arguably the ordinance would have been tailored to the Village's interest in protecting the privacy of its residents and preventing fraud. Yet, even though the Village has explained that the ordinance was adopted to serve those interests, it has never contended that it should be so narrowly interpreted. To the contrary, the Village's administration of its ordinance unquestionably demonstrates that the provisions apply to a significant number of noncommercial "canvassers" promoting a wide variety of "causes." Indeed, on the "No Solicitation Forms" provided to the residents, the canvassers include "Camp Fire Girls," "Jehovah's Witnesses," "Political Candidates," "Trick or Treaters during Halloween Season," and "Persons Affiliated with Stratton Church." The ordinance unquestionably applies, not only to religious causes, but to political activity as well. It would seem to extend to "residents casually soliciting the votes of neighbors," or ringing doorbells to enlist support for employing a more efficient garbage collector.

The mere fact that the ordinance covers so much speech raises constitutional concerns. It is offensive—not only to the values protected by the First Amendment, but to the very notion of a free society—that in the context of everyday public discourse a citizen must first inform the government of her desire to speak to her neighbors and then obtain a permit to do so. Even if the issuance of permits by the mayor's office is a ministerial task that is performed promptly and at no cost to the applicant, a law requiring a permit to engage in such speech constitutes a dramatic departure from our national heritage and constitutional tradition. . . .

The breadth and unprecedented nature of this regulation does not alone render the ordinance invalid. Also central to our conclusion that the ordinance does not pass First Amendment scrutiny is that it is not tailored to the Village's stated interests. Even if the interest in preventing fraud could adequately support the ordinance insofar as it applies to commercial transactions and the solicitation of funds, that interest provides no support for its application to petitioners, to political campaigns, or to enlisting support for unpopular causes. The Village, however, argues that the ordinance is nonetheless valid because it serves the two additional interests of protecting the privacy of the resident and the prevention of crime.

With respect to the former, it seems clear that Section 107 of the ordinance, which provides for the posting of "No Solicitation" signs and which is not challenged in this case, coupled with the resident's unquestioned right to refuse to engage in conversation with unwelcome visitors, provides ample protection for the unwilling listener. The annoyance caused by an uninvited knock on the front door is the same whether or not the visitor is armed with a permit.

With respect to the latter, it seems unlikely that the absence of a permit would preclude criminals from knocking on doors and engaging in conversations not covered by the ordinance. They might, for example, ask for directions or permission to use the telephone, or pose as surveyors or census takers. Or they might register under a false name with impunity because the ordinance contains no provision for verifying an applicant's identity or organizational credentials. Moreover, the Village did not assert an interest in crime prevention below, and there is an absence of any evidence of a special crime problem related to door-to-door solicitation in the record before us.

The rhetoric used in the World War II–era opinions that repeatedly saved petitioners' coreligionists from petty prosecutions reflected the Court's evaluation of the First Amendment freedoms that are implicated in this case. The value judgment that then motivated a united democratic people fighting to defend those very freedoms from totalitarian attack is unchanged. It motivates our decision today.

☐ *Justice SCALIA, with whom Justice THOMAS joins, concurring in the judgment.*

I concur in the judgment, for many but not all of the reasons set forth in the opinion for the Court. I do not agree, for example, that one of the causes of the invalidity of Stratton's ordinance is that some people have a religious objection to applying for a permit, and others (posited by the Court) "have such firm convictions about their constitutional right to engage in uninhibited debate in the context of door-to-door advocacy, that they would prefer silence to speech licensed by a petty official."

If a licensing requirement is otherwise lawful, it is in my view not invalidated by the fact that some people will choose, for religious reasons, to forgo speech rather than observe it. That would convert an invalid free-exercise claim, see *Employment Div., Dept. of Human Resources of Ore. v. Smith*, 494 U.S. 872 (1990), into a valid free-speech claim—and a more destructive one at that. Whereas the free-exercise claim, if acknowledged, would merely exempt Jehovah's Witnesses from the licensing requirement, the free-speech claim exempts everybody, thanks to Jehovah's Witnesses.

As for the Court's fairy-tale category of "patriotic citizens," who would rather be silenced than licensed in a manner that the Constitution (but for their "patriotic" objection) would permit: If our free-speech jurisprudence is to be determined by the predicted behavior of such crackpots, we are in a sorry state indeed.

☐ *CHIEF JUSTICE REHNQUIST, dissenting.*

Stratton is a village of 278 people located along the Ohio River where the borders of Ohio, West Virginia, and Pennsylvania converge. It is strung out along a multi-lane highway connecting it with the cities of East Liverpool to the north and Steubenville and Weirton, West Virginia, to the south. One may doubt how much legal help a village of this size has available in drafting an ordinance such as the present one, but even if it had availed itself of a battery of constitutional lawyers, they would have been of little use in the town's effort. For the Court today ignores the cases on which those lawyers would have relied, and comes up with newly fashioned doctrine. This doctrine contravenes well-established precedent, renders local governments largely impotent to address the very real safety threat that canvassers pose, and may actually result in less of the door-to-door communication it seeks to protect.

More than half a century ago we recognized that canvassers, "whether selling pots or distributing leaflets, may lessen the peaceful enjoyment of a home," and that "burglars frequently pose as canvassers, either in order that they may have a pretense to discover whether a house is empty and hence ripe for burglary, or for the purpose of spying out the premises in order that they may return later." *Martin v. City of Struthers*, 319 U.S. 141 (1943). These problems continue to be associated with door-to-door canvassing, as are even graver ones.

A recent double murder in Hanover, New Hampshire, a town of approximately 7,500 that would appear tranquil to most Americans but would probably seem like a bustling town of Dartmouth College students to Stratton residents, illustrates these dangers. Two teenagers murdered a married couple of Dartmouth College professors, Half and Susanne Zantop, in the Zantop's home. Investigators have concluded, based on the confession of one of the teenagers, that the teenagers went door-to-door intent on stealing access numbers to bank debit cards and then killing their owners. Their modus operandi was to tell residents that they were conducting an environmental survey for school. They canvassed a few homes where no one answered. At another, the resident did not allow them in to conduct the "survey." They were allowed into the Zantop home. After conducting the phony environmental survey, they stabbed the Zantops to death.

In order to reduce these very grave risks associated with canvassing, the 278 "'little people'" of Stratton, who, unlike petitioners, do not have a team of attorneys at their ready disposal, enacted the ordinance at issue here. The residents did not prohibit door-to-door communication, they simply required that canvassers obtain a permit before going door-to-door. And the village does not have the discretion to reject an applicant who completes the application.

The town had little reason to suspect that the negligible burden of having to obtain a permit runs afoul of the First Amendment. For over 60 years, we have categorically stated that a permit requirement for door-to-door canvassers, which gives no discretion to the issuing authority, is constitutional. The District Court and Court of Appeals, relying on our cases, upheld the ordinance. . . .

The double murder in Hanover described above is but one tragic example of the crime threat posed by door-to-door canvassing. . . .

What is more, the Court soon forgets both the privacy and crime interests. It finds the ordinance too broad because it applies to a "significant number of noncommercial 'canvassers.'" But noncommercial canvassers, for example, those purporting to conduct environmental surveys for school, violate no trespassing signs and engage in burglaries and violent crimes just as easily as commercial canvassers can. . . .

The next question is whether the ordinance serves the important interests of protecting privacy and preventing fraud and crime. With respect to the interest in protecting privacy, the Court concludes that "[t]he annoyance caused by an uninvited knock on the front door is the same whether or not the visitor is armed with a permit." True, but that misses the key point: the permit requirement results in fewer uninvited knocks. Those who have complied with the permit requirement are less likely to visit residences with no trespassing signs, as it is much easier for the authorities to track them down.

The Court also fails to grasp how the permit requirement serves Stratton's interest in preventing crime. We have approved of permit requirements for those engaging in protected First Amendment activity because of a common-sense recognition that their existence both deters and helps detect wrongdoing. . . .

A discretionless permit requirement for canvassers does not violate the First Amendment. Today, the Court elevates its concern with what is, at most, a negligible burden on door-to-door communication above this established proposition. Ironically, however, today's decision may result in less of the door-to-door communication that the Court extols. As the Court recognizes, any homeowner may place a "No Solicitation" sign on his or her property, and it is a crime to violate that sign. In light of today's decision depriving Stratton residents of the degree of accountability and safety that the permit requirement provides, more and more residents may decide to place these signs in their yards and cut off door-to-door communication altogether.

B | *Obscenity, Pornography, and Offensive Speech*

In its 2001–2002 term the Court continued to grapple with how to decide First Amendment challenges to the exclusionary zoning of adult entertainment businesses. As in prior cases, the issue of justifying such zoning restrictions based on the "secondary effects" of adult-oriented businesses continued to fragment the justices. In *City of Los Angeles v. Alameda Books, Inc.* (2002) (excerpted below), only a plurality joined Justice O'Connor's opinion for the Court, upholding an ordinance prohibiting more than one adult establishment from operating at the same location. Justices Scalia and Kennedy filed concurring opinions. Justice Souter filed a dissent, which Justices Stevens, Ginsburg, and Breyer joined.

In *Ashcroft v. Free Speech Coalition* (2002) (excerpted below) the Court struck down sections of the Child Pornography Prevention Act of 1996 that made it a crime to create, distribute, or possess "virtual child pornography" generated by computer images of young adults or simulated images, rather than of actual children. In doing so, the justices split six-and-a-half to two-and-a-half with Chief Justice Rehnquist and Justice

Scalia dissenting, and Justice O'Connor filing a separate opinion in part concurring and dissenting.

City of Los Angeles v. Alameda Books, Inc.
535 U.S. 425, 122 S.Ct. 1728 (2002)

Los Angeles enacted an ordinance prohibiting "the establishment or maintenance of more than one adult entertainment business in the same building, structure or portion thereof." The owners of two adult establishments, each operating a bookstore and a video arcade in the same building, were found in violation of the ordinance and challenged its constitutionality. A federal district court held that the prohibition was a content-based regulation of speech and failed to survive strict scrutiny. The Court of Appeals for the Ninth Circuit affirmed, though on different grounds. The city appealed that decision and the Supreme Court granted review.

The appellate court was reversed in a five-to-four decision. Justice O'Connor delivered the opinion for the Court. Justices Scalia and Kennedy filed concurring opinions. Justice Souter filed a dissenting opinion, which Justices Stevens, Ginsburg, and Breyer joined.

□ *Justice O'CONNOR announced the judgment of the Court and delivered an opinion, in which THE CHIEF JUSTICE, Justice SCALIA, and Justice THOMAS join.*

In 1977, the city of Los Angeles conducted a comprehensive study of adult establishments and concluded that concentrations of adult businesses are associated with higher rates of prostitution, robbery, assaults, and thefts in surrounding communities. Accordingly, the city enacted an ordinance prohibiting the establishment, substantial enlargement, or transfer of ownership of an adult arcade, bookstore, cabaret, motel, theater, or massage parlor or a place for sexual encounters within 1,000 feet of another such enterprise or within 500 feet of any religious institution, school, or public park.

There is evidence that the intent of the city council when enacting this prohibition was not only to disperse distinct adult establishments housed in separate buildings, but also to disperse distinct adult businesses operated under common ownership and housed in a single structure. The ordinance the city enacted, however, directed that "[t]he distance between any two adult entertainment businesses shall be measured in a straight line . . . from the closest exterior structural wall of each business." Subsequent to enactment, the city realized that this method of calculating distances created a loophole permitting the concentration of multiple adult enterprises in a single structure.

Concerned that allowing an adult-oriented department store to replace a strip of adult establishments could defeat the goal of the original ordinance, the city council amended Section 12.70(C) by adding a prohibition on "the establishment or maintenance of more than one adult entertainment business in the same building, structure or portion thereof." . . .

In *Renton v. Playtime Theatres, Inc.* [475 U.S. 41 (1986)], this Court considered the validity of a municipal ordinance that prohibited any adult movie theater from locating within 1,000 feet of any residential zone, family dwelling, church, park, or school. Our analysis of the ordinance proceeded in three steps. First, we found that the ordinance did not ban adult theaters altogether, but merely required that they be distanced from certain sensitive locations. The ordinance was properly analyzed, therefore, as a time, place, and manner regulation. We next considered whether the ordinance was content neutral or content based. If the regulation were content based, it would be considered presumptively invalid and subject to strict scrutiny. We held, however, that the Renton ordinance was aimed not at the content of the films shown at adult theaters, but rather at the secondary effects of such theaters on the surrounding community, namely at crime rates, property values, and the quality of the city's neighborhoods. Therefore, the ordinance was deemed content neutral. Finally, given this finding, we stated that the ordinance would be upheld so long as the city of Renton showed that its ordinance was designed to serve a substantial government interest and that reasonable alternative avenues of communication remained available. We concluded that Renton had met this burden, and we upheld its ordinance.

The Court of Appeals applied the same analysis to evaluate the Los Angeles ordinance challenged in this case. First, the Court of Appeals found that the Los Angeles ordinance was not a complete ban on adult entertainment establishments, but rather a sort of adult zoning regulation, which *Renton* considered a time, place, and manner regulation. The Court of Appeals turned to the second step of the *Renton* analysis, but did not draw any conclusions about whether the Los Angeles ordinance was content based. It explained that, even if the Los Angeles ordinance were content neutral, the city had failed to demonstrate, as required by the third step of the *Renton* analysis, that its prohibition on multiple-use adult establishments was designed to serve its substantial interest in reducing crime. The Court of Appeals noted that the primary evidence relied upon by Los Angeles to demonstrate a link between combination adult businesses and harmful secondary effects was the 1977 study conducted by the city's planning department. The Court of Appeals found, however, that the city could not rely on that study because it did not "suppor[t] a reasonable belief that [the] combination [of] businesses . . . produced harmful secondary effects of the type asserted."

The central component of the 1977 study is a report on city crime patterns provided by the Los Angeles Police Department. That report indicated that, during the period from 1965 to 1975, certain crime rates grew much faster in Hollywood, which had the largest concentration of adult establishments in the city, than in the city of Los Angeles as a whole. For example, robberies increased 3 times faster and prostitution 15 times faster in Hollywood than citywide. . . .

The Court of Appeals found that the 1977 study did not reasonably support the inference that a concentration of adult operations within a single adult establishment produced greater levels of criminal activity because the study focused on the effect that a concentration of establishments—not a concentration of operations within a single establishment—had on crime rates. The Court of Appeals pointed out that the study treated combination adult bookstore/arcades as single establishments and did not study the effect of any separate-standing adult bookstore or arcade.

The Court of Appeals misunderstood the implications of the 1977 study. While the study reveals that areas with high concentrations of adult establishments are associated with high crime rates, areas with high concentrations of adult establishments are also areas with high concentrations of adult operations, albeit each in separate establishments. It was therefore consistent with the findings of the 1977 study, and thus reasonable, for Los Angeles to suppose that a concentration of adult establishments is correlated with high crime rates because a concentration of operations in one locale draws, for example, a greater concentration of adult consumers to the neighborhood, and a high density of such consumers either attracts or generates criminal activity. The assumption behind this theory is that having a number of adult operations in one single adult establishment draws the same dense foot traffic as having a number of distinct adult establishments in close proximity, much as minimalls and department stores similarly attract the crowds of consumers. Under this view, it is rational for the city to infer that reducing the concentration of adult operations in a neighborhood, whether within separate establishments or in one large establishment, will reduce crime rates. . . .

The error that the Court of Appeals made is that it required the city to prove that its theory about a concentration of adult operations attracting crowds of customers, much like a minimall or department store does, is a necessary consequence of the 1977 study. For example, the Court of Appeals refused to allow the city to draw the inference that "the expansion of an adult bookstore to include an adult arcade would increase" business activity and "produce the harmful secondary effects identified in the Study." . . . The Court of Appeals simply replaced the city's theory—that having many different operations in close proximity attracts crowds—with its own—that the size of an operation attracts crowds. If the Court of Appeals' theory is correct, then inventory limits make more sense. If the city's theory is correct, then a prohibition on the combination of businesses makes more sense. Both theories are consistent with the data in the 1977 study. The Court of Appeals' analysis, however, implicitly requires the city to prove that its theory is the only one that can plausibly explain the data because only in this manner can the city refute the Court of Appeals' logic. . . .

In *Renton*, we specifically refused to set such a high bar for municipalities that want to address merely the secondary effects of protected speech. We held that a municipality may rely on any evidence that is "reasonably believed to be relevant" for demonstrating a connection between speech and a substantial, independent government interest. . . .

Accordingly, we reverse the Court of Appeals' judgment granting summary judgment to respondents and remand the case for further proceedings. It is so ordered.

□ *Justice SCALIA, concurring.*

I join the plurality opinion because I think it represents a correct application of our jurisprudence concerning regulation of the "secondary effects" of pornographic speech. As I have said elsewhere, however, in a case such as this our First Amendment traditions make "secondary effects" analysis quite unnecessary. The Constitution does not prevent those communities that wish to do so from regulating, or indeed entirely suppressing, the business of pandering sex.

☐ *Justice SOUTER, with whom Justice STEVENS and Justice GINSBURG join, and with whom Justice BREYER joins, dissenting.*

In 1977, the city of Los Angeles studied sections of the city with high and low concentrations of adult business establishments catering to the market for the erotic. The city found no certain correlation between the location of those establishments and depressed property values, but it did find some correlation between areas of higher concentrations of such business and higher crime rates. On that basis, Los Angeles followed the examples of other cities in adopting a zoning ordinance requiring dispersion of adult establishments. . . .

The city subsequently amended its ordinance to forbid clusters of such businesses at one address, as in a mall. The city has, in turn, taken a third step to apply this amendment to prohibit even a single proprietor from doing business in a traditional way that combines an adult bookstore, selling books, magazines, and videos, with an adult arcade, consisting of open viewing booths, where potential purchasers of videos can view them for a fee.

From a policy of dispersing adult establishments, the city has thus moved to a policy of dividing them in two. The justification claimed for this application of the new policy remains, however, the 1977 survey, as supplemented by the authority of one decided case on regulating adult arcades in another State. The case authority is not on point and the 1977 survey provides no support for the breakup policy. Its evidentiary insufficiency bears emphasis and is the principal reason that I respectfully dissent from the Court's judgment today.

This ordinance stands or falls on the results of what our cases speak of as intermediate scrutiny, generally contrasted with the demanding standard applied under the First Amendment to a content-based regulation of expression. The variants of middle-tier tests cover a grab-bag of restrictive statutes, with a corresponding variety of justifications. While spoken of as content neutral, these regulations are not uniformly distinct from the content-based regulations calling for scrutiny that is strict, and zoning of businesses based on their sales of expressive adult material receives mid-level scrutiny, even though it raises a risk of content-based restriction. It is worth being clear, then, on how close to a content basis adult business zoning can get, and why the application of a middle-tier standard to zoning regulation of adult bookstores calls for particular care.

Because content-based regulation applies to expression by very reason of what is said, it carries a high risk that expressive limits are imposed for the sake of suppressing a message that is disagreeable to listeners or readers, or the government. A restriction based on content survives only on a showing of necessity to serve a legitimate and compelling governmental interest, combined with least-restrictive narrow tailoring to serve it; since merely protecting listeners from offense at the message is not a legitimate interest of the government, see *Cohen v. California*, 403 U.S. 15 (1971), strict scrutiny leaves few survivors.

The comparatively softer intermediate scrutiny is reserved for regulations justified by something other than content of the message, such as a straightforward restriction going only to the time, place, or manner of speech or other expression. It is easy to see why review of such a regulation may be relatively relaxed. No one has to disagree with any message to find something wrong with a loudspeaker at three in the morning; the sentiment may not provoke, but being blasted out of a sound sleep does. In such a case, we ask simply whether the regulation is "narrowly tailored to serve a significant governmental interest, and . . . leave[s] open ample alternative channels for communication of the information." *Clark v. Community for Creative Non-Violence*, 468 U.S. 288 (1984). A middle-tier standard is also applied to limits on expression through action that is otherwise subject to regulation for non-expressive purposes, the best known example being the prohibition on destroying draft cards as an act of protest, *United States v. O'Brien*, 391 U.S. 367 (1968); here a regulation passes muster "if it furthers an important or substantial governmental interest . . . unrelated to the suppression of free expression" by a restriction "no greater than is essential to the furtherance of that interest." As mentioned already, yet another middle-tier variety is zoning restriction as a means of responding to the "secondary effects" of adult businesses, principally crime and declining property values in the neighborhood. *Renton v. Playtime Theatres, Inc.*, 475 U.S. 41 (1986).

Although this type of land-use restriction has even been called a variety of time, place, or manner regulation, equating a secondary-effects zoning regulation with a mere regulation of time, place, or manner jumps over an important difference between them. A restriction on loudspeakers has no obvious relationship to the substance of what is broadcast, while a zoning regulation of businesses in adult expression just as obviously does. And while it may be true that an adult business is burdened only because of its secondary effects, it is clearly burdened only if its expressive products have adult content. Thus, the Court has recognized that this kind of regulation, though called content neutral, occupies a kind of limbo between full-blown, content-based restrictions and regulations that apply without any reference to the substance of what is said.

It would in fact make sense to give this kind of zoning regulation a First Amendment label of its own, and if we called it content correlated, we would not only describe it for what it is, but keep alert to a risk of content-based regulation that it poses. The risk lies in the fact that when a law applies selectively only to speech of particular content, the more precisely the content is identified, the greater is the opportunity for government censorship. Adult speech refers not merely to sexually explicit content, but to speech reflecting a favorable view of being explicit about sex and a favorable view of the practices it depicts; a restriction on adult content is thus also a restriction turning on a particular viewpoint, of which the government may disapprove.

This risk of viewpoint discrimination is subject to a relatively simple safeguard, however. If combating secondary effects of property devaluation and crime is truly the reason for the regulation, it is possible to show by empirical evidence that the effects exist, that they are caused by the expressive activity subject to the zoning, and that the zoning can be expected either to ameliorate them or to enhance the capacity of the government to combat them (say, by concentrating them in one area), without suppressing the expressive activity itself. This capacity of zoning regulation to address the practical problems without eliminating the speech is, after all, the only possible excuse for speaking of secondary-effects zoning as akin to time, place, or manner regulations. . . .

The lesson is that the lesser scrutiny applied to content-correlated zoning restrictions is no excuse for a government's failure to provide a factual demonstration for claims it makes about secondary effects; on the contrary, this is what demands the demonstration. In this case, however, the government has not shown that bookstores containing viewing booths, isolated from other adult establishments, increase crime or produce other negative secondary effects in surrounding neighborhoods, and we are thus left without substantial justification for viewing the city's First Amendment restriction as content correlated but not simply content based. By the same token, the city has failed to show any causal relationship between the breakup policy and elimination or regulation of secondary effects. . . .

If we take the city's breakup policy at its face, enforcing it will mean that in every case two establishments will operate instead of the traditional one. Since the city presumably does not wish merely to multiply adult establishments, it makes sense to ask what offsetting gain the city may obtain from its new breakup policy. The answer may lie in the fact that two establishments in place of one will entail two business overheads in place of one: two monthly rents, two electricity bills, two payrolls. Every month business will be more expensive than it used to be, perhaps even twice as much. That sounds like a good strategy for driving out expressive adult businesses. It sounds, in other words, like a policy of content-based regulation.

I respectfully dissent.

Ashcroft v. Free Speech Coalition
535 U.S. 234, 122 S.CT. 1389 (2002)

In 1996 Congress enacted the Child Pornography Prevention Act (CPPA), making it a crime to create, distribute or possess "virtual child pornography" generated by computer images of young adults rather than actual children. The constitutionality of the law was challenged by the Free Speech Coalition—a coalition of artists, photographers, and adult entertainment businesses. A federal district court upheld its provisions but the Court of Appeals for the Ninth Circuit reversed and found that the CPPA violated the First Amendment. Attorney General John D. Ashcroft appealed that decision and the Supreme Court granted review.

The decision of the appellate court was affirmed in a vote of six and a half to two and a half. Justice Kennedy delivered the opinion for the Court. Justice Thomas filed a concurring opinion, indicating that a more narrowly drawn statute might pass constitutional muster. Chief Justice Rehnquist filed a dissenting opinion, which Justice Scalia joined. Justice O'Connor filed a separate opinion, in part concurring and in part dissenting.

☐ *Justice KENNEDY delivered the opinion of the Court.*

We consider in this case whether the Child Pornography Prevention Act of 1996 (CPPA) abridges the freedom of speech. . . . By prohibiting child pornography that does not depict an actual child, the statute goes beyond *New York v. Ferber*, 458 U.S. 747 (1982), which distinguished child pornography from other sexually explicit speech because of the State's interest in protecting the children exploited by the production process. As a general rule, pornography can be banned only if obscene, but under *Ferber*, pornography showing minors can be proscribed whether or not the images are obscene under the definition set forth in *Miller v. California*, 413 U.S. 15 (1973). . . .

The CPPA, however, is not directed at speech that is obscene; Congress has proscribed those materials through a separate statute. Like the law in *Ferber*, the CPPA seeks to reach beyond obscenity, and it makes no attempt to conform to the *Miller* standard. For instance, the statute would reach visual depictions, such as movies, even if they have redeeming social value.

The principal question to be resolved, then, is whether the CPPA is constitutional where it proscribes a significant universe of speech that is neither obscene under *Miller* nor child pornography under *Ferber*.

Before 1996, Congress defined child pornography as the type of depictions at issue in *Ferber*, images made using actual minors. The CPPA retains that prohibition at 18 U.S.C. Sec. 2256(8)(A) and adds three other prohibited categories of speech, of which the first, Sec. 2256(8)(B), and the third, Sec. 2256(8)(D), are at issue in this case. Section 2256(8)(B) prohibits "any visual depiction, including any photograph, film, video, picture, or computer or computer-generated image or picture" that "is, or appears to be, of a minor engaging in sexually explicit conduct." The prohibition on "any visual depiction" does not depend at all on how the image is produced. The section captures a range of depictions, sometimes called "virtual child pornography," which include computer-generated images, as well as images produced by more traditional means. For instance, the literal terms of the statute embrace a Renaissance painting depicting a scene from classical mythology, a "picture" that "appears to be of a minor engaging in sexually explicit conduct." The statute also prohibits Hollywood movies, filmed without any child actors, if a jury believes an actor "appears to be" a minor engaging in "actual or simulated . . . sexual intercourse."

These images do not involve, let alone harm, any children in the production process; but Congress decided the materials threaten children in other, less direct, ways. Pedophiles might use the materials to encourage children to participate in sexual activity. Furthermore, pedophiles might "whet their own sexual appetites" with the pornographic images, "thereby increasing the creation and distribution of child pornography and the sexual abuse and exploitation of actual children." Under these rationales, harm flows from the content of the images, not from the means of their production. In addition, Congress identified another problem created by computer-generated images: Their existence can make it harder to prosecute pornographers who do use real minors. As imaging technology improves, Congress found, it becomes more difficult to prove that a particular picture was produced using actual children.

Section 2256(8)(C) prohibits a more common and lower tech means of creating virtual images, known as computer morphing. Rather than creating original images, pornographers can alter innocent pictures of real children so that the children appear to be engaged in sexual activity. Although morphed images may fall within the definition of virtual child pornography, they implicate the interests of real children and are in that sense closer to the images in *Ferber*. Respondents do not challenge this provision, and we do not consider it.

Respondents do challenge Sec. 2256(8)(D). Like the text of the "appears to be" provision, the sweep of this provision is quite broad. Section 2256(8)(D) defines child pornography to include any sexually explicit image that was "advertised, promoted, presented, described, or distributed in such a manner that conveys the impression" it depicts "a minor engaging in sexually explicit conduct." The statute is not so limited in its reach, however, as it punishes even those possessors who took no part in pandering. . . .

The CPPA's penalties are indeed severe. A first offender may be imprisoned for 15 years. A repeat offender faces a prison sentence of not less than 5 years and not more than 30 years in prison. While even minor punishments can chill protected speech, this case provides a textbook example of why we permit facial challenges to statutes that burden expression. With these severe penalties in force, few legitimate movie producers or book publishers, or few other speakers in any capacity, would risk distributing images in or near the uncertain reach of this law. . . .

Under *Miller v. California* the Government must prove that the work, taken as a whole, appeals to the prurient interest, is patently offensive in light of community standards, and lacks serious literary, artistic, political, or scientific value. The CPPA, however, extends to images that appear to depict a minor engaging in sexually explicit activity without regard to the *Miller* requirements. The materials need not appeal to the prurient interest. Any depiction of sexually explicit activity, no matter how it is presented, is proscribed. The CPPA applies to a picture in a psychology manual, as well as a movie depicting the horrors of sexual abuse. It is not necessary, moreover, that the image be patently offensive. Pictures of what appear to be 17-year-olds engaging in sexually explicit activity do not in every case contravene community standards.

The CPPA prohibits speech despite its serious literary, artistic, political, or scientific value. The statute proscribes the visual depiction of an idea—that of teenagers engaging in sexual activity—that is a fact of modern society and has been a theme in art and literature throughout the ages. Under the CPPA, images are prohibited so long as the persons appear to be under 18 years of age. This is higher than the legal age for marriage in many States, as well as the age at which persons may consent to sexual relations.

Both themes—teenage sexual activity and the sexual abuse of children—have inspired countless literary works. William Shakespeare created the most famous pair of teenage lovers, one of whom is just 13 years of age. See *Romeo and Juliet*, act I, sc. 2, l. 9 ("She hath not seen the change of fourteen years"). In the drama, Shakespeare portrays the relationship as something splendid and innocent, but not juvenile. The work has inspired no less than 40 motion pictures, some of which suggest that the teenagers consummated their relationship. Shakespeare may not have written sexually explicit scenes for the Elizabethan audience, but were modern directors to adopt a less conventional approach, that fact alone would not compel the conclusion that the work was obscene. . . .

In contrast to the speech in *Ferber*, speech that itself is the record of sexual abuse, the CPPA prohibits speech that records no crime and creates no victims by its production. Virtual child pornography is not "intrinsically related" to the sexual abuse of children, as were the materials in *Ferber*. While the Government asserts that the images can lead to actual instances of child abuse, the causal link is contingent and indirect. The harm does not necessarily follow from the speech, but depends upon some unquantified potential for subsequent criminal acts.

The Government says these indirect harms are sufficient because, as *Ferber* acknowledged, child pornography rarely can be valuable speech. This argument, however, suffers from two flaws. First, *Ferber's* judgment about child pornography was based upon how it was made, not on what it communicated. The case reaffirmed that where the speech is neither obscene nor the product of sexual abuse, it does not fall outside the protection of the First Amendment.

The second flaw in the Government's position is that *Ferber* did not hold that child pornography is by definition without value. On the contrary, the Court recognized some works in this category might have significant value, but relied on virtual images—the very images prohibited by the CPPA—as an alternative and permissible means of expression: "[I]f it were necessary for literary or artistic value, a person over the statutory age who perhaps looked younger could be utilized. Simulation outside of the prohibition of the statute could provide another alternative." *Ferber*, then, not only referred to the distinction between actual and virtual child pornography, it relied on it as a reason supporting its holding. *Ferber* provides no support for a statute that eliminates the distinction and makes the alternative mode criminal as well.

The CPPA, for reasons we have explored, is inconsistent with *Miller* and finds no support in *Ferber*. The Government seeks to justify its prohibitions in other ways. It argues that the CPPA is necessary because pedophiles may use virtual child pornography to seduce children. There are many things innocent in themselves, however, such as cartoons, video games, and candy, that might be used for immoral purposes, yet we would not expect those to be prohibited because they can be misused. The Government, of course, may punish adults who provide unsuitable materials to children, see *Ginsberg v. New York*, 390 U.S. 629 (1968), and it may enforce criminal penalties for unlawful solicitation. The precedents establish, however, that speech within the rights of adults to hear may not be silenced completely in an attempt to shield children from it. *Butler v. Michigan*, 352 U.S. 380 (1957).

Here, the Government wants to keep speech from children not to protect them from its content but to protect them from those who would commit other crimes. The principle, however, remains the same: The Government cannot ban speech fit for adults simply because it may fall into the hands of children. The evil in question depends upon the actor's unlawful conduct, conduct defined as criminal quite apart from any link to the speech in question. This establishes that the speech ban is not narrowly drawn. The objective is to prohibit illegal conduct, but this restriction goes well beyond that interest by restricting the speech available to law-abiding adults. . . .

In sum, Sec. 2256(8)(B) covers materials beyond the categories recognized in *Ferber* and *Miller*, and the reasons the Government offers in support of limiting the freedom of speech have no justification in our precedents or in the law of the First Amendment. The provision abridges the freedom to engage in a substantial amount of lawful speech. For this reason, it is overbroad and unconstitutional.

Respondents challenge Sec. 2256(8)(D) as well. This provision bans depictions of sexually explicit conduct that are "advertised, promoted, presented, described, or distributed in such a manner that conveys the impression that the material is or contains a visual depiction of a minor engaging in sexually explicit conduct." The parties treat the section as nearly identical to the provision prohibiting materials that appear to be child pornography. In the Government's view, the difference between the two is that "the 'conveys the impression' provision requires the jury to assess the material at issue in light of the manner in which it is promoted."

We disagree with this view. The CPPA prohibits sexually explicit materials that "conve[y] the impression" they depict minors. While that phrase may sound

like the "appears to be" prohibition in Sec. 2256(8)(B), it requires little judgment about the content of the image. Under Sec. 2256(8)(D), the work must
be sexually explicit, but otherwise the content is irrelevant. Even if a film contains no sexually explicit scenes involving minors, it could be treated as child
pornography if the title and trailers convey the impression that the scenes
would be found in the movie. The determination turns on how the speech
is presented, not on what is depicted. While the legislative findings address at
length the problems posed by materials that look like child pornography, they
are silent on the evils posed by images simply pandered that way.

The Government does not offer a serious defense of this provision, and
the other arguments it makes in support of the CPPA do not bear on Sec.
2256(8)(D). . . .

The CPPA does more than prohibit pandering. It prohibits possession of
material described, or pandered, as child pornography by someone earlier in
the distribution chain. The provision prohibits a sexually explicit film containing no youthful actors, just because it is placed in a box suggesting a prohibited movie. Possession is a crime even when the possessor knows the movie
was mislabeled. The First Amendment requires a more precise restriction. For
this reason, Sec. 2256(8)(D) is substantially overbroad and in violation of the
First Amendment.

For the reasons we have set forth, the prohibitions of Sections 2256(8)(B)
and 2256(8)(D) are overbroad and unconstitutional. . . .

□ *CHIEF JUSTICE REHNQUIST, with whom Justice SCALIA joins in part,
dissenting.*

Congress has a compelling interest in ensuring the ability to enforce prohibitions of actual child pornography, and we should defer to its findings that rapidly
advancing technology soon will make it all but impossible to do so.

I also agree with Justice O'CONNOR that serious First Amendment
concerns would arise were the Government ever to prosecute someone for
simple distribution or possession of a film with literary or artistic value, such
as "Traffic" or "American Beauty." I write separately, however, because the
Child Pornography Prevention Act of 1996 (CPPA) need not be construed
to reach such materials. . . .

Other than computer generated images that are virtually indistinguishable from real children engaged in sexually explicit conduct, the CPPA can
be limited so as not to reach any material that was not already unprotected
before the CPPA. The CPPA's definition of "sexually explicit conduct" is
quite explicit in this regard. It makes clear that the statute only reaches "visual
depictions." . . . I think the definition reaches only the sort of "hard core of
child pornography" that we found without protection in *Ferber.* So construed,
the CPPA bans visual depictions of youthful looking adult actors engaged in
actual sexual activity; mere suggestions of sexual activity, such as youthful
looking adult actors squirming under a blanket, are more akin to written
descriptions than visual depictions, and thus fall outside the purview of the
statute. . . .

To the extent the CPPA prohibits possession or distribution of materials
that "convey the impression" of a child engaged in sexually explicit conduct,
that prohibition can and should be limited to reach "the sordid business of
pandering" which lies outside the bounds of First Amendment protection.
Ginsburg v. United States, 383 U.S. 463 (1966). . . .

For these reasons, I would construe the CPPA in a manner consistent with the First Amendment, reverse the Court of Appeals' judgment, and uphold the statute in its entirety.

☐ *Justice O'CONNOR, with whom THE CHIEF JUSTICE and Justice SCALIA join, concurring in the judgment and dissenting in part.*

Because the Government may already prohibit obscenity without violating the First Amendment, see *Miller v. California* (1973), what the Government asks this Court to rule is that it may also prohibit youthful-adult and virtual-adult pornography that is merely indecent without violating that Amendment. Although such pornography looks like the material at issue in *New York v. Ferber*, no children are harmed in the process of creating such pornography. Therefore, *Ferber* does not support the Government's ban on youthful-adult and virtual-child pornography. . . .

I also agree with the Court's decision to strike down the CPPA's ban on material presented in a manner that "conveys the impression" that it contains pornographic depictions of actual children ("actual-child pornography"). The Government fails to explain how this ban serves any compelling state interest. . . .

Finally, I agree with the Court that the CPPA's ban on youthful-adult pornography is overbroad. . . .

I disagree with the Court, however, that the CPPA's prohibition of virtual-child pornography is overbroad. . . . Although Section 2256(8)(B) does not distinguish between youthful-adult and virtual-child pornography, the CPPA elsewhere draws a line between these two classes of speech. The statute provides an affirmative defense for those who produce, distribute, or receive pornographic images of individuals who are actually adults, Sec. 2252A(c), but not for those with pornographic images that are wholly computer generated. This is not surprising given that the legislative findings enacted by Congress contain no mention of youthful-adult pornography. Those findings focus explicitly only on actual-child pornography and virtual-child pornography. Drawing a line around, and striking just, the CPPA's ban on youthful-child pornography not only is consistent with Congress' understanding of the categories of speech encompassed by Section 2256(8)(B), but also preserves the CPPA's prohibition of the material that Congress found most dangerous to children.

In sum, I would strike down the CPPA's ban on material that "conveys the impression" that it contains actual-child pornography, but uphold the ban on pornographic depictions that "appea[r] to be" of minors so long as it is not applied to youthful-adult pornography.

D | *Commercial Speech*

In *Thompson v. Western States Medical Center* (2002) (excerpted below), the Court struck down a section of a federal statute that forbid advertising for "compound drugs," thereby continuing its trend toward extending greater and greater First Amendment protection for commercial speech. However, the justices split five to four, with the chief justice and Justices

Breyer, Stevens, and Ginsburg dissenting from Justice O'Connor's opinion for the Court.

Thompson v. Western States Medical Center
535 U.S. 357, 122 S.Ct. 1497 (2002)

The pertinent facts are discussed by Justice O'Connor in her opinion for the Court. Justice Thomas filed a brief concurring opinion. Justice Breyer filed a dissent, which Chief Justice Rehnquist and Justices Stevens and Ginsburg joined.

□ *Justice O'CONNOR delivered the opinion of the Court.*

Section 503A of the Food and Drug Administration Modernization Act of 1997 (FDAMA) exempts "compounded drugs" from the Food and Drug Administration's standard drug approval requirements as long as the providers of those drugs abide by several restrictions, including that they refrain from advertising or promoting particular compounded drugs. Respondents, a group of licensed pharmacies that specialize in compounding drugs, sought to enjoin enforcement of the subsections of the Act dealing with advertising and solicitation, arguing that those provisions violate the First Amendment's free speech guarantee. The District Court agreed with respondents and granted their motion for summary judgment, holding that the provisions do not meet the test for acceptable government regulation of commercial speech set forth in *Central Hudson Gas & Elec. Corp. v. Public Serv. Comm'n of N.Y.*, 447 U.S. 557 (1980). . . . The Court of Appeals for the Ninth Circuit affirmed. . . . We conclude, as did the courts below, that Section 503A's provisions regarding advertisement and promotion amount to unconstitutional restrictions on commercial speech, and we therefore affirm. . . .

The Federal Food, Drug, and Cosmetic Act of 1938 (FDCA) regulates drug manufacturing, marketing, and distribution. For approximately the first 50 years after the enactment of the FDCA, the FDA generally left regulation of compounding to the States. Pharmacists continued to provide patients with compounded drugs without applying for FDA approval of those drugs. The FDA eventually became concerned, however, that some pharmacists were manufacturing and selling drugs under the guise of compounding, thereby avoiding the FDCA's new drug requirements. In 1992, in response to this concern, the FDA issued a Compliance Policy Guide, which announced that . . . it was FDA policy to permit pharmacists to compound drugs after receipt of a valid prescription for an individual patient or to compound drugs in "very limited quantities" before receipt of a valid prescription if they could document a history of receiving valid prescriptions "generated solely within an established professional practitioner–patient–pharmacy relationship" and if they maintained the prescription on file as required by state law. Compounding in such circumstances was permitted as long as the pharmacy's activities did not raise "the kinds of concerns normally associated with a manufacturer."

The Guide listed nine examples of activities that the FDA believed raised such concerns and that would therefore be considered by the agency in determining whether to bring an enforcement action. These activities included: "[s]oliciting business (e.g., promoting, advertising, or using salespersons) to compound specific drug products, product classes, or therapeutic classes of drug products"; "[c]ompounding, regularly, or in inordinate amounts, drug products that are commercially available . . . and that are essentially generic copies of commercially available, FDA–approved drug products"; using commercial scale manufacturing or testing equipment to compound drugs; offering compounded drugs at wholesale; and "[d]istributing inordinate amounts of compounded products out of state."

Congress turned portions of this policy into law when it enacted the FDAMA in 1997. The FDAMA, which amends the FDCA, exempts compounded drugs from the FDCA's "new drug" requirements and other requirements provided the drugs satisfy a number of restrictions. . . . [M]ost relevant for this litigation, the prescription must be "unsolicited," and the pharmacy, licensed pharmacist, or licensed physician compounding the drug may "not advertise or promote the compounding of any particular drug, class of drug, or type of drug." The pharmacy, licensed pharmacist, or licensed physician may, however, "advertise and promote the compounding service." . . .

Although commercial speech is protected by the First Amendment, not all regulation of such speech is unconstitutional. In *Central Hudson*, we articulated a test for determining whether a particular commercial speech regulation is constitutionally permissible. Under that test we ask as a threshold matter whether the commercial speech concerns unlawful activity or is misleading. If so, then the speech is not protected by the First Amendment. If the speech concerns lawful activity and is not misleading, however, we next ask "whether the asserted governmental interest is substantial." If it is, then we "determine whether the regulation directly advances the governmental interest asserted," and, finally, "whether it is not more extensive than is necessary to serve that interest." Each of these latter three inquiries must be answered in the affirmative for the regulation to be found constitutional. . . .

The Government does not attempt to defend the FDAMA's speech-related provisions under the first prong of the *Central Hudson* test; i.e., it does not argue that the prohibited advertisements would be about unlawful activity or would be misleading. Instead, the Government argues that the FDAMA satisfies the remaining three prongs of the *Central Hudson* test.

The Government asserts that three substantial interests underlie the FDAMA. The first is an interest in "preserv[ing] the effectiveness and integrity of the FDCA's new drug approval process and the protection of the public health that it provides." The second is an interest in "preserv[ing] the availability of compounded drugs for those individual patients who, for particularized medical reasons, cannot use commercially available products that have been approved by the FDA." Finally, the Government argues that "[a]chieving the proper balance between those two independently compelling but competing interests is itself a substantial governmental interest." . . .

The Government seems to believe that without advertising it would not be possible to market a drug on a large enough scale to make safety and efficacy testing economically feasible. The Government thus believes that conditioning an exemption from the FDA approval process on refraining from advertising is an ideal way to permit compounding and yet also guarantee that compounding is not conducted on such a scale as to undermine the

FDA approval process. Assuming it is true that drugs cannot be marketed on a large scale without advertising, the FDAMA's prohibition on advertising compounded drugs might indeed "directly advanc[e]" the Government's interests. Even assuming that it does, however, the Government has failed to demonstrate that the speech restrictions are "not more extensive than is necessary to serve [those] interest[s]." In previous cases addressing this final prong of the *Central Hudson* test, we have made clear that if the Government could achieve its interests in a manner that does not restrict speech, or that restricts less speech, the Government must do so.

Several non-speech-related means of drawing a line between compounding and large-scale manufacturing might be possible here. First, it seems that the Government could use the very factors the FDA relied on to distinguish compounding from manufacturing in its 1992 Compliance Policy Guide. For example, the Government could ban the use of "commercial scale manufacturing or testing equipment for compounding drug products." It could prohibit pharmacists from compounding more drugs in anticipation of receiving prescriptions than in response to prescriptions already received. It could prohibit pharmacists from "[o]ffering compounded drugs at wholesale to other state licensed persons or commercial entities for resale." Alternately, it could limit the amount of compounded drugs, either by volume or by numbers of prescriptions, that a given pharmacist or pharmacy sells out of State. . . .

The Government has not offered any reason why these possibilities, alone or in combination, would be insufficient to prevent compounding from occurring on such a scale as to undermine the new drug approval process. Indeed, there is no hint that the Government even considered these or any other alternatives. . . .

If the Government's failure to justify its decision to regulate speech were not enough to convince us that the FDAMA's advertising provisions were unconstitutional, the amount of beneficial speech prohibited by the FDAMA would be. Forbidding the advertisement of compounded drugs would affect pharmacists other than those interested in producing drugs on a large scale. It would prevent pharmacists with no interest in mass-producing medications, but who serve clienteles with special medical needs, from telling the doctors treating those clients about the alternative drugs available through compounding. For example, a pharmacist serving a children's hospital where many patients are unable to swallow pills would be prevented from telling the children's doctors about a new development in compounding that allowed a drug that was previously available only in pill form to be administered another way. Forbidding advertising of particular compounded drugs would also prohibit a pharmacist from posting a notice informing customers that if their children refuse to take medications because of the taste, the pharmacist could change the flavor, and giving examples of medications where flavoring is possible. The fact that the FDAMA would prohibit such seemingly useful speech even though doing so does not appear to directly further any asserted governmental objective confirms our belief that the prohibition is unconstitutional.

☐ *Justice BREYER, with whom THE CHIEF JUSTICE, Justice STEVENS, and Justice GINSBURG join, dissenting.*

In my view, the advertising restriction "directly advances" the statute's important safety objective. That objective, as the Court concedes, is to confine the sale of untested, compounded, drugs to where they are medically needed. But to do so the statute must exclude from the area of permitted drug sales both (1) those drugs that traditional drug manufacturers might supply after testing—typically drugs capable of being produced in large amounts, and (2) those compounded drugs sought by patients who may not clearly need them—including compounded drugs produced in small amounts.

The majority's discussion focuses upon the first exclusionary need, but it virtually ignores the second. It describes the statute's objective simply as drawing a "line" that will "distinguish compounded drugs produced on such a small scale that they could not undergo safety and efficacy testing from drugs produced and sold on a large enough scale that they could undergo such testing and therefore must do so." This description overlooks the need for a second line—a line that will distinguish (1) sales of compounded drugs to those who clearly need them from (2) sales of compounded drugs to those for whom a specially tailored but untested drug is a convenience but not a medical necessity. That is to say, the statute, in seeking to confine distribution of untested tailored drugs, must look both at the amount supplied (to help decide whether ordinary manufacturers might provide a tested alternative) and at the nature of demand (to help separate genuine need from simple convenience).

This second intermediate objective is logically related to Congress' primary end—the minimizing of safety risks. The statute's basic exemption from testing requirements inherently creates risks simply by placing untested drugs in the hands of the consumer. Where an individual has a specific medical need for a specially tailored drug those risks are likely offset. But where an untested drug is a convenience, not a necessity, that offset is unlikely to be present. . . .

I do not deny that the statute restricts the circulation of some truthful information. It prevents a pharmacist from including in an advertisement the information that "this pharmacy will compound Drug X." Nonetheless, this Court has not previously held that commercial advertising restrictions automatically violate the First Amendment. Rather, the Court has applied a more flexible test. It has examined the restriction's proportionality, the relation between restriction and objective, the fit between ends and means. In doing so, the Court has asked whether the regulation of commercial speech "directly advances" a "substantial" governmental objective and whether it is "more extensive than is necessary" to achieve those ends. It has done so because it has concluded that, from a constitutional perspective, commercial speech does not warrant application of the Court's strictest speech-protective tests. And it has reached this conclusion in part because restrictions on commercial speech do not often repress individual self-expression; they rarely interfere with the functioning of democratic political processes; and they often reflect a democratically determined governmental decision to regulate a commercial venture in order to protect, for example, the consumer, the public health, individual safety, or the environment. . . .

The Court, in my view, gives insufficient weight to the Government's regulatory rationale, and too readily assumes the existence of practical alternatives. It thereby applies the commercial speech doctrine too strictly. . . . For these reasons, I dissent.

F | *Regulating the Broadcast and Cable Media, and the Internet*

In a challenge to the Child Online Protection Act of 1998, in *Ashcroft v. American Civil Liberties Union* (2002) (excerpted below), the Court held that the law's use of "community standards" to define what material in cyberspace is "harmful to minors" does not necessarily violate the First Amendment. However, the Court also allowed the law to remain enjoined from going into effect until other questions about its impact on free speech are resolved. Justice Thomas delivered the opinion for the Court and Justice Stevens dissented.

However, in *United States v. American Library Association* (excerpted below), a plurality of the Court upheld the Children's Internet Protection Act of 2001, which requires public libraries that receive federal funding to install pornography filters on all computers providing Internet access. Writing for the Court, Chief Justice Rehnquist held that the limitations on access to the Internet were no greater for library patrons than those on access to books that for whatever reason librarians chose not to acquire. The law also authorizes, but does not require, librarians to unblock Internet sites at the request of adult users. Two justices—Justices Kennedy and Breyer—in concurring opinions indicated that the law might still not survive First Amendment challenges if it proved unduly burdensome on adult library patrons' access to the Internet. Justices Stevens, Souter, and Ginsburg dissented.

Ashcroft v. American Civil Liberties Union
535 U.S. 564, 122 S.CT. 1700 (2002)

Following the Supreme Court's invalidation of the Communications Decency Act (CDA) of 1996 in *Reno v. American Civil Liberties Union*, 521 U.S. 844 (1997) (excerpted in Vol. 1, Ch. 5), in 1998 Congress enacted the Child Online Protection Act (COPA), prohibiting any person from "knowingly and with knowledge of the character of the material, in interstate or foreign commerce by means of the World Wide Web, making any communication for commercial purposes that is available to any minor and that includes any material that is harmful to minors." Congress limited COPA's scope in at least three ways. First, while the CDA applied to communications over the Internet as a whole, including, for example, e-mail messages, COPA applies only to material displayed on the World

Wide Web. Second, unlike the CDA, COPA covers only communications made "for commercial purposes." And third, whereas the CDA prohibited "indecent" and "patently offensive" communications, COPA restricts only the narrower category of "material that is harmful to minors."

Drawing on the three-part test for obscenity set forth in *Miller v. California*, 413 U.S. 15 (1973) (excerpted in Vol. 1, Ch. 5), COPA defines "material that is harmful to minors" as "any communication, picture, image, graphic image file, article, recording, writing, or other matter of any kind that is obscene or that—(A) the average person, applying contemporary community standards, would find, taking the material as a whole and with respect to minors, is designed to appeal to, or is designed to pander to, the prurient interest; (B) depicts, describes, or represents, in a manner patently offensive with respect to minors, an actual or simulated sexual act or sexual contact, an actual or simulated normal or perverted sexual act, or a lewd exhibition of the genitals or post-pubescent female breast; and (C) taken as a whole, lacks serious literary, artistic, political, or scientific value for minors." A civil penalty of up to $50,000 may be imposed for each violation of the statute. Criminal penalties consist of up to six months in prison and a maximum fine of $50,000. An additional fine of $50,000 may be imposed for any intentional violation of the statute.

One month before COPA was scheduled to go into effect, the American Civil Liberties Union (ACLU) challenged the constitutionality of the act. A federal district court granted a motion for a preliminary injunction, barring the government from enforcing the Act until the merits of claims could be adjudicated. Subsequently, the district court concluded that the ACLU was likely to establish at trial that COPA could not withstand strict scrutiny because, among other reasons, it had not been shown to be the least restrictive means of preventing minors from accessing "harmful to minors" material. Attorney General John Ashcroft appealed the district court's ruling, and the U.S. Court of Appeals for the Third Circuit affirmed. That decision was in turn appealed to the Supreme Court, which granted review.

The Court vacated and remanded the appellate court's decision. Justice Thomas delivered the opinion for the Court. Justices O'Connor, Kennedy, and Breyer filed concurring opinions. Justice Stevens filed a dissent.

□ *Justice THOMAS delivered the opinion of the Court with respect to Parts I, II, and IV, an opinion with respect to Parts III-A, III-C, and III-D, in which THE CHIEF JUSTICE and Justice SCALIA join, and an opinion with respect to Part III-B, in which THE CHIEF JUSTICE, Justice O'CONNOR, and Justice SCALIA join.*

This case presents the narrow question whether the Child Online Protection Act's (COPA or Act) use of "community standards" to identify "material that is harmful to minors" violates the First Amendment. We hold that this aspect of COPA does not render the statute facially unconstitutional. . . .

■ II

[T]his Court in *Miller* [*v. California* (1973)] set forth the governing three-part test for assessing whether material is obscene and thus unprotected by the First Amendment: "(a) Whether 'the average person, applying contemporary community standards' would find that the work, taken as a whole, appeals to the prurient interest; (b) whether the work depicts or describes, in a patently offensive way, sexual conduct specifically defined by the applicable state law; and (c) whether the work, taken as a whole, lacks serious literary, artistic, political, or scientific value." *Miller* adopted the use of "community standards" from *Roth* [*v. United States*, 354 U.S. 476 (1957)], which repudiated an earlier approach for assessing objectionable material. . . . The Court preserved the use of community standards in formulating the *Miller* test, explaining that they furnish a valuable First Amendment safeguard: "The primary concern . . . is to be certain that . . . [material] will be judged by its impact on an average person, rather than a particularly susceptible or sensitive person—or indeed a totally insensitive one."

■ III

The Court of Appeals, however, concluded that this Court's prior community standards jurisprudence "has no applicability to the Internet and the Web" because "Web publishers are currently without the ability to control the geographic scope of the recipients of their communications." We therefore must decide whether this technological limitation renders COPA's reliance on community standards constitutionally infirm.

B

Because juries would apply different standards across the country, and Web publishers currently lack the ability to limit access to their sites on a geographic basis, the Court of Appeals feared that COPA's "community standards" component would effectively force all speakers on the Web to abide by the "most puritan" community's standards. And such a requirement, the Court of Appeals concluded, "imposes an overreaching burden and restriction on constitutionally protected speech."

In evaluating the constitutionality of the CDA, this Court expressed a similar concern over that statute's use of community standards to identify patently offensive material on the Internet. We noted that "the 'community standards' criterion as applied to the Internet means that any communication available to a nationwide audience will be judged by the standards of the community most likely to be offended by the message." *Reno* [*v. ACLU* (1997)].

The Court of Appeals below relied heavily on this observation, stating that it was "not persuaded that the Supreme Court's concern with respect to the 'community standards' criterion has been sufficiently remedied by Congress in COPA."

The CDA's use of community standards to identify patently offensive material, however, was particularly problematic in light of that statute's unprecedented breadth and vagueness. The statute covered communications depicting or describing "sexual or excretory activities or organs" that were "patently offensive as measured by contemporary community standards"—a standard somewhat similar to the second prong of *Miller's* three-prong test. But the CDA did not include any limiting terms resembling *Miller's* additional two prongs.

COPA, by contrast, does not appear to suffer from the same flaw because it applies to significantly less material than did the CDA and defines the harmful-to-minors material restricted by the statute in a manner parallel to the *Miller* definition of obscenity. To fall within the scope of COPA, works must not only "depict, describe, or represent, in a manner patently offensive with respect to minors," particular sexual acts or parts of the anatomy, they must also be designed to appeal to the prurient interest of minors and "taken as a whole, lack serious literary, artistic, political, or scientific value for minors."

These additional two restrictions substantially limit the amount of material covered by the statute. Material appeals to the prurient interest, for instance, only if it is in some sense erotic. Of even more significance, however, is COPA's exclusion of material with serious value for minors. In *Reno*, we emphasized that the serious value "requirement is particularly important because, unlike the 'patently offensive' and 'prurient interest' criteria, it is not judged by contemporary community standards." This is because "the value of [a] work [does not] vary from community to community based on the degree of local acceptance it has won." Rather, the relevant question is "whether a reasonable person would find . . . value in the material, taken as a whole." Thus, the serious value requirement "allows appellate courts to impose some limitations and regularity on the definition by setting, as a matter of law, a national floor for socially redeeming value."

C

When the scope of an obscenity statute's coverage is sufficiently narrowed by a "serious value" prong and a "prurient interest" prong, we have held that requiring a speaker disseminating material to a national audience to observe varying community standards does not violate the First Amendment. In *Hamling v. United States*, 418 U.S. 87 (1974), this Court considered the constitutionality of applying community standards to the determination of whether material is obscene under the federal statute prohibiting the mailing of obscene material. Although this statute does not define obscenity, the petitioners in *Hamling* were tried and convicted under the definition of obscenity set forth in *Book Named "John Cleland's Memoirs of a Woman of Pleasure" v. Attorney General of Mass.*, 383 U.S. 413 (1966), which included both a "prurient interest" requirement and a requirement that prohibited material be " 'utterly without redeeming social value.' " . . .

While Justice KENNEDY and Justice STEVENS question the applicability of this Court's community standards jurisprudence to the Internet, we do not believe that the medium's "unique characteristics" justify adopting a different approach than that set forth in *Hamling and Sable [Communications of Cal., Inc. v. FCC*, 492 U.S. 115 (1989)]. If a publisher chooses to send its material into a particular community, this Court's jurisprudence teaches that it is the publisher's responsibility to abide by that community's standards. The publisher's burden does not change simply because it decides to distribute its material to every community in the Nation. Nor does it change because the publisher may wish to speak only to those in a "community where avant garde culture is the norm," but nonetheless utilizes a medium that transmits its speech from coast to coast. If a publisher wishes for its material to be judged only by the standards of particular communities, then it need only take the simple step of utilizing a medium that enables it to target the release of its material into those communities. . . .

■ IV

The scope of our decision today is quite limited. We hold only that COPA's reliance on community standards to identify "material that is harmful to minors" does not by itself render the statute substantially overbroad for purposes of the First Amendment. We do not express any view as to whether COPA suffers from substantial overbreadth for other reasons, whether the statute is unconstitutionally vague, or whether the District Court correctly concluded that the statute likely will not survive strict scrutiny analysis once adjudication of the case is completed below. While respondents urge us to resolve these questions at this time, prudence dictates allowing the Court of Appeals to first examine these difficult issues. . . . [T]he Government remains enjoined from enforcing COPA absent further action by the Court of Appeals or the District Court. For the foregoing reasons, we vacate the judgment of the Court of Appeals and remand the case for further proceedings.

□ *Justice O'CONNOR, concurring in part and concurring in the judgment.*

I agree with Justice KENNEDY that, given Internet speakers' inability to control the geographic location of their audience, expecting them to bear the burden of controlling the recipients of their speech, as we did in *Hamling* and *Sable*, may be entirely too much to ask, and would potentially suppress an inordinate amount of expression. For these reasons, adoption of a national standard is necessary in my view for any reasonable regulation of Internet obscenity.

Our precedents do not forbid adoption of a national standard. Local community-based standards originated with *Miller v. California*. . . . Later, in *Jenkins v. Georgia*, 418 U.S. 153 (1974), we confirmed that "*Miller* approved the use of [instructions based on local standards]; it did not mandate their use." The instructions we approved in that case charged the jury with applying "community standards" without designating any particular "community." In holding that a State may define the obscenity standard by stating the *Miller* standard without further specification, *Jenkins* left open the possibility that jurors would apply any number of standards, including a national standard, in evaluating material's obscenity.

To be sure, the Court in *Miller* also stated that a national standard might be "unascertainable" and "unrealistic." But where speech on the Internet is concerned, I do not share that skepticism. It is true that our Nation is diverse, but many local communities encompass a similar diversity. For instance, in *Miller* itself, the jury was instructed to consider the standards of the entire State of California, a large (today, it has a population of greater than 33 million people) and diverse State that includes both Berkeley and Bakersfield. If the *Miller* Court believed generalizations about the standards of the people of California were possible, and that jurors would be capable of assessing them, it is difficult to believe that similar generalizations are not also possible for the Nation as a whole. Moreover, the existence of the Internet, and its facilitation of national dialogue, has itself made jurors more aware of the views of adults in other parts of the United States. . . .

□ *Justice BREYER, concurring in part and concurring in the judgment.*

I write separately because I believe that Congress intended the statutory word "community" to refer to the Nation's adult community taken as a whole, not to geographically separate local areas. The statutory language does not explicitly describe the specific "community" to which it refers. It says only that the "average person, applying contemporary community standards" must find that the "material as a whole and with respect to minors, is designed to appeal to, or is designed to pander to, the prurient interest. . . ." In the statute's legislative history, however, Congress made clear that it did not intend this ambiguous statutory phrase to refer to separate standards that might differ significantly among different communities. . . .

I join the judgment of the Court vacating the opinion of the Court of Appeals and remanding for consideration of the statute as a whole. Unlike Justice THOMAS, however, I would not assume that the Act is narrow enough to render the national variation in community standards unproblematic. Indeed, if the District Court correctly construed the statute across its other dimensions, then the variation in community standards might well justify enjoining enforcement of the Act. I would leave that question to the Court of Appeals in the first instance.

□ *Justice KENNEDY, concurring in part and concurring in the judgment.*

[T]he Court of Appeals was correct to focus on COPA's incorporation of varying community standards; and it may have been correct as well to conclude that in practical effect COPA imposes the most puritanical community standard on the entire country. On the other hand, it is neither realistic nor beyond constitutional doubt for Congress, in effect, to impose the community standards of Maine or Mississippi on Las Vegas and New York. In striking down COPA's predecessor, the *Reno* Court identified this precise problem, and if the *Hamling* and *Sable* Courts did not find the problem fatal, that is because those cases involved quite different media. The national variation in community standards constitutes a particular burden on Internet speech.

□ *Justice STEVENS, dissenting.*

Appeals to prurient interests are commonplace on the Internet, as in older media. Many of those appeals lack serious value for minors as well as adults. Some are offensive to certain viewers but welcomed by others. For decades, our cases have recognized that the standards for judging their acceptability vary from viewer to viewer and from community to community. Those cases developed the requirement that communications should be protected if they do not violate contemporary community standards. In its original form, the community standard provided a shield for communications that are offensive only to the least tolerant members of society. Thus, the Court "has emphasized on more than one occasion that a principal concern in requiring that a judgment be made on the basis of 'contemporary community standards' is to assure that the material is judged neither on the basis of each juror's personal opinion, nor by its effect on a particularly sensitive or insensitive person or group." *Hamling v. United States.* In the context of the Internet, however, community standards become a sword, rather than a shield. If a prurient appeal is offensive in a puritan village, it may be a crime to post it on the World Wide Web. . . .

We have recognized that the State has a compelling interest in protecting minors from harmful speech, *Sable Communications of Cal., Inc. v. FCC,* and on one occasion we upheld a restriction on indecent speech that was made available to the general public, because it could be accessed by minors, *FCC v. Pacifica Foundation,* 438 U.S. 726 (1978). Our decision in that case was influenced by the distinctive characteristics of the broadcast medium, as well as the expertise of the agency, and the narrow scope of its order. On the other hand, we have repeatedly rejected the position that the free speech rights of adults can be limited to what is acceptable for children. Petitioner relies on our decision in *Ginsberg v. New York,* 390 U.S. 629 (1968), for the proposition that Congress can prohibit the display of materials that are harmful to minors. But the statute upheld in *Ginsberg* prohibited selling indecent materials directly to children, whereas the speech implicated here is simply posted on a medium that is accessible to both adults and children. Like the restriction on indecent "dial-a-porn" numbers invalidated in *Sable,* the prohibition against mailing advertisements for contraceptives invalidated in *Bolger,* and the ban against selling adult books found impermissible in *Butler* [*v. Michigan,* 352 U.S. 380 (1957)], COPA seeks to limit protected speech that is not targeted at children, simply because it can be obtained by them while surfing the Web. In evaluating the overbreadth of such a statute, we should be mindful of Justice FRANKFURTER's admonition not to "burn the house to roast the pig," *Butler.*

COPA not only restricts speech that is made available to the general public, it also covers a medium in which speech cannot be segregated to avoid communities where it is likely to be considered harmful to minors. The Internet presents a unique forum for communication because information, once posted, is accessible everywhere on the network at once. The speaker cannot control access based on the location of the listener, nor can it choose the pathways through which its speech is transmitted. . . .

If the material were forwarded through the mails, as in *Hamling,* or over the telephone, as in *Sable,* the sender could avoid destinations with the most restrictive standards. . . . Given the undisputed fact that a provider who posts material on the Internet cannot prevent it from entering any geographic community, a law that criminalizes a particular communication in just a handful of destinations effectively prohibits transmission of that message to all of the 176.5 million Americans that have access to the Internet. In light of this fundamental difference in technologies, the rules applicable to the mass mailing of an obscene montage or to obscene dial-a-porn should not be used to judge the legality of messages on the World Wide Web. . . .

[C]ommunity standards originally served as a shield to protect speakers from the least tolerant members of society. By aggregating values at the community level, the *Miller* test eliminated the outliers at both ends of the spectrum and provided some predictability as to what constitutes obscene speech. But community standards also serve as a shield to protect audience members, by allowing people to self-sort based on their preferences. Those who abhor and those who tolerate sexually explicit speech can seek out like-minded people and settle in communities that share their views on what is acceptable for themselves and their children. This sorting mechanism, however, does not exist in cyberspace; the audience cannot self-segregate. As a result, in the context of the Internet this shield also becomes a sword, because the community that wishes to live without certain material not only rids itself, but the entire Internet of the offending speech.

In sum, I would affirm the judgment of the Court of Appeals and therefore respectfully dissent.

United States v. American Library Association
123 S.Ct. 2297 (2003)

Congress authorized federal funding for public libraries to acquire and to provide access to the Internet under an E-rate program under the Telecommunications Act of 1996 and the Library Services and Technology Act (LSTA). Subsequently, Congress was lobbied to enact the Children's Internet Protection Act (CIPA) of 2001. Under that law, public libraries may not receive federal funding for Internet access unless they install software to block obscene or pornographic images and prevent minors from assessing such materials. The statute authorizes, but does not require, librarians to unblock Internet sites at the request of adult users. It also neither specifies what kind of filters libraries should install nor provides standards and procedures for unblocking Internet sites at the request of adult users. The American Library Association and a number of other organizations and individuals challenged the constitutionality of the law. A federal district court ruled that the law ran afoul of the First Amendment and blocked its enforcement. The government appealed.

The lower court's decision was reversed. Chief Justice Rehnquist delivered the opinion of the Court, which only Justices O'Connor, Scalia, and Thomas joined. Justices Kennedy and Breyer filed opinions concurring in the judgment. Justices Stevens and Souter filed dissenting opinions, which Justice Ginsburg joined.

☐ *CHIEF JUSTICE REHNQUIST announced the judgment of the Court and delivered an opinion, in which Justice O'CONNOR, Justice SCALIA, and Justice THOMAS joined.*

By connecting to the Internet, public libraries provide patrons with a vast amount of valuable information. But there is also an enormous amount of pornography on the Internet, much of which is easily obtained. The accessibility of this material has created serious problems for libraries, which have found that patrons of all ages, including minors, regularly search for online pornography. Some patrons also expose others to pornographic images by leaving them displayed on Internet terminals or printed at library printers.

Upon discovering these problems, Congress became concerned that the E-rate and LSTA programs were facilitating access to illegal and harmful pornography. Congress learned that adults "us[e] library computers to access pornography that is then exposed to staff, passersby, and children," and that "minors acces[s] child and adult pornography in libraries."

But Congress also learned that filtering software that blocks access to pornographic Web sites could provide a reasonably effective way to prevent such uses of library resources. By 2000, before Congress enacted CIPA, almost 17% of public libraries used such software on at least some of their Internet terminals, and 7% had filters on all of them. A library can set such software to block categories of material, such as "Pornography" or "Violence." When a patron tries to view a site that falls within such a category, a screen appears indicating that the site is blocked. But a filter set to block pornography may sometimes block other sites that present neither obscene nor pornographic material, but that nevertheless trigger the filter. To minimize this problem, a library can set its software to prevent the blocking of material that falls into categories like "Education," "History," and "Medical." A library may also add or delete specific sites from a blocking category, and anyone can ask companies that furnish filtering software to unblock particular sites. Responding to this information, Congress enacted CIPA. . . .

Congress has wide latitude to attach conditions to the receipt of federal assistance in order to further its policy objectives. *South Dakota v. Dole*, 483 U.S. 203 (1987). But Congress may not "induce" the recipient "to engage in activities that would themselves be unconstitutional." To determine whether libraries would violate the First Amendment by employing the filtering software that CIPA requires, we must first examine the role of libraries in our society.

Public libraries pursue the worthy missions of facilitating learning and cultural enrichment. To this end, libraries collect only those materials deemed to have "requisite and appropriate quality."

We have held in two analogous contexts that the government has broad discretion to make content-based judgments in deciding what private speech to make available to the public. In *Arkansas Ed. Television Comm'n v. Forbes*, 523 U.S. 666 (1998), we held that public forum principles do not generally apply to a public television station's editorial judgments regarding the private speech it presents to its viewers. Recognizing a broad right of public access "would [also] risk implicating the courts in judgments that should be left to the exercise of journalistic discretion."

Similarly, in *National Endowment for Arts v. Finley*, 524 U.S. 569 (1998), we upheld an art funding program that required the National Endowment for the Arts (NEA) to use content-based criteria in making funding decisions. We explained that "[a]ny content-based considerations that may be taken into account in the grant-making process are a consequence of the nature of arts funding."

The principles underlying *Forbes* and *Finley* also apply to a public library's exercise of judgment in selecting the material it provides to its patrons. Just as forum analysis and heightened judicial scrutiny are incompatible with the role of public television stations and the role of the NEA, they are also incompatible with the discretion that public libraries must have to fulfill their traditional missions. Public library staffs necessarily consider content in making collection decisions and enjoy broad discretion in making them.

The public forum principles on which the District Court relied are out of place in the context of this case. Internet access in public libraries is neither a "traditional" nor a "designated" public forum. First, this resource—which did not exist until quite recently—has not "immemorially been held in trust for the use of the public and, time out of mind, . . . been used for purposes of assembly, communication of thoughts between citizens, and discussing public questions."

Nor does Internet access in a public library satisfy our definition of a "designated public forum." To create such a forum, the government must make an affirmative choice to open up its property for use as a public forum.

The situation here is very different. A public library does not acquire Internet terminals in order to create a public forum for Web publishers to express themselves, any more than it collects books in order to provide a public forum for the authors of books to speak. It provides Internet access, not to "encourage a diversity of views from private speakers," but for the same reasons it offers other library resources: to facilitate research, learning, and recreational pursuits by furnishing materials of requisite and appropriate quality. . . .

Moreover, because of the vast quantity of material on the Internet and the rapid pace at which it changes, libraries cannot possibly segregate, item by item, all the Internet material that is appropriate for inclusion from all that is not. While a library could limit its Internet collection to just those sites it found worthwhile, it could do so only at the cost of excluding an enormous amount of valuable information that it lacks the capacity to review. Given that tradeoff, it is entirely reasonable for public libraries to reject that approach and instead exclude certain categories of content, without making individualized judgments that everything they do make available has requisite and appropriate quality. . . .

Because public libraries' use of Internet filtering software does not violate their patrons' First Amendment rights, CIPA does not induce libraries to violate the Constitution, and is a valid exercise of Congress' spending power. Nor does CIPA impose an unconstitutional condition on public libraries.

☐ *Justice KENNEDY, concurring in the judgment.*

If on the request of an adult user, a librarian will unblock filtered material or disable the Internet software filter without significant delay, there is little to this case. The Government represents this is indeed the fact. . . .

If some libraries do not have the capacity to unblock specific Web sites or to disable the filter or if it is shown that an adult user's election to view constitutionally protected Internet material is burdened in some other substantial way, that would be the subject for an as-applied challenge, not the facial challenge made in this case.

There are, of course, substantial Government interests at stake here. The interest in protecting young library users from material inappropriate for minors is legitimate, and even compelling, as all Members of the Court appear to agree. Given this interest, and the failure to show that the ability of adult library users to have access to the material is burdened in any significant degree, the statute is not unconstitutional on its face. For these reasons, I concur in the judgment of the Court.

☐ *Justice STEVENS, dissenting.*

The unchallenged findings of fact made by the District Court reveal fundamental defects in the filtering software that is now available or that will be available in the foreseeable future. Because the software relies on key words or phrases to block undesirable sites, it does not have the capacity to exclude a precisely defined category of images. Given the quantity and ever-changing character of Web sites offering free sexually explicit material, it is inevitable that a substantial amount of such material will never be blocked. Because of this "underblocking," the statute will provide parents with a false sense of security without really solving the problem that motivated its enactment. Conversely, the software's reliance on words to identify undesirable sites necessarily results in the blocking of thousands of pages that "contain content that is completely innocuous for both adults and minors, and that no rational person could conclude matches the filtering companies' category definitions, such as 'pornography' or 'sex.'" In my judgment, a statutory blunderbuss that mandates this vast amount of "overblocking" abridges the freedom of speech protected by the First Amendment. . . .

The plurality incorrectly argues that the statute does not impose "an unconstitutional condition on public libraries." Ante, at 17. On the contrary, it impermissibly conditions the receipt of Government funding on the restriction of significant First Amendment rights. . . .

☐ *Justice SOUTER, with whom Justice GINSBURG joins, dissenting.*

Like the other Members of the Court, I have no doubt about the legitimacy of governmental efforts to put a barrier between child patrons of public libraries and the raw offerings on the Internet otherwise available to them there, and if the only First Amendment interests raised here were those of children, I would uphold application of the Act. We have said that the governmental interest in "shielding" children from exposure to indecent material is "compelling," *Reno v. American Civil Liberties Union*, 521 U.S. 844 (1997), and I do not think that the awkwardness a child might feel on asking for an unblocked terminal is any such burden as to affect constitutionality. . . .

The question for me, then, is whether a local library could itself constitutionally impose these restrictions on the content otherwise available to an adult patron through an Internet connection, at a library terminal provided for public use. The answer is no. A library that chose to block an adult's Internet access to material harmful to children (and whatever else the undiscriminating filter might interrupt) would be imposing a content-based restriction on communication of material in the library's control that an adult could otherwise lawfully see. This would simply be censorship. True, the censorship would not necessarily extend to every adult, for an intending Internet user might convince a librarian that he was a true researcher or had a "lawful purpose" to obtain everything the library's terminal could provide. But as to those who did not qualify for discretionary unblocking, the censorship would be complete and, like all censorship by an agency of the Government, presumptively invalid owing to strict scrutiny in implementing the Free Speech Clause of the First Amendment. . . .

■ IN COMPARATIVE PERSPECTIVE

The Australian High Court's Ruling on Libel and the Internet

Dow Jones & Company Inc. v. Gutnick
[2002] HCA 56, 10 December 2002, M3/2002

The high court of Australia ruled that Joseph Gutnick of Melbourne could sue Dow Jones & Company, a publisher in New Jersey, for libel in Victoria, where libel laws are very strict in permitting plaintiffs to sue based on their interpretation of an offending passage and forbidding defendants from countering that a more benign reading was plausible. A *Barron's* article reported: "Some of Gutnick's business dealings with religious charities raise uncomfortable questions. A *Barron's* investigation found that several charities traded heavily in stocks promoted by Gutnick. Although the charities profited, other investors were left with heavy losses. . . . In addition, Gutnick has had dealings with Nachum Goldberg, who is currently serving five years in an Australian prison for tax evasion that involved charities." Dow Jones attorneys argued that the case should be brought in the United States, where *Barron's* is published. A group of publishers and Internet companies—including Amazon.com, Yahoo, The Associated Press, CNN, and the *New York Times*—intervened in support of Dow Jones.

Chief Justice GLEESON and Justices McHUGH, GUMMOW, and HAYNE.

The appellant, Dow Jones & Company Inc. ("Dow Jones"), prints and publishes the *Wall Street Journal* newspaper and *Barron's* magazine. Since 1996, Dow Jones has operated WSJ.com, a subscription news site on the World Wide Web. . . .

The edition of *Barron's* Online for 28 October 2000 (and the equivalent edition of the magazine which bore the date 30 October 2000) contained an article entitled "Unholy Gains" in which several references were made to the respondent, Mr. Joseph Gutnick.

Mr. Gutnick contends that part of the article defamed him. He has brought an action in the Supreme Court of Victoria against Dow Jones claiming damages for defamation. Mr. Gutnick lives in Victoria. He has his business headquarters there. Although he conducts business outside Australia, including in the United States of America, and has made significant contributions to charities in the United States and Israel, much of his social and business life could be said to be focused in Victoria. . . .

The principal issue debated in the appeal to this Court was where was the material of which Mr. Gutnick complained published? Was it published in Victoria? . . .

The World Wide Web is but one particular service available over the Internet. It enables a document to be stored in such a way on one computer connected to the Internet that a person using another computer connected to the Internet can request and receive a copy of the document. . . .

The principal burden of the argument advanced by Dow Jones on the hearing of the appeal in this Court was that articles published on *Barron's* Online were published in South Brunswick, New Jersey, when they became available on the servers which it maintained at that place. . . .

To the extent that the suggested rule would require reference only to the law of the place in which the server is located, it is a rule that would evidently be convenient to the party putting material on a web server. But that does not conclude debate. The convenience of one party is important to it, but how would such a rule fit with other, no less relevant, considerations? In particular, how would it fit with the nature of the competing rights and interests which an action for defamation must accommodate?

It is necessary to begin by making the obvious point that the law of defamation seeks to strike a balance between, on the one hand, society's interest in freedom of speech and the free exchange of information and ideas (whether or not that information and those ideas find favour with any particular part of society) and, on the other hand, an individual's interest in maintaining his or her reputation in society free from unwarranted slur or damage. The way in which those interests are balanced differs from society to society. . . .

Harm to reputation is done when a defamatory publication is comprehended by the reader, the listener, or the observer. Until then, no harm is done by it. This being so it would be wrong to treat publication as if it were a unilateral act on the part of the publisher alone. It is not. It is a bilateral act—in which the publisher makes it available and a third party has it available for his or her comprehension. . . .

If the place in which the publisher acts and the place in which the publication is presented in comprehensible form are in two different jurisdictions, where is the tort of defamation committed? That question is not to be answered by an uncritical application of some general rule that intentional torts are committed where the tortfeasor acts or that they are committed in the place where the last event necessary to make the actor liable takes place. Nor does it require an uncritical adoption of what has come to be known in the United States as the "single publication" rule, a rule which has been rejected by the Court of Appeal of New South Wales. . . .

In the course of argument much emphasis was given to the fact that the advent of the World Wide Web is a considerable technological advance. So it is. But the problem of widely disseminated communications is much older than the Internet and the World Wide Web. The law has had to grapple with such cases ever since newspapers and magazines came to be distributed to large numbers of people over wide geographic areas. Radio and television presented the same kind of problem as was presented by widespread dissemination of printed material, although international transmission of material was made easier by the advent of electronic means of communication.

It was suggested that the World Wide Web was different from radio and television because the radio or television broadcaster could decide how far the signal was to be broadcast. It must be recognised, however, that satellite broadcasting now permits very wide dissemination of radio and television and it may, therefore, be doubted that it is right to say that the World Wide Web has a uniquely broad reach. It is no more or less ubiquitous than some television services. In the end, pointing to the breadth or depth of reach of particular forms of communication may tend to obscure one basic fact. However broad may be the reach of any particular means of communication, those who make information accessible by a particular method do so knowing of the reach that their information may have. In particular, those who post information on the World Wide Web do so knowing that the information they make available is available to all and sundry without any geographic restriction.

Because publication is an act or event to which there are at least two parties, the publisher and a person to whom material is published, publication to numerous persons may have as many territorial connections as there are those to whom particular words are published. It is only if one starts from a premise that the publication of particular words is necessarily a singular event which is to be located by reference only to the conduct of the publisher that it would be right to attach no significance to the territorial connections provided by the several places in which the publication is available for comprehension. . . .

In defamation, the same considerations that require rejection of locating the tort by reference only to the publisher's conduct, lead to the conclusion that, ordinarily, defamation is to be located at the place where the damage to reputation occurs. Ordinarily that will be where the material which is alleged to be defamatory is available in comprehensible form assuming, of course, that the person defamed has in that place a reputation which is thereby damaged. It is only when the material is in comprehensible form that the damage to reputation is done and it is damage to reputation which is the principal focus of defamation, not any quality of the defendant's conduct. In the case of material on the World Wide Web, it is not available in comprehensible form until downloaded onto the computer of a person who has used a web browser to pull the material from the web server. It is where that person downloads the material that the damage to reputation may be done. Ordinarily then, that will be the place where the tort of defamation is committed. . . .

[T]he spectre which Dow Jones sought to conjure up in the present appeal, of a publisher forced to consider every article it publishes on the World Wide Web against the defamation laws of every country from Afghanistan to Zimbabwe is seen to be unreal when it is recalled that in all except the most unusual of cases, identifying the person about whom material is to be published will readily identify the defamation law to which that person may resort.

H | *Symbolic Speech and Speech-Plus-Conduct*

In its 2001–2002 term the Court upheld Chicago's ordinance requiring permits for public assemblies in *Thomas v. Chicago Park District*, 534 U.S. 316 (2002). The ordinance requires obtaining a permit to "conduct a public assembly, parade, picnic, or other event involving more than fifty individuals," or to engage in any activity "creat[ing] or emit[ing] any Amplified Sound." The Court of Appeals for the Seventh Circuit rejected the petitioner's argument that the ordinance was unconstitutionally vague and a prior restraint on free speech. The Supreme Court affirmed that the ordinance was a content-neutral time, place, and manner regulation of the use of public forums and was "subject to effective judicial review."

Virginia v. Black
123 S.Ct. 1536 (2003)

In 1998, Barry Elton Black led a Ku Klux Klan rally at which a 25-foot cross was burned on private property with the owner's permission, but which was clearly visible to nearby homeowners and motorists on a state road. He was convicted, under Virginia's 50-year-old law making cross burning a crime, and fined $2,500. Also in 1998, Richard J. Elliott and Jonathan O'Mara burned a cross on the yard of James Jubilee, an

African American, because they were angry with him. Both were convicted and sentenced to 90 days in jail and fined $2,500. On appeal in
2001, the Virginia Supreme Court overturned their convictions and struck
down the state's law in holding that it ran afoul of the First Amendment's guarantee for freedom of expression. The state appealed and the
Supreme Court granted *certiorari.*

Justice O'Connor's opinion for the Court commanded only a plurality, but by a vote of six to three the Court held that a properly drafted
law punishing cross burning would survive a First Amendment challenge.
Justice O'Connor's opinion, joined by Chief Justice Rehnquist and
Justices Stevens and Breyer, held that states may make it a crime to burn
a cross because it is "a particularly virulent form of intimidation." Justice
Scalia, in a separate opinion in part concurring and dissenting, and Justice Thomas, in a dissenting opinion, agreed. However, Justice O'Connor
also ruled that Virginia's law was unconstitutional because a section of
the law dealing with jury instructions permitting an inference of intent
to intimidate invited juries to ignore "all of the contextual factors that
are necessary to decide whether a particular cross burning [was] intended to intimidate" instead of to express a political message. Justice
Scalia disagreed with that part of her analysis and holding in contending
that under the statute a jury could be properly instructed and the inference of intimidation rebutted. In his dissent, Justice Thomas contented
that the plurality went too far and that cross burning could never receive First Amendment protection because its sole message was one of
terror and lawlessness. Justice Souter, joined by Justices Kennedy and
Ginsburg, filed another separate opinion in part concurring and dissenting. These three justices agreed that Virginia's law was unconstitutional,
but maintained that the First Amendment forbids all content-based regulations of speech. Cross burning, in their view, was inherently symbolic
and might convey not only a message of terror but also of political
ideology. Accordingly, they would have held that any law punishing
cross burning could not survive First Amendment scrutiny.

☐ *Justice O'CONNOR announced the judgment of the Court and delivered the
opinion of the Court with respect to Parts I, II, and III, and an opinion with respect to
Parts IV and V, in which THE CHIEF JUSTICE, Justice STEVENS, and Justice
BREYER join.*

In this case we consider whether the Commonwealth of Virginia's statute
banning cross burning with "an intent to intimidate a person or group of
persons" violates the First Amendment. We conclude that while a State,
consistent with the First Amendment, may ban cross burning carried out
with the intent to intimidate, the provision in the Virginia statute treating any
cross burning as prima facie evidence of intent to intimidate renders the
statute unconstitutional in its current form. . . .

■ II

Cross burning originated in the 14th century as a means for Scottish tribes to signal each other. . . . Cross burning in this country, however, long ago became unmoored from its Scottish ancestry. Burning a cross in the United States is inextricably intertwined with the history of the Ku Klux Klan.

The first Ku Klux Klan began in Pulaski, Tennessee, in the spring of 1866. Although the Ku Klux Klan started as a social club, it soon changed into something far different. The Klan fought Reconstruction and the corresponding drive to allow freed blacks to participate in the political process. Soon the Klan imposed "a veritable reign of terror" throughout the South. The Klan employed tactics such as whipping, threatening to burn people at the stake, and murder. The Klan's victims included blacks, southern whites who disagreed with the Klan and "carpetbagger" northern whites.

The activities of the Ku Klux Klan prompted legislative action at the national level. . . . Congress passed what is now known as the Ku Klux Klan Act. President Grant used these new powers to suppress the Klan in South Carolina, the effect of which severely curtailed the Klan in other States as well. By the end of Reconstruction in 1877, the first Klan no longer existed.

The genesis of the second Klan began in 1905, with the publication of Thomas Dixon's *The Clansmen: An Historical Romance of the Ku Klux Klan.* Dixon's book was a sympathetic portrait of the first Klan, depicting the Klan as a group of heroes "saving" the South from blacks and the "horrors" of Reconstruction. Although the first Klan never actually practiced cross burning, Dixon's book depicted the Klan burning crosses to celebrate the execution of former slaves. Cross burning thereby became associated with the first Ku Klux Klan. When D. W. Griffith turned Dixon's book into the movie *The Birth of a Nation* in 1915, the association between cross burning and the Klan became indelible. In addition to the cross burnings in the movie, a poster advertising the film displayed a hooded Klansman riding a hooded horse, with his left hand holding the reins of the horse and his right hand holding a burning cross above his head. Soon thereafter, in November 1915, the second Klan began.

From the inception of the second Klan, cross burnings have been used to communicate both threats of violence and messages of shared ideology. The first initiation ceremony occurred on Stone Mountain near Atlanta, Georgia. While a 40-foot cross burned on the mountain, the Klan members took their oaths of loyalty. This cross burning was the second recorded instance in the United States. The first known cross burning in the country had occurred a little over one month before the Klan initiation, when a Georgia mob celebrated the lynching of Leo Frank by burning a "gigantic cross" on Stone Mountain that was "visible throughout" Atlanta. . . .

The Klan continued to use cross burnings to intimidate after World War II. . . . The decision of this Court in *Brown v. Board of Education*, 347 U.S. 483 (1954), along with the civil rights movement of the 1950s and 1960s, sparked another outbreak of Klan violence. These acts of violence included bombings, beatings, shootings, stabbings, and mutilations. Members of the Klan burned crosses on the lawns of those associated with the civil rights movement, assaulted the Freedom Riders, bombed churches, and murdered blacks as well as whites whom the Klan viewed as sympathetic toward the civil rights movement.

Throughout the history of the Klan, cross burnings have also remained potent symbols of shared group identity and ideology. The burning cross became a symbol of the Klan itself and a central feature of Klan gatherings. . . .

To this day, regardless of whether the message is a political one or whether the message is also meant to intimidate, the burning of a cross is a "symbol of hate." And while cross burning sometimes carries no intimidating message, at other times the intimidating message is the only message conveyed. For example, when a cross burning is directed at a particular person not affiliated with the Klan, the burning cross often serves as a message of intimidation, designed to inspire in the victim a fear of bodily harm. Moreover, the history of violence associated with the Klan shows that the possibility of injury or death is not just hypothetical. The person who burns a cross directed at a particular person often is making a serious threat, meant to coerce the victim to comply with the Klan's wishes unless the victim is willing to risk the wrath of the Klan. Indeed, as the cases of respondents Elliott and O'Mara indicate, individuals without Klan affiliation who wish to threaten or menace another person sometimes use cross burning because of this association between a burning cross and violence.

In sum, while a burning cross does not inevitably convey a message of intimidation, often the cross burner intends that the recipients of the message fear for their lives. And when a cross burning is used to intimidate, few if any messages are more powerful.

▪ III

The First Amendment affords protection to symbolic or expressive conduct as well as to actual speech. See, e.g., *R. A. V. v. City of St. Paul*, 505 U.S. [377 (1992)]; *Texas v. Johnson*, [491 U.S. 397 (1989)]; *United States v. O'Brien*, 391 U.S. 367 (1968); *Tinker v. Des Moines Independent Community School Dist.*, 393 U.S. 503 (1969).

The protections afforded by the First Amendment, however, are not absolute and we have long recognized that the government may regulate certain categories of expression consistent with the Constitution. See, e.g., *Chaplinsky v. New Hampshire*, 315 U.S. 568 (1942) ("There are certain well-defined and narrowly limited classes of speech, the prevention and punishment of which has never been thought to raise any Constitutional problem").

We have consequently held that fighting words—"those personally abusive epithets which, when addressed to the ordinary citizen, are, as a matter of common knowledge, inherently likely to provoke violent reaction"—are generally proscribable under the First Amendment. *Cohen v. California*, 403 U.S. 15 (1971). Furthermore, "the constitutional guarantees of free speech and free press do not permit a State to forbid or proscribe advocacy of the use of force or of law violation except where such advocacy is directed to inciting or producing imminent lawless action and is likely to incite or produce such action." *Brandenburg v. Ohio*, 395 U.S. 444 (1969). And the First Amendment also permits a State to ban a "true threat." *Watts v. United States*, 394 U.S. 705 (1969); accord, *R. A. V.* ("[T]hreats of violence are outside the First Amendment").

"True threats" encompass those statements where the speaker means to communicate a serious expression of an intent to commit an act of unlawful violence to a particular individual or group of individuals. The speaker need not actually intend to carry out the threat. Rather, a prohibition on true threats "protect[s] individuals from the fear of violence" and "from the disruption that fear engenders," in addition to protecting people "from the possibility that the threatened violence will occur." Intimidation in the constitutionally proscribable sense of the word is a type of true threat, where a speaker directs a threat to a person or group of persons with the intent of placing the victim in fear of bodily harm or death. . . .

The fact that cross burning is symbolic expression, however, does not resolve the constitutional question. The Supreme Court of Virginia relied upon *R. A. V.* to conclude that once a statute discriminates on the basis of this type of content, the law is unconstitutional. We disagree.

In *R. A. V.*, we held that a local ordinance that banned certain symbolic conduct, including cross burning, when done with the knowledge that such conduct would " 'arouse anger, alarm or resentment in others on the basis of race, color, creed, religion or gender' " was unconstitutional. We held that the ordinance did not pass constitutional muster because it discriminated on the basis of content by targeting only those individuals who "provoke violence" on a basis specified in the law.

We did not hold in *R. A. V.* that the First Amendment prohibits all forms of content-based discrimination within a proscribable area of speech. Rather, we specifically stated that some types of content discrimination did not violate the First Amendment. Indeed, we noted that it would be constitutional to ban only a particular type of threat: "[T]he Federal Government can criminalize only those threats of violence that are directed against the President . . . since the reasons why threats of violence are outside the First Amendment . . . have special force when applied to the person of the President." And a State may "choose to prohibit only that obscenity which is the most patently offensive in its prurience—i.e., that which involves the most lascivious displays of sexual activity." Consequently, while the holding of *R. A. V.* does not permit a State to ban only obscenity based on "offensive political messages," or "only those threats against the President that mention his policy on aid to inner cities" the First Amendment permits content discrimination "based on the very reasons why the particular class of speech at issue . . . is proscribable."

Similarly, Virginia's statute does not run afoul of the First Amendment insofar as it bans cross burning with intent to intimidate. Unlike the statute at issue in *R. A. V.*, the Virginia statute does not single out for opprobrium only that speech directed toward "one of the specified disfavored topics." It does not matter whether an individual burns a cross with intent to intimidate because of the victim's race, gender, or religion, or because of the victim's "political affiliation, union membership, or homosexuality." . . .

The First Amendment permits Virginia to outlaw cross burnings done with the intent to intimidate because burning a cross is a particularly virulent form of intimidation. Instead of prohibiting all intimidating messages, Virginia may choose to regulate this subset of intimidating messages in light of cross burning's long and pernicious history as a signal of impending violence. Thus, just as a State may regulate only that obscenity which is the most obscene due to its prurient content, so too may a State choose to prohibit only those forms of intimidation that are most likely to inspire fear of bodily harm. A ban on cross burning carried out with the intent to intimidate is fully consistent with our holding in *R. A. V.* and is proscribable under the First Amendment.

■ **IV**

The Supreme Court of Virginia ruled in the alternative that Virginia's cross-burning statute was unconstitutionally overbroad due to its provision stating that "[a]ny such burning of a cross shall be prima facie evidence of an intent to intimidate a person or group of persons." . . . In this Court, as in the Supreme Court of Virginia, respondents do not argue that the prima facie evidence provision is unconstitutional as applied to any one of them. Rather, they contend that the provision is unconstitutional on its face. . . .

As construed by the jury instruction, the prima facie provision strips away the very reason why a State may ban cross burning with the intent to intimidate. The prima facie evidence provision permits a jury to convict in every cross-burning case in which defendants exercise their constitutional right not to put on a defense. And even where a defendant like Black presents a defense, the prima facie evidence provision makes it more likely that the jury will find an intent to intimidate regardless of the particular facts of the case. The provision permits the Commonwealth to arrest, prosecute, and convict a person based solely on the fact of cross burning itself. . . .

As the history of cross burning indicates, a burning cross is not always intended to intimidate. Rather, sometimes the cross burning is a statement of ideology, a symbol of group solidarity. . . . Thus, "[b]urning a cross at a political rally would almost certainly be protected expression." *R. A. V.* . . .

The prima facie provision makes no effort to distinguish among these different types of cross burnings. It does not distinguish between a cross burning done with the purpose of creating anger or resentment and a cross burning done with the purpose of threatening or intimidating a victim. It does not distinguish between a cross burning at a public rally or a cross burning on a neighbor's lawn. It does not treat the cross burning directed at an individual differently from the cross burning directed at a group of like-minded believers. It allows a jury to treat a cross burning on the property of another with the owner's acquiescence in the same manner as a cross burning on the property of another without the owner's permission. To this extent I agree with Justice SOUTER that the prima facie evidence provision can "skew jury deliberations toward conviction in cases where the evidence of intent to intimidate is relatively weak and arguably consistent with a solely ideological reason for burning." . . .

For these reasons, the prima facie evidence provision, as interpreted through the jury instruction and as applied in Barry Black's case, is unconstitutional on its face. . . . Unlike Justice SCALIA, we refuse to speculate on whether any interpretation of the prima facie evidence provision would satisfy the First Amendment. Rather, all we hold is that because of the interpretation of the prima facie evidence provision given by the jury instruction, the provision makes the statute facially invalid at this point. . . .

■ **V**

With respect to Barry Black, we agree with the Supreme Court of Virginia that his conviction cannot stand, and we affirm the judgment of the Supreme Court of Virginia. With respect to Elliott and O'Mara, we vacate the judgment of the Supreme Court of Virginia, and remand the case for further proceedings. It is so ordered.

☐ *Justice STEVENS, concurring.*

Cross burning with "an intent to intimidate" unquestionably qualifies as the kind of threat that is unprotected by the First Amendment. For the reasons stated in the separate opinions that Justice WHITE and I wrote in *R. A. V.* that simple proposition provides a sufficient basis for upholding the basic prohibition in the Virginia statute even though it does not cover other types of threatening expressive conduct. With this observation, I join Justice O'CONNOR's opinion.

☐ *Justice THOMAS, dissenting.*

Although I agree with the majority's conclusion that it is constitutionally permissible to "ban . . . cross burning carried out with intent to intimidate," I believe that the majority errs in imputing an expressive component to the activity in question. In my view, whatever expressive value cross burning has, the legislature simply wrote it out by banning only intimidating conduct undertaken by a particular means. A conclusion that the statute prohibiting cross burning with intent to intimidate sweeps beyond a prohibition on certain conduct into the zone of expression overlooks not only the words of the statute but also reality. . . .

Virginia's experience has been no exception. In Virginia, though facing widespread opposition in 1920s, the KKK developed localized strength in the southeastern part of the State, where there were reports of scattered raids and floggings. Although the KKK was disbanded at the national level in 1944, a series of cross burnings in Virginia took place between 1949 and 1952. . . .

That in the early 1950s the people of Virginia viewed cross burning as creating an intolerable atmosphere of terror is not surprising: Although the cross took on some religious significance in the 1920s when the Klan became connected with certain southern white clergy, by the postwar period it had reverted to its original function "as an instrument of intimidation." . . .

It strains credulity to suggest that a state legislature that adopted a litany of segregationist laws self-contradictorily intended to squelch the segregationist message. Even for segregationists, violent and terroristic conduct, the Siamese twin of cross burning, was intolerable. The ban on cross burning with intent to intimidate demonstrates that even segregationists understood the difference between intimidating and terroristic conduct and racist expression. It is simply beyond belief that, in passing the statute now under review, the Virginia legislature was concerned with anything but penalizing conduct it must have viewed as particularly vicious.

Accordingly, this statute prohibits only conduct, not expression. And, just as one cannot burn down someone's house to make a political point and then seek refuge in the First Amendment, those who hate cannot terrorize and intimidate to make their point. In light of my conclusion that the statute here addresses only conduct, there is no need to analyze it under any of our First Amendment tests.

Even assuming that the statute implicates the First Amendment, in my view, the fact that the statute permits a jury to draw an inference of intent to intimidate from the cross burning itself presents no constitutional problems. Therein lies my primary disagreement with the plurality. . . .

Because the prima facie clause here is an inference, not an irrebuttable presumption, there is all the more basis under our Due Process precedents to sustain this statute. . . .

Moreover, even in the First Amendment context, the Court has upheld such regulations where conduct that initially appears culpable, ultimately results in dismissed charges. A regulation of pornography is one such example. While possession of child pornography is illegal, *New York v. Ferber*, 458 U.S. 747 (1982), possession of adult pornography, as long as it is not obscene, is allowed, *Miller v. California*, 413 U.S. 15 (1973). As a result, those pornographers trafficking in images of adults who look like minors, may be not only deterred but also arrested and prosecuted for possessing what a jury might find to be legal materials. This "chilling" effect has not, however, been a cause for grave concern with respect to overbreadth of such statutes among the members of this Court. . . .

Because I would uphold the validity of this statute, I respectfully dissent.

☐ *Justice SCALIA, with whom Justice THOMAS joins, concurring in part, concurring in the judgment in part, and dissenting in part.*

I agree with the Court that, under our decision in *R. A. V.,* a State may, without infringing the First Amendment, prohibit cross burning carried out with the intent to intimidate. Accordingly, I join Parts I–III of the Court's opinion. I also agree that we should vacate and remand the judgment of the Virginia Supreme Court so that that Court can have an opportunity authoritatively to construe the prima-facie-evidence provision of Section 18.2-423. I write separately, however, to describe what I believe to be the correct interpretation of Sec. 18.2-423, and to explain why I believe there is no justification for the plurality's apparent decision to invalidate that provision on its face.

In order to determine whether this component of the statute violates the Constitution, it is necessary, first, to establish precisely what the presentation of prima facie evidence accomplishes. . . . [P]resentation of evidence that a defendant burned a cross in public view is automatically sufficient, on its own, to support an inference that the defendant intended to intimidate only until the defendant comes forward with some evidence in rebuttal.

The question presented, then, is whether, given this understanding of the term "prima facie evidence," the cross-burning statute is constitutional. The Virginia Supreme Court answered that question in the negative. It stated that "[Sec.] 18.2-423 sweeps within its ambit for arrest and prosecution, both protected and unprotected speech." "The enhanced probability of prosecution under the statute chills the expression of protected speech sufficiently to render the statute overbroad."

This approach toward overbreadth analysis is unprecedented. We have never held that the mere threat that individuals who engage in protected conduct will be subject to arrest and prosecution suffices to render a statute overbroad. Rather, our overbreadth jurisprudence has consistently focused on whether the prohibitory terms of a particular statute extend to protected conduct; that is, we have inquired whether individuals who engage in protected conduct can be convicted under a statute, not whether they might be subject to arrest and prosecution. . . .

In deeming Sec. 18.2-423 facially invalid, the plurality presumably means to rely on some species of overbreadth doctrine. But it must be a rare species indeed. . . . The class of persons that the plurality contemplates could impermissibly be convicted under Sec. 18.2-423 includes only those individuals who (1) burn a cross in public view, (2) do not intend to intimidate, (3) are nonetheless charged and prosecuted, and (4) refuse to present a defense. ("The prima facie evidence provision permits a jury to convict in every cross-burning case in which defendants exercise their constitutional right not to put on a defense.")

Conceding (quite generously, in my view) that this class of persons exists, it cannot possibly give rise to a viable facial challenge, not even with the aid of our First Amendment overbreadth doctrine.

I believe the prima-facie-evidence provision in Virginia's cross-burning statute is constitutionally unproblematic. . . .

□ *Justice SOUTER, with whom Justice KENNEDY and Justice GINSBURG join, concurring in the judgment in part and dissenting in part.*

I agree with the majority that the Virginia statute makes a content-based distinction within the category of punishable intimidating or threatening expression, the very type of distinction we considered in *R. A. V.* I disagree that any exception should save Virginia's law from unconstitutionality under the holding in *R. A. V.* or any acceptable variation of it.

As the majority points out, the burning cross can broadcast threat and ideology together, ideology alone, or threat alone, as was apparently the choice of respondents Elliott and O'Mara.

The issue is whether the statutory prohibition restricted to this symbol falls within one of the exceptions to *R. A. V.*'s general condemnation of limited content-based proscription within a broader category of expression proscribable generally. Because of the burning cross's extraordinary force as a method of intimidation, the *R. A. V.* exception most likely to cover the statute is the first of the three mentioned there, which the *R. A. V.* opinion called an exception for content discrimination on a basis that "consists entirely of the very reason the entire class of speech at issue is proscribable." *R. A. V.* This is the exception the majority speaks of here as covering statutes prohibiting "particularly virulent" proscribable expression.

I do not think that the Virginia statute qualifies for this virulence exception as *R. A. V.* explained it. The statute fits poorly with the illustrative examples given in *R. A. V.*, none of which involves communication generally associated with a particular message, and in fact, the majority's discussion of a special virulence exception here moves that exception toward a more flexible conception than the version in *R. A. V.* I will reserve judgment on that doctrinal development, for even on a pragmatic conception of *R. A. V.* and its exceptions the Virginia statute could not pass muster, the most obvious hurdle being the statute's prima facie evidence provision. That provision is essential to understanding why the statute's tendency to suppress a message disqualifies it from any rescue by exception from *R. A. V.*'s general rule. . . .

[N]o content-based statute should survive even under a pragmatic recasting of *R. A. V.* without a high probability that no "official suppression of ideas is afoot," *R. A. V.* I believe the prima facie evidence provision stands in the way of any finding of such a high probability here. . . .

As I see the likely significance of the evidence provision, its primary effect is to skew jury deliberations toward conviction in cases where the evidence of intent to intimidate is relatively weak and arguably consistent with a solely ideological reason for burning. To understand how the provision may work, recall that the symbolic act of burning a cross, without more, is consistent with both intent to intimidate and intent to make an ideological statement free of any aim to threaten. One can tell the intimidating instance from the wholly ideological one only by reference to some further circumstance. In the real world, of course, and in real-world prosecutions, there will always be further circumstances, and the factfinder will always learn something more than the isolated fact of cross burning. Sometimes those circumstances will show an intent to intimidate, but sometimes they will be at least equivocal, as in cases where a white supremacist group burns a cross at an initiation ceremony or political rally visible to the public. In such a case, if the factfinder is aware of the prima facie evidence provision, as the jury was in respondent Black's case, the provision will have the practical effect of tilting the jury's thinking in favor of the prosecution. What is significant is not that the provision permits a factfinder's conclusion that the defendant acted with proscribable and punishable intent without any further indication, because some such indication will almost always be presented. What is significant is that the provision will encourage a factfinder to err on the side of a finding of intent to intimidate when the evidence of circumstances fails to point with any clarity either to the criminal intent or to the permissible one. . . . The provision will thus tend to draw nonthreatening ideological expression within the ambit of the prohibition of intimidating expression, as Justice O'CONNOR notes.

To the extent the prima facie evidence provision skews prosecutions, then, it skews the statute toward suppressing ideas. Thus, the appropriate way to consider the statute's prima facie evidence term, in my view, is not as if it were an overbroad statutory definition amenable to severance or a narrowing construction. The question here is not the permissible scope of an arguably overbroad statute, but the claim of a clearly content-based statute to an exception from the general prohibition of content-based proscriptions, an exception that is not warranted if the statute's terms show that suppression of ideas may be afoot. Accordingly, the way to look at the prima facie evidence provision is to consider it for any indication of what is afoot. And if we look at the provision for this purpose, it has a very obvious significance as a mechanism for bringing within the statute's prohibition some expression that is doubtfully threatening though certainly distasteful. . . .

I conclude that the statute under which all three of the respondents were prosecuted violates the First Amendment, since the statute's content-based distinction was invalid at the time of the charged activities, regardless of whether the prima facie evidence provision was given any effect in any respondent's individual case. In my view, severance of the prima facie evidence provision now could not eliminate the unconstitutionality of the whole statute at the time of the respondents' conduct. I would therefore affirm the judgment of the Supreme Court of Virginia vacating the respondents' convictions and dismissing the indictments. Accordingly, I concur in the Court's judgment as to respondent Black and dissent as to respondents Elliott and O'Mara.

6

FREEDOM FROM AND
OF RELIGION

In its 2003–2004 term the Court will consider again the issue of public subsidies for religion that places the tensions between the (dis)establishment clause and the free exercise clause, along with the free speech clause, into bold relief. *Locke v. Davey*, No. 01-1315, appeals the decision of the Court of Appeals for the Ninth Circuit that struck down Washington's constitutional provision barring public funding for religious instruction. Thirty-six other states have similar proscriptions against public financial support for religion. These provisions are known as "Blaine amendments," after the sponsor of a failed effort to attach such an amendment to the federal Constitution in 1875. Joshua Davey, a student at Northwest College, a Christian college, challenged the denial of a state scholarship because he was pursuing a degree in theology. Davey had been awarded a scholarship under the state's Promise Scholarships program for students who have excellent high school grades, who have low- and middle-class family incomes, and who attend a state-accredited college. Under the program, students may attend state-accredited religious schools, but they may not use their scholarships to pursue religious instruction.

Davey's scholarship was withdrawn by the state's Higher Education Coordinating Board (HECB) after he declared his intent to pursue a degree in theology. The HECB defended its decision on the ground that Davey's use of the scholarship for that purpose violated the state's constitutional provision for and the First Amendment provision for "the separation of church and state." Davey's attorney countered that the denial of the scholarship violated his First Amendment right to the free exercise of religion. A federal district court rejected Davey's claim, but on appeal was reversed. The Ninth Circuit held that the scholarship program created a "fiscal forum," analogous to a "public forum" for free speech, and just as religious speech may not be excluded from a public forum, the benefits of a fiscal forum "may not be denied on account of religion." Governor Gary Locke appealed that decision and the Court granted review.

A | *The (Dis)Establishment of Religion*

Zelman v. Simmons-Harris
536 U.S. 639, 122 S.Ct. 2460 (2002)

In 1995, Cleveland, Ohio's low-income inner-city schools were declared to be in crisis and placed under state control. Subsequently, Ohio adopted a "Pilot Project Scholarship Program," providing school vouchers of up to $2,250 to send inner-city children to schools outside the Cleveland school district. About 96 percent of the money went to religious schools. A group of taxpayers challenged the constitutionality of the program for violating the First Amendment's separation of government from religion. A federal district held the voucher program unconstitutional and the Court of Appeals for the Sixth Circuit affirmed that decision.

The appellate court's decision was reversed on a vote of five to four. Chief Justice Rehnquist delivered the opinion of the Court. Justices O'Connor and Thomas issued concurring opinions. Justices Stevens, Breyer, and Souter filed dissenting opinions, and Justice Ginsburg joined the latter's dissent.

□ *CHIEF JUSTICE REHNQUIST delivered the opinion of the Court.*

The Establishment Clause of the First Amendment, applied to the States through the Fourteenth Amendment, prevents a State from enacting laws that have the "purpose" or "effect" of advancing or inhibiting religion. *Agostini v. Felton*, 521 U.S. 203 (1997). There is no dispute that the program challenged here was enacted for the valid secular purpose of providing educational assistance to poor children in a demonstrably failing public school system. Thus, the question presented is whether the Ohio program nonetheless has the forbidden "effect" of advancing or inhibiting religion.

To answer that question, our decisions have drawn a consistent distinction between government programs that provide aid directly to religious schools, *Mitchell v. Helms*, 530 U.S. 793 (2000); *Agostini*; *Rosenberger v. Rector and Visitors of Univ. of Va.*, 515 U.S. 819 (1995), and programs of true private choice, in which government aid reaches religious schools only as a result of the genuine and independent choices of private individuals, *Mueller v. Allen*, 463 U.S. 388 (1983); *Witters v. Washington Dept. of Servs. for Blind*, 474 U.S. 481 (1986); *Zobrest v. Catalina Foothills School Dist.*, 509 U.S. 1 (1993). While our jurisprudence with respect to the constitutionality of direct aid programs has "changed significantly" over the past two decades, our jurisprudence with respect to true private choice programs has remained consistent and unbroken. Three times we have confronted Establishment Clause challenges to neutral government programs that provide aid directly to a broad class of individuals, who, in turn, direct the aid to religious schools or institutions of their own choosing. Three times we have rejected such challenges.

In *Mueller*, we rejected an Establishment Clause challenge to a Minnesota program authorizing tax deductions for various educational expenses, including private school tuition costs, even though the great majority of the program's beneficiaries (96%) were parents of children in religious schools. . . .

In *Witters*, we used identical reasoning to reject an Establishment Clause challenge to a vocational scholarship program that provided tuition aid to a student studying at a religious institution to become a pastor. . . .

Finally, in *Zobrest*, we applied *Mueller* and *Witters* to reject an Establishment Clause challenge to a federal program that permitted sign-language interpreters to assist deaf children enrolled in religious schools. Reviewing our earlier decisions, we stated that "government programs that neutrally provide benefits to a broad class of citizens defined without reference to religion are not readily subject to an Establishment Clause challenge." Looking once again to the challenged program as a whole, we observed that the program "distributes benefits neutrally to any child qualifying as 'disabled.'" Its "primary beneficiaries," we said, were "disabled children, not sectarian schools." . . .

Mueller, Witters, and *Zobrest* thus make clear that where a government aid program is neutral with respect to religion, and provides assistance directly to a broad class of citizens who, in turn, direct government aid to religious schools wholly as a result of their own genuine and independent private choice, the program is not readily subject to challenge under the Establishment Clause. A program that shares these features permits government aid to reach religious institutions only by way of the deliberate choices of numerous individual recipients. The incidental advancement of a religious mission, or the perceived endorsement of a religious message, is reasonably attributable to the individual recipient, not to the government, whose role ends with the disbursement of benefits.

We believe that the program challenged here is a program of true private choice, consistent with *Mueller, Witters*, and *Zobrest*, and thus constitutional. . . .

Respondents suggest that even without a financial incentive for parents to choose a religious school, the program creates a "public perception that the State is endorsing religious practices and beliefs." But we have repeatedly recognized that no reasonable observer would think a neutral program of private choice, where state aid reaches religious schools solely as a result of the numerous independent decisions of private individuals, carries with it the imprimatur of government endorsement. The argument is particularly misplaced here since "the reasonable observer in the endorsement inquiry must be deemed aware" of the "history and context" underlying a challenged program. *Good News Club v. Milford Central School*, 533 U.S. 98 (2001). Any objective observer familiar with the full history and context of the Ohio program would reasonably view it as one aspect of a broader undertaking to assist poor children in failed schools, not as an endorsement of religious schooling in general. . . .

Respondents and Justice SOUTER claim that even if we do not focus on the number of participating schools that are religious schools, we should attach constitutional significance to the fact that 96% of scholarship recipients have enrolled in religious schools. They claim that this alone proves parents lack genuine choice, even if no parent has ever said so. We need not consider this argument in detail, since it was flatly rejected in *Mueller*, where we found it irrelevant that 96% of parents taking deductions for tuition expenses paid tuition at religious schools. Indeed, we have recently found it irrelevant even to the constitutionality of a direct aid program that a vast majority of program benefits went to religious schools. . . .

Respondents finally claim that we should look to *Committee for Public Ed. & Religious Liberty v. Nyquist*, 413 U.S. 756 (1973), to decide these cases. We disagree for two reasons. First, the program in *Nyquist* was quite different from the program challenged here. *Nyquist* involved a New York program that gave a package of benefits exclusively to private schools and the parents of private school enrollees. Although the program was enacted for ostensibly secular purposes, we found that its "function" was "unmistakably to provide desired financial support for nonpublic, sectarian institutions." Its genesis, we said, was that private religious schools faced "increasingly grave fiscal problems." The program thus provided direct money grants to religious schools.

Second, were there any doubt that the program challenged in *Nyquist* is far removed from the program challenged here, we expressly reserved judgment with respect to "a case involving some form of public assistance (e.g., scholarships) made available generally without regard to the sectarian-nonsectarian, or public-nonpublic nature of the institution benefited." That, of course, is the very question now before us, and it has since been answered, first in *Mueller*. To the extent the scope of *Nyquist* has remained an open question in light of these later decisions, we now hold that *Nyquist* does not govern neutral educational assistance programs that, like the program here, offer aid directly to a broad class of individual recipients defined without regard to religion.

In sum, the Ohio program is entirely neutral with respect to religion. It provides benefits directly to a wide spectrum of individuals, defined only by financial need and residence in a particular school district. It permits such individuals to exercise genuine choice among options public and private, secular and religious. The program is therefore a program of true private choice. In keeping with an unbroken line of decisions rejecting challenges to similar programs, we hold that the program does not offend the Establishment Clause. The judgment of the Court of Appeals is reversed. It is so ordered.

□ *Justice O'CONNOR, concurring.*

While I join the Court's opinion, I write separately for two reasons. First, although the Court takes an important step, I do not believe that today's decision, when considered in light of other longstanding government programs that impact religious organizations and our prior Establishment Clause jurisprudence, marks a dramatic break from the past. Second, given the emphasis the Court places on verifying that parents of voucher students in religious schools have exercised "true private choice," I think it is worth elaborating on the Court's conclusion that this inquiry should consider all reasonable educational alternatives to religious schools that are available to parents. To do otherwise is to ignore how the educational system in Cleveland actually functions.

These cases are different from prior indirect aid cases in part because a significant portion of the funds appropriated for the voucher program reach religious schools without restrictions on the use of these funds. The share of public resources that reach religious schools is not, however, as significant as respondents suggest. Data from the 1999–2000 school year indicate that 82 percent of schools participating in the voucher program were religious and that 96 percent of participating students enrolled in religious schools (46 of 56 private schools in the program are religiously affiliated; 3,637 of 3,765 voucher students attend religious private schools), but these data are incomplete. These statistics do not take into account all of the reasonable educational choices that may be available to students in Cleveland public schools. When one considers the option to attend community schools, the percentage of students enrolled in religious schools falls to 62.1 percent. If magnet schools are included in the mix, this percentage falls to 16.5 percent.

Even these numbers do not paint a complete picture. The Cleveland program provides voucher applicants from low-income families with up to $2,250 in tuition assistance and provides the remaining applicants with up to $1,875 in tuition assistance. In contrast, the State provides community schools $4,518 per pupil and magnet schools, on average, $7,097 per pupil. Even if one assumes that all voucher students came from low-income families and that each voucher student used up the entire $2,250 voucher, at most $8.2 million of public funds flowed to religious schools under the voucher program in 1999–2000. Although just over one-half as many students attended community schools as religious private schools on the state fisc, the State spent over $1 million more—$9.4 million—on students in community schools than on students in religious private schools because per-pupil aid to community schools is more than double the per-pupil aid to private schools under the voucher program. Moreover, the amount spent on religious private schools is minor compared to the $114.8 million the State spent on students in the Cleveland magnet schools.

Although $8.2 million is no small sum, it pales in comparison to the amount of funds that federal, state, and local governments already provide religious institutions. Religious organizations may qualify for exemptions from the federal corporate income tax; the corporate income tax in many States; and property taxes in all 50 States; and clergy qualify for a federal tax break on income used for housing expenses. In addition, the Federal Government provides individuals, corporations, trusts, and estates a tax deduction for charitable contributions to qualified religious groups. See §§170, 642(c). Finally, the Federal Government and certain state governments provide tax credits for educational expenses, many of which are spent on education at religious schools. . . .

Based on the reasoning in the Court's opinion, which is consistent with the realities of the Cleveland educational system, I am persuaded that the Cleveland voucher program affords parents of eligible children genuine nonreligious options and is consistent with the Establishment Clause.

□ *Justice THOMAS, concurring.*

Frederick Douglass once said that "[e]ducation . . . means emancipation. It means light and liberty. It means the uplifting of the soul of man into the glorious light of truth, the light by which men can only be made free." Today many of our inner-city public schools deny emancipation to urban minority students. Despite this Court's observation nearly 50 years ago in *Brown v. Board of Education* that "it is doubtful that any child may reasonably be expected to succeed in life if he is denied the opportunity of an education," urban children have been forced into a system that continually fails them. These cases present an example of such failures. Besieged by escalating financial problems and declining academic achievement, the Cleveland City School District was in the midst of an academic emergency when Ohio enacted its scholarship program.

The dissents and respondents wish to invoke the Establishment Clause of the First Amendment, as incorporated through the Fourteenth, to constrain a State's neutral efforts to provide greater educational opportunity for underprivileged minority students. Today's decision properly upholds the program as constitutional, and I join it in full. . . .

□ *Justice STEVENS, dissenting.*

Is a law that authorizes the use of public funds to pay for the indoctrination of thousands of grammar school children in particular religious faiths a "law respecting an establishment of religion" within the meaning of the First Amendment? In answering that question, I think we should ignore three factual matters that are discussed at length by my colleagues.

First, the severe educational crisis that confronted the Cleveland City School District when Ohio enacted its voucher program is not a matter that should affect our appraisal of its constitutionality. . . .

Second, the wide range of choices that have been made available to students within the public school system has no bearing on the question whether the State may pay the tuition for students who wish to reject public education entirely and attend private schools that will provide them with a sectarian education. The fact that the vast majority of the voucher recipients who have entirely rejected public education receive religious indoctrination at state expense does, however, support the claim that the law is one "respecting an establishment of religion." The State may choose to divide up its public schools into a dozen different options and label them magnet schools, community schools, or whatever else it decides to call them, but the State is still required to provide a public education and it is the State's decision to fund private school education over and above its traditional obligation that is at issue in these cases.

Third, the voluntary character of the private choice to prefer a parochial education over an education in the public school system seems to me quite irrelevant to the question whether the government's choice to pay for religious indoctrination is constitutionally permissible. Today, however, the Court seems to have decided that the mere fact that a family that cannot afford a private education wants its children educated in a parochial school is a sufficient justification for this use of public funds.

For the reasons stated by Justice SOUTER and Justice BREYER, I am convinced that the Court's decision is profoundly misguided. Admittedly, in reaching that conclusion I have been influenced by my understanding of the impact of religious strife on the decisions of our forbears to migrate to this continent, and on the decisions of neighbors in the Balkans, Northern Ireland, and the Middle East to mistrust one another. Whenever we remove a brick from the wall that was designed to separate religion and government, we increase the risk of religious strife and weaken the foundation of our democracy.

I respectfully dissent.

☐ *Justice BREYER, with whom Justice STEVENS and Justice SOUTER join, dissenting.*

I join Justice SOUTER's opinion, and I agree substantially with Justice STEVENS. I write separately, however, to emphasize the risk that publicly financed voucher programs pose in terms of religiously based social conflict. I do so because I believe that the Establishment Clause concern for protecting the Nation's social fabric from religious conflict poses an overriding obstacle to the implementation of this well-intentioned school voucher program. And by explaining the nature of the concern, I hope to demonstrate why, in my view, "parental choice" cannot significantly alleviate the constitutional problem. . . .

I do not believe that the "parental choice" aspect of the voucher program sufficiently offsets the concerns I have mentioned. Parental choice cannot help the taxpayer who does not want to finance the religious education of children. It will not always help the parent who may see little real choice between inadequate nonsectarian public education and adequate education at a school whose religious teachings are contrary to his own. It will not satisfy religious minorities unable to participate because they are too few in number to support the creation of their own private schools. It will not satisfy groups whose religious beliefs preclude them from participating in a government-sponsored program, and who may well feel ignored as government funds primarily support the education of children in the doctrines of the dominant religions. And it does little to ameliorate the entanglement problems or the related problems of social division. Consequently, the fact that the parent may choose which school can cash the government's voucher check does not alleviate the Establishment Clause concerns associated with voucher programs.

The Court, in effect, turns the clock back. It adopts, under the name of "neutrality," an interpretation of the Establishment Clause that this Court rejected more than half a century ago. In its view, the parental choice that offers each religious group a kind of equal opportunity to secure government funding overcomes the Establishment Clause concern for social concord. An earlier Court found that "equal opportunity" principle insufficient; it read the Clause as insisting upon greater separation of church and state, at least in respect to primary education. See *Nyquist*. In a society composed of many different religious creeds, I fear that this present departure from the Court's earlier understanding risks creating a form of religiously based conflict potentially harmful to the Nation's social fabric. Because I believe the Establishment Clause was written in part to avoid this kind of conflict, and for reasons set forth by Justice SOUTER and Justice STEVENS, I respectfully dissent.

☐ *Justice SOUTER, with whom Justice STEVENS, Justice GINSBURG, and Justice BREYER join, dissenting.*

The applicability of the Establishment Clause to public funding of benefits to religious schools was settled in *Everson v. Board of Ed. of Ewing*, 330 U.S. 1 (1947), which inaugurated the modern era of establishment doctrine. The Court stated the principle in words from which there was no dissent: "No tax in any amount, large or small, can be levied to support any religious activities or institutions, whatever they may be called, or whatever form they may adopt to teach or practice religion." The Court has never in so many words repudiated this statement, let alone, in so many words, overruled *Everson*. . . .

How can a Court consistently leave *Everson* on the books and approve the Ohio vouchers? The answer is that it cannot. It is only by ignoring *Everson* that the majority can claim to rest on traditional law in its invocation of neutral aid provisions and private choice to sanction the Ohio law. It is, moreover, only by ignoring the meaning of neutrality and private choice themselves that the majority can even pretend to rest today's decision on those criteria.

The majority's statements of Establishment Clause doctrine cannot be appreciated without some historical perspective on the Court's announced limitations on government aid to religious education, and its repeated repudiation of limits previously set. . . .

Viewed with the necessary generality, the cases can be categorized in three groups. In the period from 1947 to 1968, the basic principle of no aid to religion through school benefits was unquestioned. Thereafter for some 15 years, the Court termed its efforts as attempts to draw a line against aid that would be divertible to support the religious, as distinct from the secular, activity of an institutional beneficiary. Then, starting in 1983, concern with divertibility was gradually lost in favor of approving aid in amounts unlikely to afford substantial benefits to religious schools, when offered evenhandedly without regard to a recipient's religious character, and when channeled to a religious institution only by the genuinely free choice of some private individual. Now, the three stages are succeeded by a fourth, in which the substantial character of government aid is held to have no constitutional significance, and the espoused criteria of neutrality in offering aid, and private choice in directing it, are shown to be nothing but examples of verbal formalism. . . .

Although it has taken half a century since *Everson* to reach the majority's twin standards of neutrality and free choice, the facts show that, in the majority's hands, even these criteria cannot convincingly legitimize the Ohio scheme.

Consider first the criterion of neutrality. As recently as two Terms ago, a majority of the Court recognized that neutrality conceived of as evenhandedness toward aid recipients had never been treated as alone sufficient to satisfy the Establishment Clause, *Mitchell* [*v. Helms*]. But at least in its limited significance, formal neutrality seemed to serve some purpose. Today, however, the majority employs the neutrality criterion in a way that renders it impossible to understand.

Neutrality in this sense refers, of course, to evenhandedness in setting eligibility as between potential religious and secular recipients of public money. Thus, for example, the aid scheme in *Witters* provided an eligible recipient with a scholarship to be used at any institution within a practically unlimited universe of schools; it did not tend to provide more or less aid depending on which one the scholarship recipient chose, and there was no indication that the maximum scholarship amount would be insufficient at secular schools. Neither did any condition of *Zobrest's* interpreter's subsidy favor religious education.

In order to apply the neutrality test, then, it makes sense to focus on a category of aid that may be directed to religious as well as secular schools, and ask whether the scheme favors a religious direction. Here, one would ask whether the voucher provisions, allowing for as much as $2,250 toward private school tuition (or a grant to a public school in an adjacent district), were written in a way that skewed the scheme toward benefiting religious schools.

This, however, is not what the majority asks. The majority looks not to the provisions for tuition vouchers, but to every provision for educational opportunity: "The program permits the participation of all schools within the district [as well as public schools in adjacent districts], religious or non-religious." The majority then finds confirmation that "participation of all schools" satisfies neutrality by noting that the better part of total state educational expenditure goes to public schools, thus showing there is no favor of religion.

The illogic is patent. If regular, public schools (which can get no voucher payments) "participate" in a voucher scheme with schools that can, and public expenditure is still predominantly on public schools, then the majority's reasoning would find neutrality in a scheme of vouchers available for private tuition in districts with no secular private schools at all. "Neutrality" as the majority employs the term is, literally, verbal and nothing more. This, indeed, is the only way the majority can gloss over the very nonneutral feature of the total scheme covering "all schools": public tutors may receive from the State no more than $324 per child to support extra tutoring (that is, the State's 90% of a total amount of $360), whereas the tuition voucher schools (which turn out to be mostly religious) can receive up to $2,250.

Why the majority does not simply accept the fact that the challenge here is to the more generous voucher scheme and judge its neutrality in relation to religious use of voucher money seems very odd. It seems odd, that is, until one recognizes that comparable schools for applying the criterion of neutrality are also the comparable schools for applying the other majority criterion, whether the immediate recipients of voucher aid have a genuinely free choice of religious and secular schools to receive the voucher money. And in applying this second criterion, the consideration of "all schools" is ostensibly helpful to the majority position.

The majority addresses the issue of choice the same way it addresses neutrality, by asking whether recipients or potential recipients of voucher aid have a choice of public schools among secular alternatives to religious schools. Again, however, the majority asks the wrong question and misapplies the criterion. The majority has confused choice in spending scholarships with choice from the entire menu of possible educational placements, most of them open to anyone willing to attend a public school. I say "confused" because the majority's new use of the choice criterion, which it frames negatively as "whether Ohio is coercing parents into sending their children to religious schools" ignores the reason for having a private choice enquiry in the first place. Cases since *Mueller* have found private choice relevant under a rule that aid to religious schools can be permissible so long as it first passes through the hands of students or parents. The majority's view that all educational choices are comparable for purposes of choice thus ignores the whole point of the choice test: it is a criterion for deciding whether indirect aid to a religious school is legitimate because it passes through private hands that can spend or use the aid in a secular school. The question is whether the private hand is genuinely free to send the money in either a secular direction or a religious one. The majority now has transformed this question about private choice in channeling aid into a question about selecting from examples of state spending (on education) including direct spending on magnet and community public schools that goes through no private hands and could never reach a religious school under any circumstance. When the choice test is transformed from where to spend the money to where to go to school, it is cut loose from its very purpose.

Defining choice as choice in spending the money or channeling the aid is, moreover, necessary if the choice criterion is to function as a limiting principle at all. If "choice" is present whenever there is any educational alternative to the religious school to which vouchers can be endorsed, then there will always be a choice and the voucher can always be constitutional, even in a system in which there is not a single private secular school as an alternative to the religious school. And because it is unlikely that any participating private religious school will enroll more pupils than the generally available public system, it will be easy to generate numbers suggesting that aid to religion is not the significant intent or effect of the voucher scheme.

That is, in fact, just the kind of rhetorical argument that the majority accepts in these cases. In addition to secular private schools (129 students), the majority considers public schools with tuition assistance (roughly 1,400 students), magnet schools (13,000 students), and community schools (1,900 students), and concludes that fewer than 20% of pupils receive state vouchers to attend religious schools. . . .

If, contrary to the majority, we ask the right question about genuine choice to use the vouchers, the answer shows that something is influencing choices in a way that aims the money in a religious direction: of 56 private schools in the district participating in the voucher program (only 53 of which accepted voucher students in 1999–2000), 46 of them are religious; 96.6% of all voucher recipients go to religious schools, only 3.4% to nonreligious ones. Unfortunately for the majority position, there is no explanation for this that suggests the religious direction results simply from free choices by parents. One answer to these statistics, for example, which would be consistent with the genuine choice claimed to be operating, might be that 96.6% of families choosing to avail themselves of vouchers choose to educate their children in schools of their own religion. This would not, in my view, render the scheme constitutional, but it would speak to the majority's choice criterion. Evidence shows, however, that almost two out of three families using vouchers to send their children to religious schools did not embrace the religion of those schools. The families made it clear they had not chosen the schools because they wished their children to be proselytized in a religion not their own, or in any religion, but because of educational opportunity.

Even so, the fact that some 2,270 students chose to apply their vouchers to schools of other religions might be consistent with true choice if the students "chose" their religious schools over a wide array of private nonreligious options, or if it could be shown generally that Ohio's program had no effect on educational choices and thus no impermissible effect of advancing religious education. But both possibilities are contrary to fact. First, even if all existing nonreligious private schools in Cleveland were willing to accept large numbers of voucher students, only a few more than the 129 currently enrolled in such schools would be able to attend, as the total enrollment at all nonreligious private schools in Cleveland for kindergarten through eighth grade is only 510 children, and there is no indication that these schools have many open seats. Second, the $2,500 cap that the program places on tuition for participating low-income pupils has the effect of curtailing the participation of nonreligious schools: "nonreligious schools with higher tuition (about $4,000) stated that they could afford to accommodate just a few voucher students." By comparison, the average tuition at participating Catholic schools in Cleveland in 1999–2000 was $1,592, almost $1,000 below the cap.

Of course, the obvious fix would be to increase the value of vouchers so that existing nonreligious private and non-Catholic religious schools would be able to enroll more voucher students, and to provide incentives for educators to create new such schools given that few presently exist. Private choice, if as robust as that available to the seminarian in *Witters*, would then be "true private choice" under the majority's criterion. But it is simply unrealistic to presume that parents of elementary and middle schoolchildren in Cleveland will have a range of secular and religious choices even arguably comparable to the statewide program for vocational and higher education in Witters. And to get to that hypothetical point would require that such massive financial support be made available to religion as to disserve every objective of the Establishment Clause even more than the present scheme does.

There is, in any case, no way to interpret the 96.6% of current voucher money going to religious schools as reflecting a free and genuine choice by the families that apply for vouchers. The 96.6% reflects, instead, the fact that too few nonreligious school desks are available and few but religious schools can afford to accept more than a handful of voucher students. And contrary to the majority's assertion, public schools in adjacent districts hardly have a financial incentive to participate in the Ohio voucher program, and none has. For the overwhelming number of children in the voucher scheme, the only alternative to the public schools is religious. And it is entirely irrelevant that the State did not deliberately design the network of private schools for the sake of channeling money into religious institutions. The criterion is one of genuinely free choice on the part of the private individuals who choose, and a Hobson's choice is not a choice, whatever the reason for being Hobsonian.

I do not dissent merely because the majority has misapplied its own law, for even if I assumed arguendo that the majority's formal criteria were satisfied on the facts, today's conclusion would be profoundly at odds with the Constitution. Proof of this is clear on two levels. The first is circumstantial, in the now discarded symptom of violation, the substantial dimension of the aid. The second is direct, in the defiance of every objective supposed to be served by the bar against establishment.

The scale of the aid to religious schools approved today is unprecedented, both in the number of dollars and in the proportion of systemic school expenditure supported. Each measure has received attention in previous cases. On one hand, the sheer quantity of aid, when delivered to a class of religious primary and secondary schools, was suspect on the theory that the greater the aid, the greater its proportion to a religious school's existing expenditures, and the greater the likelihood that public money was supporting religious as well as secular instruction. . . .

On the other hand, the Court has found the gross amount unhelpful for Establishment Clause analysis when the aid afforded a benefit solely to one individual, however substantial as to him, but only an incidental benefit to the religious school at which the individual chose to spend the State's money. When neither the design nor the implementation of an aid scheme channels a series of individual students' subsidies toward religious recipients, the relevant beneficiaries for establishment purposes, the Establishment Clause is unlikely to be implicated. The majority's reliance on the observations of five Members of the Court in *Witters* as to the irrelevance of substantiality of aid in that case is therefore beside the point in the matter before us, which involves considerable sums of public funds systematically distributed through thousands of students attending religious elementary and middle schools in the city of Cleveland. . . .

It is virtually superfluous to point out that every objective underlying the prohibition of religious establishment is betrayed by this scheme, but something has to be said about the enormity of the violation. I anticipated these objectives earlier in discussing *Everson*, which cataloged them, the first being respect for freedom of conscience. Jefferson described it as the idea that no one "shall be compelled to . . . support any religious worship, place, or ministry whatsoever," A Bill for Establishing Religious Freedom.

As for the second objective, to save religion from its own corruption, Madison wrote of the "experience . . . that ecclesiastical establishments, instead of maintaining the purity and efficacy of Religion, have had a contrary operation." Memorial and Remonstrance. . . .

The risk is already being realized. In Ohio, for example, a condition of receiving government money under the program is that participating religious schools may not "discriminate on the basis of . . . religion," which means the school may not give admission preferences to children who are members of the patron faith; children of a parish are generally consigned to the same admission lotteries as non-believers. . . .

For perspective on this foot-in-the-door of religious regulation, it is well to remember that the money has barely begun to flow. Prior examples of aid, whether grants through individuals or in-kind assistance, were never significant enough to alter the basic fiscal structure of religious schools; state aid was welcome, but not indispensable. . . .

When government aid goes up, so does reliance on it; the only thing likely to go down is independence. . . .

Justice BREYER has addressed this issue in his own dissenting opinion, which I join, and here it is enough to say that the intensity of the expectable friction can be gauged by realizing that the scramble for money will energize not only contending sectarians, but taxpayers who take their liberty of conscience seriously. Religious teaching at taxpayer expense simply cannot be cordoned from taxpayer politics, and every major religion currently espouses social positions that provoke intense opposition. Not all taxpaying Protestant citizens, for example, will be content to underwrite the teaching of the Roman Catholic Church condemning the death penalty. Nor will all of America's Muslims acquiesce in paying for the endorsement of the religious Zionism taught in many religious Jewish schools, which combines "a nationalistic sentiment" in support of Israel with a "deeply religious" element. Nor will every secular taxpayer be content to support Muslim views on differential treatment of the sexes, or, for that matter, to fund the espousal of a wife's obligation of obedience to her husband, presumably taught in any schools adopting the articles of faith of the Southern Baptist Convention. Views like these, and innumerable others, have been safe in the sectarian pulpits and classrooms of this Nation not only because the Free Exercise Clause protects them directly, but because the ban on supporting religious establishment has protected free exercise, by keeping it relatively private. With the arrival of vouchers in religious schools, that privacy will go, and along with it will go confidence that religious disagreement will stay moderate.

If the divisiveness permitted by today's majority is to be avoided in the short term, it will be avoided only by action of the political branches at the state and national levels. Legislatures not driven to desperation by the problems of public education may be able to see the threat in vouchers negotiable in sectarian schools. Perhaps even cities with problems like Cleveland's will perceive the danger, now that they know a federal court will not save them from it.

My own course as a judge on the Court cannot, however, simply be to hope that the political branches will save us from the consequences of the majority's decision. *Everson's* statement is still the touchstone of sound law, even though the reality is that in the matter of educational aid the Establishment Clause has largely been read away. True, the majority has not approved vouchers for religious schools alone, or aid earmarked for religious instruction. But no scheme so clumsy will ever get before us, and in the cases that we may see, like these, the Establishment Clause is largely silenced. I do not have the option to leave it silent, and I hope that a future Court will reconsider today's dramatic departure from basic Establishment Clause principle.

7

THE FOURTH AMENDMENT GUARANTEE AGAINST UNREASONABLE SEARCHES AND SEIZURES

A | Requirements for a Warrant and Reasonable Searches and Seizures

In its 2003–2004 term, the justices will consider whether an arresting officer had probable cause to arrest a passenger in a car, which there was neither the odor of drugs nor any other indication of drug activity but in which money was found in a closed glove compartment and drugs were found hidden behind the rear armrest. The case is *Maryland v. Pringle* (No. 02-809). Joseph Pringle and two other men were traveling in a car when it was pulled over for a routine traffic stop. When the driver was retrieving the vehicle registration from the glove compartment, the officer noticed a large amount of rolled up money there. After finding no outstanding traffic violations, the officer asked the driver for permission to search the car, and found cocaine behind the armrest. All three men were arrested. Subsequently, Pringle confessed that the cocaine was his, but during his trial his attorney argued that the arrest was unlawful because it was not supported by probable cause, and therefore Pringle's confession should be suppressed as unlawful fruit of an illegal arrest. The trial judge ruled that the officer had probable cause and Pringle was convicted and sentenced to 10 years incarceration without the possibility of parole. On appeal, however, that decision was reversed and the state appealed to the Supreme Court.

B | *Exceptions to the Warrant Requirement*

The Court reaffirmed three earlier interrelated rulings, bearing on searches of citizens in public places, that the "consent" of a passenger on a bus to a request by an officer to a pat-down search for contraband, *Minnesota v. Dickerson*, 508 U.S. 366 (1993) (excerpted in Vol. 2, Ch. 7), "presupposes an innocent person" would consent, *Florida v. Bostick*, 501 U.S. 429 (1991), and that the officers are not required to inform citizens of their right to refuse, *Ohio v. Robinette*, 519 U.S. 33 (1996). Here three law enforcement officers boarded a bus in Tallahassee, Florida, which was bound for Detroit, Michigan. One sat in the driver's seat, another in the back of the bus, and the third questioned passengers. Two young men wearing jackets and baggy pants, in the summer, were questioned and consented to pat-downs, which revealed plastic bags of cocaine under their clothing. Writing for the Court in *United States v. Drayton*, 536 U.S. 194 (2002), Justice Kennedy observed:

Law enforcement officers do not violate the Fourth Amendment's prohibition of unreasonable seizures merely by approaching individuals on the street or in other public places and putting questions to them if they are willing to listen. Even when law enforcement officers have no basis for suspecting a particular individual, they may pose questions, ask for identification, and request consent to search luggage—provided they do not induce cooperation by coercive means. See *Florida v. Bostick*, 501 U.S. [429 (1991)]. If a reasonable person would feel free to terminate the encounter, then he or she has not been seized.

The Court has addressed on a previous occasion the specific question of drug interdiction efforts on buses. In *Bostick*, two police officers requested a bus passenger's consent to a search of his luggage. The passenger agreed, and the resulting search revealed cocaine in his suitcase. The Florida Supreme Court suppressed the cocaine. In doing so it adopted a per se rule that due to the cramped confines onboard a bus the act of questioning would deprive a person of his or her freedom of movement and so constitute a seizure under the Fourth Amendment.

This Court reversed. *Bostick* first made it clear that for the most part per se rules are inappropriate in the Fourth Amendment context. The proper inquiry necessitates a consideration of "all the circumstances surrounding the encounter." The Court noted next that the traditional rule, which states that a seizure does not occur so long as a reasonable person would feel free "to disregard the police and go about his business," *California v. Hodari D.*, 499 U.S. 621 (1991), is not an accurate measure of the coercive effect of a bus encounter. A passenger may not want to get off a bus if there is a risk it will depart before the opportunity to reboard. A bus rider's movements are confined in this sense, but this is the natural result of choosing to take the bus; it says nothing about whether the police conduct is coercive. The proper inquiry "is whether a reasonable person would feel free to decline the officers' requests or otherwise terminate the encounter." Finally, the Court rejected *Bostick* 's argument that he must have been seized because no reasonable person would consent to a search of luggage containing drugs. The reasonable person test, the Court explained, is objective and "presupposes an innocent person."

Justice Souter dissented and was joined by Justices Stevens and Ginsburg.

In *Kaupp v. Texas* (excerpted below) the Court reaffirmed the central principle that an illegal search and seizure, without probable cause, precludes the admission as evidence of incriminating statements made by the accused prior to arrest and reaffirmed the contours of "consent" to a search.

Kaupp v. Texas
123 S.Ct. 1843 (2003)

The facts are discussed in the decision, which was unanimous and delivered unsigned.

☐ *PER CURIAM*

This case turns on the Fourth Amendment rule that a confession "obtained by exploitation of an illegal arrest" may not be used against a criminal defendant. *Brown v. Illinois*, 422 U.S. 590 (1975). After a 14-year-old girl disappeared in January 1999, the Harris County Sheriff's Department learned she had had a sexual relationship with her 19-year-old half brother, who had been in the company of petitioner Robert Kaupp, then 17 years old, on the day of the girl's disappearance. On January 26th, deputy sheriffs questioned the brother and Kaupp at headquarters; Kaupp was cooperative and was permitted to leave, but the brother failed a polygraph examination (his third such failure). Eventually he confessed that he had fatally stabbed his half sister and placed her body in a drainage ditch. He implicated Kaupp in the crime.

Detectives immediately tried but failed to obtain a warrant to question Kaupp. Detective Gregory Pinkins nevertheless decided (in his words) to "get [Kaupp] in and confront him with what [the brother] had said." In the company of two other plain clothes detectives and three uniformed officers, Pinkins went to Kaupp's house at approximately 3 A.M. on January 27th. After Kaupp's father let them in, Pinkins, with at least two other officers, went to Kaupp's bedroom, awakened him with a flashlight, identified himself, and said, "'we need to go and talk.'" Kaupp said "'Okay.'" The two officers then handcuffed Kaupp and led him, shoeless and dressed only in boxer shorts and a T-shirt, out of his house and into a patrol car. The state points to nothing in the record indicating Kaupp was told that he was free to decline to go with the officers.

They stopped for 5 or 10 minutes where the victim's body had just been found, in anticipation of confronting Kaupp with the brother's confession, and then went on to the sheriff's headquarters. There, they took Kaupp to an interview room, removed his handcuffs, and advised him of his rights under *Miranda v. Arizona*, 384 U.S. 436 (1966). Kaupp first denied any involvement in the victim's disappearance, but 10 or 15 minutes into the interrogation, told of the brother's confession, he admitted having some part in the crime. He did not, however, acknowledge causing the fatal wound or confess to murder, for which he was later indicted.

After moving unsuccessfully to suppress his confession as the fruit of an illegal arrest, Kaupp was convicted and sentenced to 55 years' imprisonment. The State Court of Appeals affirmed the conviction by unpublished opinion, concluding that no arrest had occurred until after the confession. The state court said that Kaupp consented to go with the officers when he answered "'Okay'" to Pinkins's statement that "'we need to go and talk.'" The court saw no contrary significance in the subsequent handcuffing and removal to the patrol car, given the practice of the sheriff's department in "routinely" using handcuffs for safety purposes when transporting individuals, as officers had done with Kaupp only the day before. The court observed that "a reasonable person in [Kaupp's] position would not believe that being put in handcuffs was a significant restriction on his freedom of movement." Finally, the state court noted that Kaupp "did not resist the use of handcuffs or act in a manner consistent with anything other than full cooperation." Kaupp appealed, but the Court of Criminal Appeals of Texas denied discretionary review. We grant the motion for leave to proceed in forma pauperis, grant the petition for *certiorari*, and vacate the judgment below.

A seizure of the person within the meaning of the Fourth and Fourteenth Amendments occurs when, "taking into account all of the circumstances surrounding the encounter, the police conduct would 'have communicated to a reasonable person that he was not at liberty to ignore the police presence and go about his business.'" *Florida v. Bostick*, 501 U.S. 429 (1991). . . .

Although certain seizures may be justified on something less than probable cause, see, e.g., *Terry v. Ohio*, 392 U.S. 1 (1968), we have never "sustained against Fourth Amendment challenge the involuntary removal of a suspect from his home to a police station and his detention there for investigative purposes . . . absent probable cause or judicial authorization." *Hayes v. Florida*, 470 U.S. 811 (1985).

The state does not claim to have had probable cause here, and a straightforward application of the test just mentioned shows beyond cavil that Kaupp was arrested within the meaning of the Fourth Amendment. . . . A 17-year-old boy was awakened in his bedroom at three in the morning by at least three police officers, one of whom stated "we need to go and talk." He was taken out in handcuffs, without shoes, dressed only in his underwear in January, placed in a patrol car, driven to the scene of a crime and then to the sheriff's offices, where he was taken into an interrogation room and questioned. This evidence points to arrest even more starkly than the facts in *Dunaway v. New York*, 442 U.S. 200 (1979), where the petitioner "was taken from a neighbor's home to a police car, transported to a police station, and placed in an interrogation room." There we held it clear that the detention was "in important respects indistinguishable from a traditional arrest" and therefore required probable cause or judicial authorization to be legal. The same is, if anything, even clearer here.

Contrary reasons mentioned by the state courts are no answer to the facts. Kaupp's "'Okay'" in response to Pinkins's statement is no showing of consent under the circumstances. Pinkins offered Kaupp no choice, and a group of police officers rousing an adolescent out of bed in the middle of the night with the words "we need to go and talk" presents no option but "to go." There is no reason to think Kaupp's answer was anything more than "a mere submission to a claim of lawful authority." If reasonable doubt were possible on this point, the ensuing events would resolve it: removal from one's house in handcuffs on a January night with nothing on but underwear for a trip to a crime scene on the way to an interview room at law enforcement headquarters. . . .

Since Kaupp was arrested before he was questioned, and because the state does not even claim that the sheriff's department had probable cause to detain him at that point, well-established precedent requires suppression of the confession unless that confession was "an act of free will [sufficient] to purge the primary taint of the unlawful invasion." *Wong Sun v. United States*, 371 U.S. 471 (1963). . . .

The judgment of the State Court of Appeals is vacated, and the case is remanded for further proceedings not inconsistent with this opinion.

C | *The Special Problems of Automobiles in a Mobile Society*

In the Court's 2003–2004 term, the justices will reconsider how far police may go in searching a car incident to the arrest of the driver, in *Arizona v. Gant* (No. 02-1019). Police arrested Rodney J. Gant, on an outstanding arrest warrant, after he drove into his driveway and started walking toward his house. They subsequently found cocaine and drug paraphernalia. The Arizona Court of Appeals, however, ordered the suppression of the evidence on the ground that unless a suspect is aware of the presence of police before leaving a vehicle it may not be searched without a warrant. The state appealed that decision, contending that the subjective nature of the suspect's awareness introduced too much uncertainty into the law enforcement practice of "searches incident to arrest" and that the ruling ran contrary to the holding in *New York v. Belton*, 453 U.S. 454 (1981), which upheld warrantless searches of automobiles that are incident to an arrest.

In its 2003–2004 term the Court will also reconsider its ruling in *Indianapolis v. Edmond*, 531 U.S. 32 (2000), holding that police may not search cars at a checkpoint set up to advance a state's "general interest in crime control" and suspend the requirement of individualized suspicion of criminal activity. In *Illinois v. Lidster* (No. 02-1060) the state contends that its "informational checkpoint" is not barred by the holding in *Edmond*. The case appeals a conviction after an arrest incident to a roadblock set up for looking for information about a hit-and-run accident that occurred in the area a week before. Robert Lidster almost hit a police officer directing the roadblock and was asked out of his van. Lidster failed several sobriety tests and was arrested and convicted. His conviction, however, was reversed on appeal by state courts on the ground that his arrest lacked individualized suspicion under *Edmond*.

■ THE DEVELOPMENT OF LAW

Automobiles and Border Patrol Searches

CASE	VOTE	RULING
United States v. Arvizu, 534 U.S. 161 (2002)	9:0	Writing for the Court, Chief Justice Rehnquist held that under *Terry v. Ohio*, 392 U.S. 1 (1968),

based on "the totality of the circumstances" an experienced border patrol officer had "reasonable suspicion" to stop on an unpaved road in a remote area of Arizona an otherwise innocuous automobile, which in turn led to a search that uncovered over 100 pounds of marijuana.

D | *Other Governmental Searches in the Administrative State*

Board of Education of Independent School District No. 92 of Pottawatomie City v. Earls
536 U.S. 822, 122 S.CT. 2559 (2002)

Following the Court's upholding of random drug testing of high school athletes, in *Vernonia School District No. 47J v. Acton*, 515 U.S. 646 (1995) (excerpted in Vol. 2, Ch. 7), in 1998 the school district of Tecumseh, Oklahoma, a rural community about 40 miles from Oklahoma City, adopted a policy of requiring all middle and high school students who participate in any extracurricular activities to consent to random drug testing. Lindsay Earles, a member of the choir and the marching band, challenged the constitutionally of the policy for violating the Fourth Amendment guarantee against unreasonable searches and seizures. A federal district court rejected her claim, but the Court of Appeals for the Tenth Circuit reversed and the school board appealed.

The appellate court's decision was reversed by a five-to-four vote. Justice Thomas delivered the opinion of the Court. Justice Breyer filed a concurring opinion. Justices O'Connor and Ginsburg filed dissenting opinions, which Justices Stevens and Souter joined.

□ *Justice THOMAS delivered the opinion of the Court.*

The Fourth Amendment to the United States Constitution protects "[t]he right of the people to be secure in their persons, houses, papers, and effects, against unreasonable searches and seizures." Searches by public school officials, such as the collection of urine samples, implicate Fourth Amendment interests. See *Vernonia*; *New Jersey v. T. L. O.*, 469 U.S. 325 (1985). We must therefore review the School District's Policy for "reasonableness," which is the touchstone of the constitutionality of a governmental search.

In the criminal context, reasonableness usually requires a showing of probable cause. See, e.g., *Skinner v. Railway Labor Executives' Assn.*, 489 U.S. 602 (1989). The probable-cause standard, however, "is peculiarly related to criminal investigations" and may be unsuited to determining the reasonableness of administrative searches where the "Government seeks to prevent the development of hazardous conditions." *Treasury Employees v. Von Raab*, 489 U.S. 656 (1989).

Given that the School District's Policy is not in any way related to the conduct of criminal investigations, respondents do not contend that the School District requires probable cause before testing students for drug use. Respondents instead argue that drug testing must be based at least on some level of individualized suspicion. It is true that we generally determine the reasonableness of a search by balancing the nature of the intrusion on the individual's privacy against the promotion of legitimate governmental interests. But we have long held that "the Fourth Amendment imposes no irreducible requirement of [individualized] suspicion." *United States v. Martinez-Fuerte*, 428 U.S. 543 (1976).

Significantly, this Court has previously held that "special needs" inhere in the public school context. While schoolchildren do not shed their constitutional rights when they enter the schoolhouse, see *Tinker v. Des Moines Independent Community School Dist.*, 393 U.S. 503 (1969), "Fourth Amendment rights . . . are different in public schools than elsewhere; the 'reasonableness' inquiry cannot disregard the schools' custodial and tutelary responsibility for children." *Vernonia*. In particular, a finding of individualized suspicion may not be necessary when a school conducts drug testing.

In *Vernonia*, this Court held that the suspicionless drug testing of athletes was constitutional. Applying the principles of *Vernonia* to the somewhat different facts of this case, we conclude that Tecumseh's Policy is also constitutional.

We first consider the nature of the privacy interest allegedly compromised by the drug testing. . . . A student's privacy interest is limited in a public school environment where the State is responsible for maintaining discipline, health, and safety. Schoolchildren are routinely required to submit to physical examinations and vaccinations against disease. Securing order in the school environment sometimes requires that students be subjected to greater controls than those appropriate for adults.

Respondents argue that because children participating in nonathletic extracurricular activities are not subject to regular physicals and communal undress, they have a stronger expectation of privacy than the athletes tested in *Vernonia*. This distinction, however, was not essential to our decision in *Vernonia*, which depended primarily upon the school's custodial responsibility and authority.

In any event, students who participate in competitive extracurricular activities voluntarily subject themselves to many of the same intrusions on their privacy as do athletes. Some of these clubs and activities require occasional off-campus travel and communal undress. All of them have their own rules and requirements for participating students that do not apply to the student body as a whole.

Next, we consider the character of the intrusion imposed by the Policy. Urination is "an excretory function traditionally shielded by great privacy." *Skinner*. But the "degree of intrusion" on one's privacy caused by collecting a urine sample "depends upon the manner in which production of the urine sample is monitored." *Vernonia*.

Under the Policy, a faculty monitor waits outside the closed restroom stall for the student to produce a sample and must "listen for the normal sounds of urination in order to guard against tampered specimens and to insure an accurate chain of custody." The monitor then pours the sample into two bottles that are sealed and placed into a mailing pouch along with a consent form signed by the student. This procedure is virtually identical to that reviewed in *Vernonia*, except that it additionally protects privacy by allowing male students to produce their samples behind a closed stall. Given that we considered the method of collection in *Vernonia* a "negligible" intrusion, the method here is even less problematic. . . .

Finally, this Court must consider the nature and immediacy of the government's concerns and the efficacy of the Policy in meeting them. This Court has already articulated in detail the importance of the governmental concern in preventing drug use by schoolchildren. The drug abuse problem among our Nation's youth has hardly abated since *Vernonia* was decided in 1995. In fact, evidence suggests that it has only grown worse. As in *Vernonia*, "the necessity for the State to act is magnified by the fact that this evil is being visited not just upon individuals at large, but upon children for whom it has undertaken a special responsibility of care and direction." The health and safety risks identified in *Vernonia* apply with equal force to Tecumseh's children. Indeed, the nationwide drug epidemic makes the war against drugs a pressing concern in every school. . . .

Given the nationwide epidemic of drug use, and the evidence of increased drug use in Tecumseh schools, it was entirely reasonable for the School District to enact this particular drug testing policy. We reject the Court of Appeals' novel test that "any district seeking to impose a random suspicion-less drug testing policy as a condition to participation in a school activity must demonstrate that there is some identifiable drug abuse problem among a sufficient number of those subject to the testing, such that testing that group of students will actually redress its drug problem." Among other problems, it would be difficult to administer such a test. As we cannot articulate a threshold level of drug use that would suffice to justify a drug testing program for schoolchildren, we refuse to fashion what would in effect be a constitutional quantum of drug use necessary to show a "drug problem." . . .

We also reject respondents' argument that drug testing must presumptively be based upon an individualized reasonable suspicion of wrongdoing because such a testing regime would be less intrusive. In this context, the Fourth Amendment does not require a finding of individualized suspicion. And we decline to impose such a requirement on schools attempting to prevent and detect drug use by students. Moreover, we question whether testing based on individualized suspicion in fact would be less intrusive. Such a regime would place an additional burden on public school teachers who are already tasked with the difficult job of maintaining order and discipline. A program of individualized suspicion might unfairly target members of unpopular groups. The fear of lawsuits resulting from such targeted searches may chill enforcement of the program, rendering it ineffective in combating drug use.

Finally, we find that testing students who participate in extracurricular activities is a reasonably effective means of addressing the School District's legitimate concerns in preventing, deterring, and detecting drug use. . . . Accordingly, we reverse the judgment of the Court of Appeals. It is so ordered.

☐ *Justice O'CONNOR, with whom Justice SOUTER joins, dissenting.*

I dissented in *Vernonia School Dist. 47J v. Acton*, 515 U.S. 646 (1995), and continue to believe that case was wrongly decided. Because *Vernonia* is now this Court's precedent, and because I agree that petitioners' program fails even under the balancing approach adopted in that case, I join Justice GINSBURG's dissent.

☐ *Justice GINSBURG, with whom Justice STEVENS, Justice O'CONNOR, and Justice SOUTER join, dissenting.*

This case presents circumstances dispositively different from those of *Vernonia*. True, as the Court stresses, Tecumseh students participating in competitive extracurricular activities other than athletics share two relevant characteristics with the athletes of *Vernonia*. First, both groups attend public schools. "[O]ur decision in *Vernonia*," the Court states, "depended primarily upon the school's custodial responsibility and authority." Concern for student health and safety is basic to the school's caretaking, and it is undeniable that "drug use carries a variety of health risks for children, including death from overdose."

Those risks, however, are present for all schoolchildren. *Vernonia* cannot be read to endorse invasive and suspicionless drug testing of all students upon any evidence of drug use, solely because drugs jeopardize the life and health of those who use them. Many children, like many adults, engage in dangerous activities on their own time; that the children are enrolled in school scarcely allows government to monitor all such activities. If a student has a reasonable subjective expectation of privacy in the personal items she brings to school, surely she has a similar expectation regarding the chemical composition of her urine. Had the *Vernonia* Court agreed that public school attendance, in and of itself, permitted the State to test each student's blood or urine for drugs, the opinion in *Vernonia* could have saved many words.

The second commonality to which the Court points is the voluntary character of both interscholastic athletics and other competitive extracurricular activities. "By choosing to 'go out for the team,' [school athletes] voluntarily subject themselves to a degree of regulation even higher than that imposed on students generally." Comparably, the Court today observes, "students who participate in competitive extracurricular activities voluntarily subject themselves to" additional rules not applicable to other students. . . .

The comparison is enlightening. While extracurricular activities are "voluntary" in the sense that they are not required for graduation, they are part of the school's educational program; for that reason, the petitioner (hereinafter School District) is justified in expending public resources to make them available. Participation in such activities is a key component of school life, essential in reality for students applying to college, and, for all participants, a significant contributor to the breadth and quality of the educational experience.

Voluntary participation in athletics has a distinctly different dimension: Schools regulate student athletes discretely because competitive school sports by their nature require communal undress and, more important, expose students to physical risks that schools have a duty to mitigate. For the very reason that schools cannot offer a program of competitive athletics without intimately affecting the privacy of students, *Vernonia* reasonably analogized school athletes to "adults who choose to participate in a closely regulated industry." Industries fall within the closely regulated category when the nature of their activities requires substantial government oversight. Interscholastic athletics similarly require close safety and health regulation; a school's choir, band, and academic team do not.

In short, *Vernonia* applied, it did not repudiate, the principle that "the legality of a search of a student should depend simply on the reasonableness, under all the circumstances, of the search." *T. L. O.* Enrollment in a public school, and election to participate in school activities beyond the bare minimum that the curriculum requires, are indeed factors relevant to reasonableness, but they do not on their own justify intrusive, suspicionless searches. *Vernonia*, accordingly, did not rest upon these factors; instead, the Court performed what today's majority aptly describes as a "fact-specific balancing." Balancing of that order, applied to the facts now before the Court, should yield a result other than the one the Court announces today. . . .

Nationwide, students who participate in extracurricular activities are significantly less likely to develop substance abuse problems than are their less-involved peers. Even if students might be deterred from drug use in order to preserve their extracurricular eligibility, it is at least as likely that other students might forgo their extracurricular involvement in order to avoid detection of their drug use. Tecumseh's policy thus falls short doubly if deterrence is its aim: It invades the privacy of students who need deterrence least, and risks steering students at greatest risk for substance abuse away from extracurricular involvement that potentially may palliate drug problems.

To summarize, this case resembles *Vernonia* only in that the School Districts in both cases conditioned engagement in activities outside the obligatory curriculum on random subjection to urinalysis. The defining characteristics of the two programs, however, are entirely dissimilar. The *Vernonia* district sought to test a subpopulation of students distinguished by their reduced expectation of privacy, their special susceptibility to drug-related injury, and their heavy involvement with drug use. The Tecumseh district seeks to test a much larger population associated with none of these factors. It does so, moreover, without carefully safeguarding student confidentiality and without regard to the program's untoward effects. A program so sweeping is not sheltered by *Vernonia*; its unreasonable reach renders it impermissible under the Fourth Amendment. . . . For the reasons stated, I would affirm the judgment of the Tenth Circuit declaring the testing policy at issue unconstitutional.

8

THE FIFTH AMENDMENT
GUARANTEE AGAINST
SELF-ACCUSATION

A │ *Coerced Confessions*
and Police Interrogations

Although the Fifth Amendment guarantee against self-incrimination applies beyond criminal investigations, for example, before congressional investigating committees, in *Chavez v. Martinez*, 123 S.Ct. 1994 (2003), the Court ruled that violations of *Miranda* (excerpted in Vol. 2, Ch. 8) do not run afoul of the constitutional protection against self-incrimination in civil cases. Writing for the Court, Justice Thomas held that "a violation of the constitutional right against self-incrimination occurs only if one has been compelled to be a witness against himself in a criminal case." Oliverio Martinez had sought civil damage in a suit against Ben Chavez, a police officer who repeatedly questioned him without advising him of his *Miranda* rights and over his objections and begging to be left alone. At the time, Martinez was in the hospital being treated for a police shooting that left him blind and paralyzed. Martinez's statements were never introduced in a criminal case against him and Justice Thomas held that "the absence of a 'criminal case' in which Martinez was compelled to be a 'witness' against himself defeats his Fifth Amendment claim." Justices Stevens and Ginsburg joined a dissent by Justice Kennedy, who vigorously disagreed: "Our cases and our legal tradition establish that the self-incrimination clause is a substantive constraint on the conduct of the government, not merely an evidentiary rule governing the work of the courts."

In its 2003–2004 term the Court will reconsider the application of *Miranda* in three other cases. *Fellers v. United States* (No. 02-6320) raises the issue of the scope of a suspect's right to remain silent during a police interrogation. John Fellers, an alleged drug dealer, made a confession to police during their questioning of him in his home without first being advised of his right to remain silent. He was then taken to the police station, where he was informed of his right to remain silent, and he waived his right to an attorney and repeated his confession. Subsequently, his attorney argued that the confession should be excluded as evidence because Fellers was not advised of his rights before the first conversation and police questioning.

The justices will also revisit the issue of whether prosecutors may use physical evidence obtained by police as a result of statements made by suspects who are not given proper *Miranda* warnings, in *United States v. Patane* (No. 02-1183). The case stemmed from the arrest of Samuel Francis Patane for violating a court order to stay away from an ex-girlfriend. A police officer got as far as warning him that he had a "right to remain silent," when Patane said that he knew his rights and did not need to hear the rest of the warning. Subsequently, in response to questioning about whether he had a gun Patane told the police that he had a pistol at his house and where to locate it. As a result, Patane, who had previously been convicted for possessing drugs, was indicted for possessing a gun in violation of a federal statute making it a crime for convicted felons to possess firearms.

Patane's attorney argued that the introduction of the gun as evidence against him should be suppressed because he had not received his full *Miranda* warnings. A federal district court agreed and the Court of Appeals for the Tenth Circuit affirmed on the ground that the evidence should be suppressed because of the *Miranda* violation. The appellate court noted that prior rulings of the Supreme Court, in *Michigan v. Tucker*, 417 U.S. 433 (1974) and *Oregon v. Elstad*, 470 U.S. 298 (1985), had held such evidence may be used at trial because a violation of *Miranda* was not a constitutional violation as long as the suspect's statements were voluntary. Those prior rulings had interpreted *Miranda* warnings as merely "prophylactic" measures to ensure that confessions are voluntary. However, the appellate court reasoned that the law had been "fundamentally altered" by the ruling in *Dickerson v. United States*, 530 U.S. 428 (2000) (excerpted in Vol. 2, Ch. 8), that *Miranda* warnings are constitutionally required by the Fifth Amendment's guarantee against self-incrimination. The evidence had to be suppressed, the appellate court concluded, because *Dickerson* held "that an un-*Mirandized* statement, even if voluntary, is a Fifth Amendment violation."

Finally, in a third *Miranda*-related case, the justices will reconsider a 1985 ruling, in *Oregon v. Elstad*, on prosecutorial use of suspects' statements made prior to receiving the *Miranda* warnings and who then waive their *Miranda* rights and continue to talk, in *Missouri v. Seibert*, No. 02-1371. Patrice Siebert, suspected of murdering her son and setting fire to their trailer, was taken into police custody for interrogation. In response to an officer's questions, she made incriminating statements. After a 20-minute break in the questioning, the officer read Siebert her *Miranda* rights but she continued to make incriminating statements. After her trial and conviction for murder, Siebert appealed and claimed that the police violated her Fifth Amendment right against self-incriminating by interrogating her prior to giving her the *Miranda* warnings and questioning her in the absence of an attorney. The Missouri state supreme court agreed that her incriminating statements should have been suppressed at trial, because police had violated her *Miranda* rights, and that the failure to suppress her incriminating statements was not a harmless error.

B | *Grants of Immunity*

A sharply divided Court upheld Kansas's Sexual Abuse Treatment Program, which requires convicted sexual offenders to sign a form taking responsibility for their sexual offenses as part of their treatment, without also granting them immunity from further prosecution, in *McKune v. Lile* (excerpted below). Moreover, Justice Kennedy's opinion commanded the support of only a plurality, with Justice O'Connor concurring in the result but not in his analysis of the Fifth Amendment. Justice Stevens's dissent was joined by Justices Souter, Ginsburg, and Breyer.

McKune v. Lile
536 U.S. 24, 122 S.Ct. 2017 (2002)

Robert G. Lile was convicted in 1983 of raping a high school girl at gunpoint and was imprisoned. A few years before he was scheduled to be released, Kansas correction officers recommended that he enter a sexual abuse treatment program in which he would be required to admit his guilt and for which he would not receive immunity from any further prosecution. Lile refused, maintaining that he had had consensual sex, whereupon he was removed to a maximum security area of the prison and lost the privileges of having a television set and working for wages in the prison. Lile sued and challenged the constitutionality of Kansas's Sexual Abuse Treatment Program for violating his Fifth Amendment right against self-incrimination. A federal district court agreed with Lile, reasoning that because he had testified at his trial that the intercourse was consensual, requiring him to admit responsibility for rape could subject him to a charge of perjury, and that the loss of privileges and change in the condition of his imprisonment for refusing to incriminate himself constituted coercion in violation of the Fifth Amendment. The Court of Appeals for the Tenth Circuit affirmed and the state appealed to the Supreme Court, which granted *certiorari*.

The lower court's decision was reversed by a five-to-four vote. Justice Kennedy delivered the opinion for the Court. Justice O'Connor filed a concurring opinion and Justice Stevens issued a dissent, which Justices Souter, Ginsburg, and Breyer joined.

☐ *Justice KENNEDY announced the judgment of the Court and delivered an opinion, in which THE CHIEF JUSTICE, Justice SCALIA, and Justice THOMAS join.*

When convicted sex offenders reenter society, they are much more likely than any other type of offender to be rearrested for a new rape or sexual assault. States thus have a vital interest in rehabilitating convicted sex offenders.

Therapists and correctional officers widely agree that clinical rehabilitative programs can enable sex offenders to manage their impulses and in this way reduce recidivism.

The critical first step in the Kansas Sexual Abuse Treatment Program (SATP), therefore, is acceptance of responsibility for past offenses. This gives inmates a basis to understand why they are being punished and to identify the traits that cause such a frightening and high risk of recidivism. As part of this first step, Kansas requires each SATP participant to complete an "Admission of Responsibility" form, to fill out a sexual history form discussing their offending behavior, and to discuss their past behavior in individual and group counseling sessions.

The District Court found that the Kansas SATP is a valid "clinical rehabilitative program," supported by a "legitimate penological objective" in rehabilitation. The SATP lasts for 18 months and involves substantial daily counseling. It helps inmates address sexual addiction; understand the thoughts, feelings, and behavior dynamics that precede their offenses; and develop relapse prevention skills. Although inmates are assured of a significant level of confidentiality, Kansas does not offer legal immunity from prosecution based on any statements made in the course of the SATP. According to Kansas, however, no inmate has ever been charged or prosecuted for any offense based on information disclosed during treatment. There is no contention, then, that the program is a mere subterfuge for the conduct of a criminal investigation.

As the parties explain, Kansas' decision not to offer immunity to every SATP participant serves two legitimate state interests. First, the professionals who design and conduct the program have concluded that for SATP participants to accept full responsibility for their past actions, they must accept the proposition that those actions carry consequences. . . .

Second, while Kansas as a rule does not prosecute inmates based upon information revealed in the course of the program, the State confirms its valid interest in deterrence by keeping open the option to prosecute a particularly dangerous sex offender. Kansas is not alone in declining to offer blanket use immunity as a condition of participation in a treatment program. The Federal Bureau of Prisons and other States conduct similar sex offender programs and do not offer immunity to the participants.

The mere fact that Kansas declines to grant inmates use immunity does not render the SATP invalid. Asking at the outset whether prison administrators can or should offer immunity skips the constitutional inquiry altogether. If the State of Kansas offered immunity, the self-incrimination privilege would not be implicated. The State, however, does not offer immunity. So the central question becomes whether the State's program, and the consequences for nonparticipation in it, combine to create a compulsion that encumbers the constitutional right. If there is compulsion, the State cannot continue the program in its present form; and the alternatives, as will be discussed, defeat the program's objectives.

The SATP does not compel prisoners to incriminate themselves in violation of the Constitution. . . . The "Amendment speaks of compulsion," and the Court has insisted that the "constitutional guarantee is only that the witness not be compelled to give self-incriminating testimony." The consequences in question here—a transfer to another prison where television sets are not placed in each inmate's cell, where exercise facilities are not readily available, and where work and wage opportunities are more limited—are not ones that compel a prisoner to speak about his past crimes despite a desire to remain silent. The fact that these consequences are imposed on prisoners, rather than ordinary citizens, moreover, is important in weighing respondent's constitutional claim.

The privilege against self-incrimination does not terminate at the jailhouse door, but the fact of a valid conviction and the ensuing restrictions on liberty are essential to the Fifth Amendment analysis. A broad range of choices that might infringe constitutional rights in free society fall within the expected conditions of confinement of those who have suffered a lawful conviction. . . .

The limitation on prisoners' privileges and rights also follows from the need to grant necessary authority and capacity to federal and state officials to administer the prisons. To respect these imperatives, courts must exercise restraint in supervising the minutiae of prison life. Where, as here, a state penal system is involved, federal courts have "additional reason to accord deference to the appropriate prison authorities." . . .

[T]his Court has recognized that lawful conviction and incarceration necessarily place limitations on the exercise of a defendant's privilege against self-incrimination. See, e.g., *Baxter v. Palmigiano*, 425 U.S. 308 (1976). *Baxter* declined to extend to prison disciplinary proceedings the rule of *Griffin v. California*, 380 U.S. 609 (1965), that the prosecution may not comment on a defendant's silence at trial. As the Court explained, "[d]isciplinary proceedings in state prisons . . . involve the correctional process and important state interests other than conviction for crime." The inmate in *Baxter* no doubt felt compelled to speak in one sense of the word. The Court, considering the level of compulsion in light of the prison setting and the State's interests in rehabilitation and orderly administration, nevertheless rejected the inmate's self-incrimination claim.

In the present case, respondent's decision not to participate in the Kansas SATP did not extend his term of incarceration. Nor did his decision affect his eligibility for good-time credits or parole. Respondent instead complains that if he remains silent about his past crimes, he will be transferred from the medium-security unit—where the program is conducted—to a less desirable maximum-security unit.

No one contends, however, that the transfer is intended to punish prisoners for exercising their Fifth Amendment rights. Rather, the limitation on these rights is incidental to Kansas' legitimate penological reason for the transfer: Due to limited space, inmates who do not participate in their respective programs will be moved out of the facility where the programs are held to make room for other inmates. . . .

Respondent fails to cite a single case from this Court holding that the denial of discrete prison privileges for refusal to participate in a rehabilitation program amounts to unconstitutional compulsion. Instead, relying on the so-called penalty cases, respondent treats the fact of his incarceration as if it were irrelevant. . . .

Determining what constitutes unconstitutional compulsion involves a question of judgment: Courts must decide whether the consequences of an inmate's choice to remain silent are closer to the physical torture against which the Constitution clearly protects or the *de minimis* harms against which it does not. . . .

It is proper to consider the nexus between remaining silent and the consequences that follow. Plea bargains are not deemed to be compelled in part because a defendant who pleads not guilty still must be convicted. States may award good-time credits and early parole for inmates who accept responsibility because silence in these circumstances does not automatically mean the parole board, which considers other factors as well, will deny them parole. . . .

The Kansas SATP represents a sensible approach to reducing the serious danger that repeat sex offenders pose to many innocent persons, most often children. The State's interest in rehabilitation is undeniable. There is, furthermore, no indication that the SATP is merely an elaborate ruse to skirt the protections of the privilege against compelled self-incrimination. Rather, the program allows prison administrators to provide to those who need treatment the incentive to seek it.

□ *Justice O'CONNOR, concurring in the judgment.*

The Court today is divided on the question of what standard to apply when evaluating compulsion for the purposes of the Fifth Amendment privilege against self-incrimination in a prison setting. I write separately because, although I agree with Justice STEVENS that the Fifth Amendment compulsion standard is broader than the "atypical and significant hardship" standard we have adopted for evaluating due process claims in prisons, I do not believe that the alterations in respondent's prison conditions as a result of his failure to participate in the Sexual Abuse Treatment Program (SATP) were so great as to constitute compulsion for the purposes of the Fifth Amendment privilege against self-incrimination. I therefore agree with the plurality that the decision below should be reversed. . . .

☐ *Justice STEVENS, with whom Justice SOUTER, Justice GINSBURG, and Justice BREYER join, dissenting.*

No one could possibly disagree with the plurality's statement that "offering inmates minimal incentives to participate [in a rehabilitation program] does not amount to compelled self-incrimination prohibited by the Fifth Amendment." The question that this case presents, however, is whether the State may punish an inmate's assertion of his Fifth Amendment privilege with the same mandatory sanction that follows a disciplinary conviction for an offense such as theft, sodomy, riot, arson, or assault. Until today the Court has never characterized a threatened harm as "a minimal incentive." Nor have we ever held that a person who has made a valid assertion of the privilege may nevertheless be ordered to incriminate himself and sanctioned for disobeying such an order. This is truly a watershed case. . . .

The privilege against self-incrimination may have been born of the rack and the Star Chamber, but the Framers had a broader view of compulsion in mind when they drafted the Fifth Amendment. We know, for example, that the privilege was thought to protect defendants from the moral compulsion associated with any statement made under oath. In addition, the language of the Amendment, which focuses on a courtroom setting in which a defendant or a witness in a criminal trial invokes the privilege, encompasses the compulsion inherent in any judicial order overruling an assertion of the privilege. . . .

The plurality and Justice O'CONNOR hold that the consequences stemming from respondent's invocation of the privilege are not serious enough to constitute compulsion. The threat of transfer to Level I and a maximum-security unit is not sufficiently coercive in their view—either because the consequence is not really a penalty, just the loss of a benefit, or because it is a penalty, but an insignificant one. I strongly disagree.

It took respondent several years to acquire the status that he occupied in 1994 when he was ordered to participate in the SATP. Because of the nature of his convictions, in 1983 the Department initially placed him in a maximum-security classification. Not until 1989 did the Department change his "security classification to 'medium by exception' because of his good behavior." Thus, the sanction at issue threatens to deprive respondent of a status in the prison community that it took him six years to earn and which he had successfully maintained for five more years when he was ordered to incriminate himself.

Moreover, abruptly "busting" his custody back to Level I would impose the same stigma on him as would a disciplinary conviction for any of the most serious offenses described in petitioners' formal statement of Internal Management Policy and Procedure (IMPP). This same loss of privileges is considered serious enough by prison authorities that it is used as punishment for theft, drug abuse, assault, and possession of dangerous contraband.

The punitive consequences of the discipline include not only the dignitary and reputational harms flowing from the transfer, but a serious loss of tangible privileges as well. Because he refused to participate in the SATP, respondent's visitation rights will be restricted. He will be able to earn only $0.60 per day, as compared to Level III inmates, who can potentially earn minimum wage. His access to prison organizations and activities will be limited. He will no longer be able to send his family more than $30 per pay period. He will be prohibited from spending more than $20 per payroll period at the canteen, rather than the $140 he could spend at Level III, and he will be restricted in what property he can keep in his cell. In addition, because he will be transferred to a maximum-security unit, respondent will be forced to share a cell with three other inmates rather than one, and his movement outside the cell will be substantially curtailed.

The plurality's glib attempt to characterize these consequences as a loss of potential benefits rather than a penalty is wholly unpersuasive. The threatened transfer to Level I and to a maximum-security unit represents a significant, adverse change from the status quo. Respondent achieved his medium-security status after six years of good behavior and maintained that status during five more years. During that time, an inmate unquestionably develops settled expectations regarding the conditions of his confinement. These conditions then form the baseline against which any change must be measured, and rescinding them now surely constitutes punishment. . . .

The SATP clearly serves legitimate therapeutic purposes. The goal of the program is to rehabilitate sex offenders, and the requirement that participants complete admission of responsibility and sexual history forms may well be an important component of that process. . . .

The program's laudable goals, however, do not justify reduced constitutional protection for those ordered to participate. . . .

The plurality's willingness to sacrifice prisoners' Fifth Amendment rights is also unwarranted because available alternatives would allow the State to achieve the same objectives without impinging on inmates' privilege. The most obvious alternative is to grant participants use immunity. Petitioners have not provided any evidence that the program's therapeutic aims could not be served equally well by granting use immunity. Participants would still obtain all the therapeutic benefits of accepting responsibility and admitting past misconduct; they simply would not incriminate themselves in the process. At least one State already offers such protection [Kentucky].

The plurality contends that requiring immunity will undermine the therapeutic goals of the program because once "inmates know society will not punish them for their past offenses, they may be left with the false impression that society does not consider those crimes to be serious ones." The idea that an inmate who is confined to prison for almost 20 years for an offense could be left with the impression that his crimes are not serious or that wrongdoing does not carry consequences is absurd. Moreover, the argument starts from a false premise. Granting use immunity does not preclude prosecution; it merely prevents the State from using an inmate's own words, and the fruits thereof, against him in a subsequent prosecution. . . .

Alternatively, the State could continue to pursue its rehabilitative goals without violating participants' Fifth Amendment rights by offering inmates a voluntary program. The United States points out that an inmate's participation in the sexual offender treatment program operated by the Federal Bureau of Prisons is entirely voluntary. . . .

Through its treatment program, Kansas seeks to achieve the admirable goal of reducing recidivism among sex offenders. In the process, however, the State demands an impermissible and unwarranted sacrifice from the participants. No matter what the goal, inmates should not be compelled to forfeit the privilege against self-incrimination simply because the ends are legitimate or because they have been convicted of sex offenses. Particularly in a case like this one, in which respondent has protested his innocence all along and is being compelled to confess to a crime that he still insists he did not commit, we ought to ask ourselves—What if this is one of those rare cases in which the jury made a mistake and he is actually innocent? And in answering that question, we should consider that even members of the Star Chamber thought they were pursuing righteous ends.

I respectfully dissent.

9

THE RIGHTS TO COUNSEL AND OTHER PROCEDURAL GUARANTEES

A | *The Right to Counsel*

In *Alabama v. Shelton*, 535 U.S. 654 (2002), the Court held that the Sixth Amendment right to counsel was violated and that suspended sentences, which could result in actual imprisonment, cannot be imposed when the defendant does not have the assistance of counsel. LeReed Shelton represented himself in a case of third-degree assault. Upon conviction, he received a suspended sentence and probation. He appealed but a state court held that the Sixth Amendment is not violated unless there is a deprivation of liberty. Writing for the Court, Justice Ginsburg reversed that decision and held that a suspended sentence may not be imposed unless the defendant has been offered and provided the assistance of counsel at the trial. Justice Scalia, joined by Chief Justice Rehnquist and Justices Kennedy and Thomas, dissented and warned that the majority had imposed a new requirement and an undue burden on the states to provide the assistance of counsel.

B | Plea Bargaining and the Right to Effective Counsel

■ THE DEVELOPMENT OF LAW

Rulings on Plea Bargaining and Effective Counsel

CASE	VOTE	RULING
Mickens v. Taylor, 535 U.S. 162 (2002)	5:4	The Court rejected a death row inmate's claim that his Sixth Amendment right to effective counsel was violated by the fact that his court-appointed attorney had previously represented the murder victim. Justices Stevens, Souter, Ginsburg and Breyer dissented.
Wiggins v. Smith, 123 S.Ct. 2527 (2003)	7:2	The Court overturned a death sentence upon finding that the defendant's attorney failed to investigate and to introduce mitigating factors related to his sexual abuse by his parents and that the failure to do so violated the Sixth Amendment right to effective counsel under *Strickland v. Washington*, 466 U.S. 668 (1984).

IO

CRUEL AND UNUSUAL PUNISHMENT

A | *Noncapital Punishment*

In its 2002–2003 term the justices considered whether sentences of 25 years to life in prison under California's "three-strikes-and-you're-out" law violate the Eighth Amendment when the third strike is for a minor crime. Although about half of the states have three-strikes laws, only California's 1994 law allows misdemeanors to count as strikes. In *Ewing v. California*, 123 S.Ct. 1174 (2003), Gary Ewing, who had previous convictions for robbery, received a 25-year to life sentence for stealing three golf clubs, each valued at $399. Writing for the Court in a five-to-four ruling, Justice O'Connor held that Ewing's sentence was not grossly disproportionate and therefore did not violate the Eighth Amendment,. Justices Scalia and Thomas, concurring, disagreed that disproportional analysis has any place in Eighth Amendment jurisprudence. Justices Stevens, Souter, Ginsburg, and Breyer dissented.

B | Capital Punishment

Atkins v. Virginia
536 U.S. 304, 122 S.CT. 2242 (2002)

In *Ford v. Wainwright*, 477 U.S. 399 (1986), the Court held that the Eighth Amendment bars the execution of death-row inmates who are (or who have gone while on death row) insane. However, in *Penry v. Lynaugh*, 492 U.S. 302 (1989) (excerpted in Vol. 2, Ch. 10), a bare majority upheld the execution of an individual who was mentally retarded. In her opinion for Court, Justice O'Connor emphasized that at the time only one state banned the execution of the mentally retarded and that, even when added to the 14 states that had rejected capital punishment, this did "not provide sufficient evidence at present of a national consensus" against executing mentally retarded convicts. Subsequently, 17 other states of the 38 that impose the death penalty enacted laws barring executions of the mentally retarded. And opponents of the death penalty continued to raise the issue in an effort to persuade the Court to reconsider the matter.

In 1998, Daryl Renard Atkins, who has an IQ of 59—that of a nine- to twelve-year-old—was convicted and sentenced to death for participating in the robbery and murder of a U.S. airman in Virginia. The Virginia Supreme Court affirmed his sentence. This decision was appealed to the Supreme Court. Notably, a number of friend-of-court briefs highlighted the controversy and urged the Court to abandon its earlier ruling; among those filing *amicus* briefs were the European Union, the U.S. Catholic Conference, and the American Psychological Association.

The state supreme court's decision was reversed by a six-to-three vote. Justice Stevens delivered the opinion of the Court. Chief Justice Rehnquist and Justice Scalia filed dissenting opinions, which Justice Thomas joined.

☐ *Justice STEVENS delivered the opinion of the Court.*

Those mentally retarded persons who meet the law's requirements for criminal responsibility should be tried and punished when they commit crimes. Because of their disabilities in areas of reasoning, judgment, and control of their impulses, however, they do not act with the level of moral culpability that characterizes the most serious adult criminal conduct. Moreover, their impairments can jeopardize the reliability and fairness of capital proceedings against mentally retarded defendants. Presumably for these reasons, in the 13 years since we decided *Penry v. Lynaugh*, 492 U.S. 302 (1989), the American public, legislators, scholars, and judges have deliberated over the question whether the death penalty should ever be imposed on a mentally retarded criminal. The consensus reflected in those deliberations informs our answer to the question presented by this case: whether such executions are "cruel and unusual punishments" prohibited by the Eighth Amendment to the Federal Constitution. . . .

The Eighth Amendment succinctly prohibits "excessive" sanctions. . . . A claim that punishment is excessive is judged not by the standards that prevailed in 1685 when Lord Jeffreys presided over the "Bloody Assizes" or when the Bill of Rights was adopted, but rather by those that currently prevail. As CHIEF JUSTICE WARREN explained in his opinion in *Trop v. Dulles*, 356 U.S. 86 (1958): "The basic concept underlying the Eighth Amendment is nothing less than the dignity of man. . . . The Amendment must draw its meaning from the evolving standards of decency that mark the progress of a maturing society."

Proportionality review under those evolving standards should be informed by "objective factors to the maximum possible extent." We have pinpointed that the "clearest and most reliable objective evidence of contemporary values is the legislation enacted by the country's legislatures." *Penry*. Relying in part on such legislative evidence, we have held that death is an impermissibly excessive punishment for the rape of an adult woman, *Coker v. Georgia*, 433 U.S. 584 (1977), or for a defendant who neither took life, attempted to take life, nor intended to take life, *Enmund v. Florida*, 458 U.S. 782 (1982). In *Coker*, we focused primarily on the then-recent legislation that had been enacted in response to our decision 10 years earlier in *Furman v. Georgia*, 408 U.S. 238 (1972) (*per curiam*), to support the conclusion that the "current judgment," though "not wholly unanimous," weighed very heavily on the side of rejecting capital punishment as a "suitable penalty for raping an adult woman." The "current legislative judgment" relevant to our decision in *Enmund* was less clear than in *Coker* but "nevertheless weigh[ed] on the side of rejecting capital punishment for the crime at issue." . . .

Guided by our approach in these cases, we shall first review the judgment of legislatures that have addressed the suitability of imposing the death penalty on the mentally retarded and then consider reasons for agreeing or disagreeing with their judgment.

The parties have not called our attention to any state legislative consideration of the suitability of imposing the death penalty on mentally retarded offenders prior to 1986. In that year, the public reaction to the execution of a mentally retarded murderer in Georgia apparently led to the enactment of the first state statute prohibiting such executions. In 1988, when Congress enacted legislation reinstating the federal death penalty, it expressly provided that a "sentence of death shall not be carried out upon a person who is mentally retarded." In 1989, Maryland enacted a similar prohibition. It was in that year that we decided *Penry*, and concluded that those two state enactments, "even when added to the 14 States that have rejected capital punishment completely, do not provide sufficient evidence at present of a national consensus."

Much has changed since then. [S]tate legislatures across the country began to address the issue. In 1990 Kentucky and Tennessee enacted statutes similar to those in Georgia and Maryland, as did New Mexico in 1991, and Arkansas, Colorado, Washington, Indiana, and Kansas in 1993 and 1994. In 1995, when New York reinstated its death penalty, it emulated the Federal Government by expressly exempting the mentally retarded. Nebraska followed suit in 1998.

There appear to have been no similar enactments during the next two years, but in 2000 and 2001 six more States—South Dakota, Arizona, Connecticut, Florida, Missouri, and North Carolina—joined the procession. The Texas Legislature unanimously adopted a similar bill, and bills have passed at least one house in other States, including Virginia and Nevada.

It is not so much the number of these States that is significant, but the consistency of the direction of change. Given the well-known fact that anti-crime legislation is far more popular than legislation providing protections for persons guilty of violent crime, the large number of States prohibiting the execution of mentally retarded persons (and the complete absence of States passing legislation reinstating the power to conduct such executions) provides powerful evidence that today our society views mentally retarded offenders as categorically less culpable than the average criminal. . . .

To the extent there is serious disagreement about the execution of mentally retarded offenders, it is in determining which offenders are in fact retarded. In this case, for instance, the Commonwealth of Virginia disputes that Atkins suffers from mental retardation. Not all people who claim to be mentally retarded will be so impaired as to fall within the range of mentally retarded offenders about whom there is a national consensus. As was our approach in *Ford v. Wainwright*, with regard to insanity, "we leave to the State[s] the task of developing appropriate ways to enforce the constitutional restriction upon its execution of sentences." . . .

[O]ur death penalty jurisprudence provides two reasons consistent with the legislative consensus that the mentally retarded should be categorically excluded from execution. First, there is a serious question as to whether either justification that we have recognized as a basis for the death penalty applies to mentally retarded offenders. *Gregg v. Georgia*, 428 U.S. 153 (1976), identified "retribution and deterrence of capital crimes by prospective offenders" as the social purposes served by the death penalty. Unless the imposition of the death penalty on a mentally retarded person "measurably contributes to one or both of these goals, it 'is nothing more than the purposeless and needless imposition of pain and suffering,' and hence an unconstitutional punishment." *Enmund*.

With respect to retribution—the interest in seeing that the offender gets his "just deserts"—the severity of the appropriate punishment necessarily depends on the culpability of the offender. Since Gregg, our jurisprudence has consistently confined the imposition of the death penalty to a narrow category of the most serious crimes. For example, in *Godfrey v. Georgia*, 446 U.S. 420 (1980), we set aside a death sentence because the petitioner's crimes did not reflect "a consciousness materially more 'depraved' than that of any person guilty of murder." If the culpability of the average murderer is insufficient to justify the most extreme sanction available to the State, the lesser culpability of the mentally retarded offender surely does not merit that form of retribution. Thus, pursuant to our narrowing jurisprudence, which seeks to ensure that only the most deserving of execution are put to death, an exclusion for the mentally retarded is appropriate.

With respect to deterrence—the interest in preventing capital crimes by prospective offenders—"it seems likely that 'capital punishment can serve as a deterrent only when murder is the result of premeditation and deliberation,'" *Enmund*. Exempting the mentally retarded from that punishment will not affect the "cold calculus that precedes the decision" of other potential murderers. Indeed, that sort of calculus is at the opposite end of the spectrum from behavior of mentally retarded offenders. . . . Nor will exempting the mentally retarded from execution lessen the deterrent effect of the death penalty with respect to offenders who are not mentally retarded. Such individuals are unprotected by the exemption and will continue to face the threat of execution. Thus, executing the mentally retarded will not measurably further the goal of deterrence. . . .

The judgment of the Virginia Supreme Court is reversed and the case is remanded for further proceedings not inconsistent with this opinion. It is so ordered.

☐ *Justice SCALIA, with whom the CHIEF JUSTICE and Justice THOMAS join, dissenting.*

Today's decision is the pinnacle of our Eighth Amendment death-is-different jurisprudence. Not only does it, like all of that jurisprudence, find no support in the text or history of the Eighth Amendment; it does not even have support in current social attitudes regarding the conditions that render an otherwise just death penalty inappropriate. Seldom has an opinion of this Court rested so obviously upon nothing but the personal views of its members. . . .

The Court makes no pretense that execution of the mildly mentally retarded would have been considered "cruel and unusual" in 1791. Only the severely or profoundly mentally retarded, commonly known as "idiots," enjoyed any special status under the law at that time. They, like lunatics, suffered a "deficiency in will" rendering them unable to tell right from wrong. W. Blackstone, *Commentaries on the Laws of England* (1769). Due to their incompetence, idiots were "excuse[d] from the guilt, and of course from the punishment, of any criminal action committed under such deprivation of the senses." Instead, they were often committed to civil confinement or made wards of the State, thereby preventing them from "go[ing] loose, to the terror of the king's subjects." Mentally retarded offenders with less severe impairments—those who were not "idiots"—suffered criminal prosecution and punishment, including capital punishment.

The Court is left to argue, therefore, that execution of the mildly retarded is inconsistent with the "evolving standards of decency that mark the progress of a maturing society." *Trop v. Dulles.* Before today, our opinions consistently emphasized that Eighth Amendment judgments regarding the existence of social "standards" "should be informed by objective factors to the maximum possible extent" and "should not be, or appear to be, merely the subjective views of individual Justices." *Coker v. Georgia.*

The Court pays lipservice to these precedents as it miraculously extracts a "national consensus" forbidding execution of the mentally retarded from the fact that 18 States—less than half (47%) of the 38 States that permit capital punishment (for whom the issue exists)—have very recently enacted legislation barring execution of the mentally retarded. Even that 47% figure is a distorted one. If one is to say, as the Court does today, that all executions of the mentally retarded are so morally repugnant as to violate our national "standards of decency," surely the "consensus" it points to must be one that has set its righteous face against all such executions. Not 18 States, but only seven—18% of death penalty jurisdictions—have legislation of that scope. Eleven of those that the Court counts enacted statutes prohibiting execution of mentally retarded defendants convicted after, or convicted of crimes committed after, the effective date of the legislation; those already on death row, or consigned there before the statute's effective date, or even (in those States using the date of the crime as the criterion of retroactivity) tried in the future for murders committed many years ago, could be put to death. That is not a statement of absolute moral repugnance, but one of current preference between two tolerable approaches. . . .

But let us accept, for the sake of argument, the Court's faulty count. That bare number of States alone—18—should be enough to convince any reasonable person that no "national consensus" exists. How is it possible that agreement among 47% of the death penalty jurisdictions amounts to "consensus"? Our prior cases have generally required a much higher degree of agreement before finding a punishment cruel and unusual on "evolving standards" grounds. . . .

Moreover, a major factor that the Court entirely disregards is that the legislation of all 18 States it relies on is still in its infancy. The oldest of the statutes is only 14 years old; five were enacted last year; over half were enacted within the past eight years. Few, if any, of the States have had sufficient experience with these laws to know whether they are sensible in the long term. . . .

The Court's thrashing about for evidence of "consensus" includes reliance upon the margins by which state legislatures have enacted bans on execution of the retarded. Presumably, in applying our Eighth Amendment "evolving-standards-of-decency" jurisprudence, we will henceforth weigh not only how many States have agreed, but how many States have agreed by how much. Of course if the percentage of legislators voting for the bill is significant, surely the number of people represented by the legislators voting for the bill is also significant: the fact that 49% of the legislators in a State with a population of 60 million voted against the bill should be more impressive than the fact that 90% of the legislators in a state with a population of 2 million voted for it. (By the way, the population of the death penalty States that exclude the mentally retarded is only 44% of the population of all death penalty States.) This is quite absurd. . . .

But the Prize for the Court's Most Feeble Effort to fabricate "national consensus" must go to its appeal (deservedly relegated to a footnote) to the views of assorted professional and religious organizations, members of the so-called "world community," and respondents to opinion polls. I agree with the CHIEF JUSTICE that the views of professional and religious organizations and the results of opinion polls are irrelevant. Equally irrelevant are the practices of the "world community," whose notions of justice are (thankfully) not always those of our people. . . .

Today's opinion adds one more to the long list of substantive and procedural requirements impeding imposition of the death penalty imposed under this Court's assumed power to invent a death-is-different jurisprudence. None of those requirements existed when the Eighth Amendment was adopted, and some of them were not even supported by current moral consensus. . . .

This newest invention promises to be more effective than any of the others in turning the process of capital trial into a game. One need only read the definitions of mental retardation adopted by the American Association of Mental Retardation and the American Psychiatric Association to realize that the symptoms of this condition can readily be feigned. And whereas the capital defendant who feigns insanity risks commitment to a mental institution until he can be cured (and then tried and executed), *Jones v. United States,* 463 U.S. 354 (1983), the capital defendant who feigns mental retardation risks nothing at all. The mere pendency of the present case has brought us petitions by death row inmates claiming for the first time, after multiple habeas petitions, that they are retarded. . . .

☐ *CHIEF JUSTICE REHNQUIST, with whom Justice SCALIA and Justice THOMAS join, dissenting.*

I agree with Justice SCALIA that the Court's assessment of the current legislative judgment regarding the execution of defendants like petitioner more resembles a post hoc rationalization for the majority's subjectively preferred result rather than any objective effort to ascertain the content of an evolving standard of decency. I write separately, however, to call attention to the defects in the Court's decision to place weight on foreign laws, the views of professional and religious organizations, and opinion polls in reaching its conclusion. The Court's suggestion that these sources are relevant to the constitutional question finds little support in our precedents and, in my view, is antithetical to considerations of federalism, which instruct that any "permanent prohibition upon all units of democratic government must [be apparent] in the operative acts (laws and the application of laws) that the people have approved." *Stanford v. Kentucky*, 492 U.S. 361 (1989).

[T]wo sources—the work product of legislatures and sentencing jury determinations—ought to be the sole indicators by which courts ascertain the contemporary American conceptions of decency for purposes of the Eighth Amendment. They are the only objective indicia of contemporary values firmly supported by our precedents. More importantly, however, they can be reconciled with the undeniable precepts that the democratic branches of government and individual sentencing juries are, by design, better suited than courts to evaluating and giving effect to the complex societal and moral considerations that inform the selection of publicly acceptable criminal punishments.

In reaching its conclusion today, the Court . . . adverts to the fact that other countries have disapproved imposition of the death penalty for crimes committed by mentally retarded offenders (citing the Brief for The European Union as *Amicus Curiae* in *McCarver v. North Carolina*, O. T. 2001, No. 00—8727). I fail to see, however, how the views of other countries regarding the punishment of their citizens provide any support for the Court's ultimate determination. While it is true that some of our prior opinions have looked to "the climate of international opinion," *Coker*, to reinforce a conclusion regarding evolving standards of decency; we have since explicitly rejected the idea that the sentencing practices of other countries could "serve to establish the first Eighth Amendment prerequisite, that [a] practice is accepted among our people." *Stanford* (emphasizing that "American conceptions of decency . . . are dispositive"). . . .

There are strong reasons for limiting our inquiry into what constitutes an evolving standard of decency under the Eighth Amendment to the laws passed by legislatures and the practices of sentencing juries in America. Here, the Court goes beyond these well-established objective indicators of contemporary values. It finds "further support to [its] conclusion" that a national consensus has developed against imposing the death penalty on all mentally retarded defendants in international opinion, the views of professional and religious organizations, and opinion polls not demonstrated to be reliable. Believing this view to be seriously mistaken, I dissent.

■ THE DEVELOPMENT OF LAW

Post–Furman *Rulings on Capital Punishment*

CASE	VOTE	RULING
Kelly v. South Carolina, 534 U.S. 246 (2002)	5:4	Writing for the Court, Justice Souter held that, when prosecutors introduce evidence showing

future violent propensities of a convict, due process requires a jury instruction that, instead of a death sentence, a sentence of lifetime imprisonment would be imposed without the possibility of parole.

| *Mickens v. Taylor*, 535 U.S. 162 (2002) | 5:4 | The Court rejected a death row inmate's claim that his Sixth Amendment right to effective |

counsel was violated, and his murder conviction tainted, by the fact that his court-appointed attorney had previously represented the murder victim. Writing for the Court, Justice Scalia observed that it made "little policy sense" to presume that the verdict was unreliable because the trial judge had not inquired into the potential for conflict of interest. Justices Stevens, Souter, Ginsburg, and Breyer dissented.

| *Ring v. Arizona*, 536 U.S. 584 (2002) | 7:2 | Writing for the Court, Justice Ginsburg struck Arizona's law and those in four other states—Colo- |

rado, Idaho, Montana, and Nebraska—permitting judges alone, and not juries, to decide whether "aggravating" factors in a murder warrant the imposition of capital punishment. That death-penalty statute was deemed to violate the Sixth Amendment right to a jury trial and to its determination of the facts in a case. In so ruling, the Court extended *Apprendi v. New Jersey*, 530 U.S. 466 (2000), which invalidated a state law permitting judges to hand down longer sentences for "hate crimes," and overturned a prior decision. Chief Justice Rehnquist and Justice O'Connor dissented.

| *United States v. Bass*, 536 U.S. 516 (2002) | 9:0 | In a two-page unsigned opinion, the Court rejected a racial bias claim against the government's |

seeking a death sentence on the ground that statistics showing that 80 percent of federal death penalty prosecutions involve minority defendants does not establish differential treatment in cases similar to those of other black defendants. Under *United States v. Armstrong*, 517 U.S. 456 (1996), defendants claiming selective prosecution must show evidence of both discriminatory intent and effect. Here, in response to the government's notice of intent to seek the death penalty, the defendant filed a motion to dismiss or, alternatively, for discovery of information relating to the government's capital charging practices. He did so on the basis of a 2000 Department of Justice study that found that "blacks [are charged] with a death-eligible offense more than twice as often as [the government] charges whites" and that plea bargains are made with white more often than with black defendants. A federal district court granted the motion and was affirmed by an appellate court. The Supreme Court reversed in holding that "raw statistics regarding overall charges say nothing about charges brought against similarly situated defendants" and fail to establish discriminatory intent in charges of capital punishment.

Sattazahn v. Pennsylvania,   5:4   Justice Scalia held that a death
123 S.Ct. 732 (2003)   row inmate did not suffer double
jeopardy as a result of a judge's sentencing him to life imprisonment, after the jury became deadlocked on a death sentence, and a second jury in a subsequent trial unanimously imposed the death penalty. Justices Stevens, Souter, Ginsburg, and Breyer dissented.

Miller-El v. Cockrell,   8:1   Justice Kennedy held that a death
123 S.Ct. 1029 (2003)   row inmate should be allowed
to apply for a writ of *habeas corpus* based on a claim that the prosecutor's office was historically "suffused with bias" in excluding blacks from juries. Justice Thomas dissented on the ground that evidence of historical bias was "entirely circumstantial" and not "clear and convincing."

II

THE RIGHT OF PRIVACY

B | *Privacy and Personal Autonomy*

Lawrence v. Texas
123 S.CT. 2472 (2003)

On the night of September 17, 1998, the Harris County Texas police department received a frantic call from someone who claimed that there was a man with a gun "going crazy" in the Houston apartment of John Geddes Lawrence. Officers responded and arrived and entered the apartment. They found no intruder, but instead found Lawrence and Tyron Garner engaged in sodomy. They arrested them for violating the state's "homosexual conduct" law, which makes it a misdemeanor for any person to engage "in deviant sexual intercourse with another individual of the same sex." A few weeks later, Lawrence and Garner were tried and found guilty of "deviant homosexual conduct," and each was fined $200. They appealed and challenged the statute's constitutionality. A three-judge appeals panel ruled two to one that the convictions "impermissibly discriminate on the basis of sex" and violated the Equal Rights Amendment of the state constitution. But in March 2001, the full Texas Court of Appeals reversed and upheld the state's "homosexual conduct" law. Lawrence appealed that decision to the Texas Court of Criminal Appeals, which denied review, and subsequently filed an appeal to the U.S. Supreme Court, which granted review.

The state court's decision was reversed by a vote of six to three. Justice Kennedy delivered the opinion of the Court. Justice O'Connor filed a concurring opinion. Justices Scalia and Thomas filed dissenting opinions, which Chief Justice Rehnquist joined.

☐ *Justice KENNEDY delivered the opinion of the Court.*

Liberty protects the person from unwarranted government intrusions into a dwelling or other private places. In our tradition the State is not omnipresent in the home. And there are other spheres of our lives and existence, outside the home, where the State should not be a dominant presence. Freedom extends beyond spatial bounds. Liberty presumes an autonomy of self that includes freedom of thought, belief, expression, and certain intimate conduct. The instant case involves liberty of the person both in its spatial and more transcendent dimensions.

The question before the Court is the validity of a Texas statute making it a crime for two persons of the same sex to engage in certain intimate sexual conduct. . . .

We conclude the case should be resolved by determining whether the petitioners were free as adults to engage in the private conduct in the exercise of their liberty under the Due Process Clause of the Fourteenth Amendment to the Constitution. For this inquiry we deem it necessary to reconsider the Court's holding in *Bowers* [*v. Hardwick*, 478 U.S. 186 (1986)].

There are broad statements of the substantive reach of liberty under the Due Process Clause in earlier cases, including *Pierce v. Society of Sisters*, 268 U.S. 510 (1925), and *Meyer v. Nebraska*, 262 U.S. 390 (1923); but the most pertinent beginning point is our decision in *Griswold v. Connecticut*, 381 U.S. 479 (1965).

In *Griswold* the Court invalidated a state law prohibiting the use of drugs or devices of contraception and counseling or aiding and abetting the use of contraceptives. The Court described the protected interest as a right to privacy and placed emphasis on the marriage relation and the protected space of the marital bedroom.

After *Griswold* it was established that the right to make certain decisions regarding sexual conduct extends beyond the marital relationship. In *Eisenstadt v. Baird*, 405 U.S. 438 (1972), the Court invalidated a law prohibiting the distribution of contraceptives to unmarried persons. The case was decided under the Equal Protection Clause, but with respect to unmarried persons, the Court went on to state the fundamental proposition that the law impaired the exercise of their personal rights.

The opinions in *Griswold* and *Eisenstadt* were part of the background for the decision in *Roe v. Wade*, 410 U.S. 113 (1973). As is well known, the case involved a challenge to the Texas law prohibiting abortions, but the laws of other States were affected as well. Although the Court held the woman's rights were not absolute, her right to elect an abortion did have real and substantial protection as an exercise of her liberty under the Due Process Clause. The Court cited cases that protect spatial freedom and cases that go well beyond it. *Roe* recognized the right of a woman to make certain fundamental decisions affecting her destiny and confirmed once more that the protection of liberty under the Due Process Clause has a substantive dimension of fundamental significance in defining the rights of the person. . . .

This was the state of the law with respect to some of the most relevant cases when the Court considered *Bowers v. Hardwick*. The facts in *Bowers* had some similarities to the instant case. A police officer, whose right to enter seems not to have been in question, observed Hardwick, in his own bedroom, engaging in intimate sexual conduct with another adult male. The conduct was in violation of a Georgia statute making it a criminal offense to engage in sodomy. One difference between the two cases is that the Georgia statute prohibited the conduct whether or not the participants were of the same sex, while the Texas statute, as we have seen, applies only to participants of the same sex. Hardwick was not prosecuted, but he brought an action in federal court to declare the state statute invalid. He alleged he was a practicing homosexual and that the criminal prohibition violated rights guaranteed to him by the Constitution. The Court, in an opinion by Justice WHITE, sustained the Georgia law. Chief Justice BURGER and Justice POWELL joined the opinion of the Court and filed separate, concurring opinions. Four Justices dissented.

The Court began its substantive discussion in *Bowers* as follows: "The issue presented is whether the Federal Constitution confers a fundamental right upon homosexuals to engage in sodomy and hence invalidates the laws of the many States that still make such conduct illegal and have done so for a very long time." That statement, we now conclude, discloses the Court's own failure to appreciate the extent of the liberty at stake. To say that the issue in *Bowers* was simply the right to engage in certain sexual conduct demeans the claim the individual put forward, just as it would demean a married couple were it to be said marriage is simply about the right to have sexual intercourse. The laws involved in *Bowers* and here are, to be sure, statutes that purport to do no more than prohibit a particular sexual act. Their penalties and purposes, though, have more far-reaching consequences, touching upon the most private human conduct, sexual behavior, and in the most private of places, the home. The statutes do seek to control a personal relationship that, whether or not entitled to formal recognition in the law, is within the liberty of persons to choose without being punished as criminals.

This, as a general rule, should counsel against attempts by the State, or a court, to define the meaning of the relationship or to set its boundaries absent injury to a person or abuse of an institution the law protects. It suffices for us to acknowledge that adults may choose to enter upon this relationship in the confines of their homes and their own private lives and still retain their dignity as free persons. When sexuality finds overt expression in intimate conduct with another person, the conduct can be but one element in a personal bond that is more enduring. The liberty protected by the Constitution allows homosexual persons the right to make this choice....

At the outset it should be noted that there is no longstanding history in this country of laws directed at homosexual conduct as a distinct matter. Beginning in colonial times there were prohibitions of sodomy derived from the English criminal laws passed in the first instance by the Reformation Parliament of 1533. The English prohibition was understood to include relations between men and women as well as relations between men and men. Thus early American sodomy laws were not directed at homosexuals as such but instead sought to prohibit nonprocreative sexual activity more generally. This does not suggest approval of homosexual conduct. It does tend to show that this particular form of conduct was not thought of as a separate category from like conduct between heterosexual persons.

Laws prohibiting sodomy do not seem to have been enforced against consenting adults acting in private. A substantial number of sodomy prosecutions and convictions for which there are surviving records were for predatory acts against those who could not or did not consent, as in the case of a minor or the victim of an assault....

The policy of punishing consenting adults for private acts was not much discussed in the early legal literature. We can infer that one reason for this was the very private nature of the conduct. Despite the absence of prosecutions, there may have been periods in which there was public criticism of homosexuals as such and an insistence that the criminal laws be enforced to discourage their practices. But far from possessing "ancient roots," *Bowers*, American laws targeting same-sex couples did not develop until the last third of the 20th century. The reported decisions concerning the prosecution of consensual, homosexual sodomy between adults for the years 1880–1995 are not always clear in the details, but a significant number involved conduct in a public place.

It was not until the 1970s that any State singled out same-sex relations for criminal prosecution, and only nine States have done so.

In summary, the historical grounds relied upon in *Bowers* are more complex than the majority opinion and the concurring opinion by Chief Justice BURGER indicate. Their historical premises are not without doubt and, at the very least, are overstated.

It must be acknowledged, of course, that the Court in *Bowers* was making the broader point that for centuries there have been powerful voices to condemn homosexual conduct as immoral. The condemnation has been shaped by religious beliefs, conceptions of right and acceptable behavior, and respect for the traditional family. For many persons these are not trivial concerns but profound and deep convictions accepted as ethical and moral principles to which they aspire and which thus determine the course of their lives. These considerations do not answer the question before us, however. The issue is whether the majority may use the power of the State to enforce these views on the whole society through operation of the criminal law. "Our obligation is to define the liberty of all, not to mandate our own moral code." *Planned Parenthood of Southeastern Pa. v. Casey*, 505 U.S. 833 (1992).

Chief Justice BURGER joined the opinion for the Court in *Bowers* and further explained his views as follows: "Decisions of individuals relating to homosexual conduct have been subject to state intervention throughout the history of Western civilization. Condemnation of those practices is firmly rooted in Judeao-Christian moral and ethical standards." As with Justice WHITE's assumptions about history, scholarship casts some doubt on the sweeping nature of the statement by Chief Justice BURGER as it pertains to private homosexual conduct between consenting adults. In all events we think that our laws and traditions in the past half century are of most relevance here. These references show an emerging awareness that liberty gives substantial protection to adult persons in deciding how to conduct their private lives in matters pertaining to sex. . . .

In *Bowers* the Court referred to the fact that before 1961 all 50 States had outlawed sodomy, and that at the time of the Court's decision 24 States and the District of Columbia had sodomy laws. Justice POWELL pointed out that these prohibitions often were being ignored, however. Georgia, for instance, had not sought to enforce its law for decades.

The sweeping references by Chief Justice BURGER to the history of Western civilization and to Judeo-Christian moral and ethical standards did not take account of other authorities pointing in an opposite direction. A committee advising the British Parliament recommended in 1957 repeal of laws punishing homosexual conduct. *The Wolfenden Report* (1963). Parliament enacted the substance of those recommendations 10 years later.

Of even more importance, almost five years before *Bowers* was decided the European Court of Human Rights considered a case with parallels to *Bowers* and to today's case. An adult male resident in Northern Ireland alleged he was a practicing homosexual who desired to engage in consensual homosexual conduct. The laws of Northern Ireland forbade him that right. He alleged that he had been questioned, his home had been searched, and he feared criminal prosecution. The court held that the laws proscribing the conduct were invalid under the European Convention on Human Rights. *Dudgeon v. United Kingdom*, 45 Eur. Ct. H. R. (1981). Authoritative in all countries that are members of the Council of Europe (21 nations then, 45 nations now), the decision is at odds with the premise in *Bowers* that the claim put forward was insubstantial in our Western civilization.

In our own constitutional system the deficiencies in *Bowers* became even more apparent in the years following its announcement. The 25 States with laws prohibiting the relevant conduct referenced in the *Bowers* decision are reduced now to 13, of which 4 enforce their laws only against homosexual conduct. In those States where sodomy is still proscribed, whether for same-sex or heterosexual conduct, there is a pattern of nonenforcement with respect to consenting adults acting in private. The State of Texas admitted in 1994 that as of that date it had not prosecuted anyone under those circumstances.

Two principal cases decided after *Bowers* cast its holding into even more doubt. In *Planned Parenthood of Southeastern Pa. v. Casey*, 505 U.S. 833 (1992), the Court reaffirmed the substantive force of the liberty protected by the Due Process Clause. The Casey decision again confirmed that our laws and tradition afford constitutional protection to personal decisions relating to marriage, procreation, contraception, family relationships, child rearing, and education. . . . Persons in a homosexual relationship may seek autonomy for these purposes, just as heterosexual persons do. The decision in *Bowers* would deny them this right.

The second post-*Bowers* case of principal relevance is *Romer v. Evans*, 517 U.S. 620 (1996). There the Court struck down class-based legislation directed at homosexuals as a violation of the Equal Protection Clause. *Romer* invalidated an amendment to Colorado's constitution which named as a solitary class persons who were homosexuals, lesbians, or bisexual either by "orientation, conduct, practices or relationships," and deprived them of protection under state antidiscrimination laws. We concluded that the provision was "born of animosity toward the class of persons affected" and further that it had no rational relation to a legitimate governmental purpose. . . .

Equality of treatment and the due process right to demand respect for conduct protected by the substantive guarantee of liberty are linked in important respects, and a decision on the latter point advances both interests. If protected conduct is made criminal and the law which does so remains unexamined for its substantive validity, its stigma might remain even if it were not enforceable as drawn for equal protection reasons. When homosexual conduct is made criminal by the law of the State, that declaration in and of itself is an invitation to subject homosexual persons to discrimination both in the public and in the private spheres. The central holding of *Bowers* has been brought in question by this case, and it should be addressed. Its continuance as precedent demeans the lives of homosexual persons. . . .

The foundations of *Bowers* have sustained serious erosion from our recent decisions in *Casey* and *Romer*. When our precedent has been thus weakened, criticism from other sources is of greater significance. In the United States criticism of *Bowers* has been substantial and continuing, disapproving of its reasoning in all respects, not just as to its historical assumptions. The courts of five different States have declined to follow it in interpreting provisions in their own state constitutions parallel to the Due Process Clause of the Fourteenth Amendment.

To the extent *Bowers* relied on values we share with a wider civilization, it should be noted that the reasoning and holding in *Bowers* have been rejected elsewhere. The European Court of Human Rights has followed not *Bowers* but its own decision in *Dudgeon v. United Kingdom*. Other nations, too, have taken action consistent with an affirmation of the protected right of homosexual adults to engage in intimate, consensual conduct. The right the petitioners seek in this case has been accepted as an integral part of human freedom in many other countries. There has been no showing that in this country the governmental interest in circumscribing personal choice is somehow more legitimate or urgent.

The doctrine of *stare decisis* is essential to the respect accorded to the judgments of the Court and to the stability of the law. It is not, however, an inexorable command. *Payne v. Tennessee*, 501 U.S. 808 (1991). In *Casey* we noted that when a Court is asked to overrule a precedent recognizing a constitutional liberty interest, individual or societal reliance on the existence of that liberty cautions with particular strength against reversing course. The holding in *Bowers*, however, has not induced detrimental reliance comparable to some instances where recognized individual rights are involved. Indeed, there has been no individual or societal reliance on *Bowers* of the sort that could counsel against overturning its holding once there are compelling reasons to do so. *Bowers* itself causes uncertainty, for the precedents before and after its issuance contradict its central holding.

The rationale of *Bowers* does not withstand careful analysis. *Bowers* was not correct when it was decided, and it is not correct today. It ought not to remain binding precedent. *Bowers v. Hardwick* should be and now is overruled.

The present case does not involve minors. It does not involve persons who might be injured or coerced or who are situated in relationships where consent might not easily be refused. It does not involve public conduct or prostitution. It does not involve whether the government must give formal recognition to any relationship that homosexual persons seek to enter. The case does involve two adults who, with full and mutual consent from each other, engaged in sexual practices common to a homosexual lifestyle. The petitioners are entitled to respect for their private lives. The State cannot demean their existence or control their destiny by making their private sexual conduct a crime. Their right to liberty under the Due Process Clause gives them the full right to engage in their conduct without intervention of the government. The Texas statute furthers no legitimate state interest which can justify its intrusion into the personal and private life of the individual.

Had those who drew and ratified the Due Process Clauses of the Fifth Amendment or the Fourteenth Amendment known the components of liberty in its manifold possibilities, they might have been more specific. They did not presume to have this insight. They knew times can blind us to certain truths and later generations can see that laws once thought necessary and proper in fact serve only to oppress. As the Constitution endures, persons in every generation can invoke its principles in their own search for greater freedom.

The judgment of the Court of Appeals for the Texas Fourteenth District is reversed, and the case is remanded for further proceedings not inconsistent with this opinion.

It is so ordered.

☐ *Justice O'CONNOR, concurriong in the judgment.*

The Court today overrules *Bowers v. Hardwick.* I joined *Bowers,* and do not join the Court in overruling it. Nevertheless, I agree with the Court that Texas's statute banning same-sex sodomy is unconstitutional. Rather than relying on the substantive component of the Fourteenth Amendment's Due Process Clause, as the Court does, I base my conclusion on the Fourteenth Amendment's Equal Protection Clause. . . .

The statute at issue here makes sodomy a crime only if a person "engages in deviate sexual intercourse with another individual of the same sex." Sodomy between opposite-sex partners, however, is not a crime in Texas. That is, Texas treats the same conduct differently based solely on the participants. Those harmed by this law are people who have a same-sex sexual orientation and thus are more likely to engage in behavior prohibited by Section 21.06. The Texas statute makes homosexuals unequal in the eyes of the law by making particular conduct—and only that conduct—subject to criminal sanction. It appears that prosecutions under Texas's sodomy law are rare.

And the effect of Texas's sodomy law is not just limited to the threat of prosecution or consequence of conviction. Texas's sodomy law brands all homosexuals as criminals. . . .

This case raises a different issue than *Bowers*: whether, under the Equal Protection Clause, moral disapproval is a legitimate state interest to justify by itself a statute that bans homosexual sodomy, but not heterosexual sodomy. It is not. Moral disapproval of this group, like a bare desire to harm the group, is an interest that is insufficient to satisfy rational basis review under the Equal Protection Clause. Indeed, we have never held that moral disapproval, without any other asserted state interest, is a sufficient rationale under the Equal Protection Clause to justify a law that discriminates among groups of persons. . . .

That this law as applied to private, consensual conduct is unconstitutional under the Equal Protection Clause does not mean that other laws distinguishing between heterosexuals and homosexuals would similarly fail under rational basis review. Texas cannot assert any legitimate state interest here, such as national security or preserving the traditional institution of marriage. Unlike the moral disapproval of same-sex relations—the asserted state interest in this case—other reasons exist to promote the institution of marriage beyond mere moral disapproval of an excluded group.

A law branding one class of persons as criminal solely based on the State's moral disapproval of that class and the conduct associated with that class runs contrary to the values of the Constitution and the Equal Protection Clause, under any standard of review. I therefore concur in the Court's judgment that Texas's sodomy law banning "deviate sexual intercourse" between consenting adults of the same sex, but not between consenting adults of different sexes, is unconstitutional.

☐ *Justice SCALIA,* with whom The CHIEF JUSTICE and Justice THOMAS join, dissenting.

"Liberty finds no refuge in a jurisprudence of doubt." *Planned Parenthood of Southeastern Pa. v. Casey,* 505 U.S. 833 (1992). That was the Court's sententious response, barely more than a decade ago, to those seeking to overrule

Roe v. Wade, 410 U.S. 113 (1973). The Court's response today, to those who have engaged in a 17-year crusade to overrule *Bowers v. Hardwick*, 478 U.S. 186 (1986), is very different. The need for stability and certainty presents no barrier. . . .

I begin with the Court's surprising readiness to reconsider a decision rendered a mere 17 years ago in *Bowers v. Hardwick*. I do not myself believe in rigid adherence to *stare decisis* in constitutional cases; but I do believe that we should be consistent rather than manipulative in invoking the doctrine. Today's opinions in support of reversal do not bother to distinguish—or indeed, even bother to mention—the paean to *stare decisis* coauthored by three Members of today's majority in *Planned Parenthood v. Casey*. There, when *stare decisis* meant preservation of judicially invented abortion rights, the widespread criticism of *Roe* was strong reason to reaffirm it. Today, however, the widespread opposition to *Bowers*, a decision resolving an issue as "intensely divisive" as the issue in *Roe*, is offered as a reason in favor of overruling it. Gone, too, is any "enquiry" (of the sort conducted in *Casey*) into whether the decision sought to be overruled has "proven 'unworkable,'" *Casey*.

Today's approach to *stare decisis* invites us to overrule an erroneously decided precedent (including an "intensely divisive" decision) if: (1) its foundations have been "eroded" by subsequent decisions; (2) it has been subject to "substantial and continuing" criticism; and (3) it has not induced "individual or societal reliance" that counsels against overturning. The problem is that *Roe* itself—which today's majority surely has no disposition to overrule—satisfies these conditions to at least the same degree as *Bowers*. . . .

What a massive disruption of the current social order, therefore, the overruling of *Bowers* entails. Not so the overruling of *Roe*, which would simply have restored the regime that existed for centuries before 1973, in which the permissibility of and restrictions upon abortion were determined legislatively State-by-State. *Casey*, however, chose to base its *stare decisis* determination on a different "sort" of reliance. "[P]eople," it said, "have organized intimate relationships and made choices that define their views of themselves and their places in society, in reliance on the availability of abortion in the event that contraception should fail." This falsely assumes that the consequence of overruling *Roe* would have been to make abortion unlawful. It would not; it would merely have permitted the States to do so. Many States would unquestionably have declined to prohibit abortion, and others would not have prohibited it within six months (after which the most significant reliance interests would have expired). Even for persons in States other than these, the choice would not have been between abortion and childbirth, but between abortion nearby and abortion in a neighboring State.

To tell the truth, it does not surprise me, and should surprise no one, that the Court has chosen today to revise the standards of *stare decisis* set forth in *Casey*. It has thereby exposed *Casey*'s extraordinary deference to precedent for the result-oriented expedient that it is.

Having decided that it need not adhere to *stare decisis*, the Court still must establish that *Bowers* was wrongly decided and that the Texas statute, as applied to petitioners, is unconstitutional. . . .

Our opinions applying the doctrine known as "substantive due process" hold that the Due Process Clause prohibits States from infringing fundamental liberty interests, unless the infringement is narrowly tailored to serve a compelling state interest. We have held repeatedly, in cases the Court today does not overrule, that only fundamental rights qualify for this so-called "heightened scrutiny" protection—that is, rights which are "'deeply rooted in this Nation's history and tradition.'"

Bowers held, first, that criminal prohibitions of homosexual sodomy are not subject to heightened scrutiny because they do not implicate a "fundamental right" under the Due Process Clause. Noting that "[p]roscriptions against that conduct have ancient roots," that "[s]odomy was a criminal offense at common law and was forbidden by the laws of the original 13 States when they ratified the Bill of Rights," and that many States had retained their bans on sodomy, *Bowers* concluded that a right to engage in homosexual sodomy was not "'deeply rooted in this Nation's history and tradition.'"

The Court today does not overrule this holding. Not once does it describe homosexual sodomy as a "fundamental right" or a "fundamental liberty interest," nor does it subject the Texas statute to strict scrutiny. Instead, having failed to establish that the right to homosexual sodomy is "'deeply rooted in this Nation's history and tradition,'" the Court concludes that the application of Texas's statute to petitioners' conduct fails the rational-basis test, and overrules *Bowers*' holding to the contrary.

I shall address that rational-basis holding presently. First, however, I address some aspersions that the Court casts upon *Bowers*' conclusion that homosexual sodomy is not a "fundamental right"—even though, as I have said, the Court does not have the boldness to reverse that conclusion.

The Court's description of "the state of the law" at the time of *Bowers* only confirms that *Bowers* was right. The Court points to *Griswold v. Connecticut* (1965). But that case expressly disclaimed any reliance on the doctrine of "substantive due process," and grounded the so-called "right to privacy" in penumbras of constitutional provisions other than the Due Process Clause.

Roe v. Wade recognized that the right to abort an unborn child was a "fundamental right" protected by the Due Process Clause. The *Roe* Court, however, made no attempt to establish that this right was "'deeply rooted in this Nation's history and tradition'"; instead, it based its conclusion that "the Fourteenth Amendment's concept of personal liberty . . . is broad enough to encompass a woman's decision whether or not to terminate her pregnancy" on its own normative judgment that anti-abortion laws were undesirable. . . .

After discussing the history of antisodomy laws, the Court proclaims that, "it should be noted that there is no longstanding history in this country of laws directed at homosexual conduct as a distinct matter." This observation in no way casts into doubt the "definitive [historical] conclusion," on which *Bowers* relied: that our Nation has a longstanding history of laws prohibiting sodomy in general—regardless of whether it was performed by same-sex or opposite-sex couples. It is (as *Bowers* recognized) entirely irrelevant whether the laws in our long national tradition criminalizing homosexual sodomy were "directed at homosexual conduct as a distinct matter." Whether homosexual sodomy was prohibited by a law targeted at same-sex sexual relations or by a more general law prohibiting both homosexual and heterosexual sodomy, the only relevant point is that it was criminalized—which suffices to establish that homosexual sodomy is not a right "deeply rooted in our Nation's history and tradition." The Court today agrees that homosexual sodomy was criminalized and thus does not dispute the facts on which *Bowers* actually relied.

Next the Court makes the claim, again unsupported by any citations, that "[l]aws prohibiting sodomy do not seem to have been enforced against consenting adults acting in private." The key qualifier here is "acting in private"—since the Court admits that sodomy laws were enforced against consenting adults (although the Court contends that prosecutions were "infrequent"). I do not know what "acting in private" means; surely consensual sodomy, like heterosexual intercourse, is rarely performed on stage. If all the Court means by "acting in private" is "on private premises, with the doors closed and windows covered," it is entirely unsurprising that evidence of enforcement would be hard to come by. Surely that lack of evidence would not sustain the proposition that consensual sodomy on private premises with the doors closed and windows covered was regarded as a "fundamental right," even though all other consensual sodomy was criminalized. There are 203 prosecutions for consensual, adult homosexual sodomy reported in the West Reporting system and official state reporters from the years 1880–1995. There are also records of 20 sodomy prosecutions and 4 executions during the colonial period. *Bowers'* conclusion that homosexual sodomy is not a fundamental right "deeply rooted in this Nation's history and tradition" is utterly unassailable.

Realizing that fact, the Court instead says: "[W]e think that our laws and traditions in the past half century are of most relevance here. These references show an emerging awareness that liberty gives substantial protection to adult persons in deciding how to conduct their private lives in matters pertaining to sex." Apart from the fact that such an "emerging awareness" does not establish a "fundamental right," the statement is factually false. States continue to prosecute all sorts of crimes by adults "in matters pertaining to sex": prostitution, adult incest, adultery, obscenity, and child pornography. Sodomy laws, too, have been enforced "in the past half century," in which there have been 134 reported cases involving prosecutions for consensual, adult, homosexual sodomy. In relying, for evidence of an "emerging recognition," upon the American Law Institute's 1955 recommendation not to criminalize "'consensual sexual relations conducted in private,'" the Court ignores the fact that this recommendation was "a point of resistance in most of the states that considered adopting the Model Penal Code."

In any event, an "emerging awareness" is by definition not "deeply rooted in this Nation's history and tradition[s]," as we have said "fundamental right" status requires. Constitutional entitlements do not spring into existence because some States choose to lessen or eliminate criminal sanctions on certain behavior. Much less do they spring into existence, as the Court seems to believe, because foreign nations decriminalize conduct. The *Bowers* majority opinion never relied on "values we share with a wider civilization," but rather rejected the claimed right to sodomy on the ground that such a right was not "'deeply rooted in this Nation's history and tradition.'" *Bowers'* rational-basis holding is likewise devoid of any reliance on the views of a "wider civilization." The Court's discussion of these foreign views (ignoring, of course, the many countries that have retained criminal prohibitions on sodomy) is therefore meaningless dicta.

I turn now to the ground on which the Court squarely rests its holding: the contention that there is no rational basis for the law here under attack. This proposition is so out of accord with our jurisprudence—indeed, with the jurisprudence of any society we know—that it requires little discussion.

The Texas statute undeniably seeks to further the belief of its citizens that certain forms of sexual behavior are "immoral and unacceptable," *Bowers*—the same interest furthered by criminal laws against fornication, bigamy, adultery, adult incest, bestiality, and obscenity. *Bowers* held that this was a legitimate state interest. The Court today reaches the opposite conclusion.

The Texas statute, it says, "furthers no legitimate state interest which can justify its intrusion into the personal and private life of the individual." The Court embraces instead Justice STEVENS' declaration in his *Bowers* dissent, that "the fact that the governing majority in a State has traditionally viewed a particular practice as immoral is not a sufficient reason for upholding a law prohibiting the practice." This effectively decrees the end of all morals legislation. If, as the Court asserts, the promotion of majoritarian sexual morality is not even a legitimate state interest, none of the above-mentioned laws can survive rational-basis review.

Finally, I turn to petitioners' equal-protection challenge, which no Member of the Court save Justice O'CONNOR embraces: On its face Section 21.06(a) applies equally to all persons. Men and women, heterosexuals and homosexuals, are all subject to its prohibition of deviate sexual intercourse with someone of the same sex. To be sure, Section 21.06 does distinguish between the sexes insofar as concerns the partner with whom the sexual acts are performed: men can violate the law only with other men, and women only with other women. But this cannot itself be a denial of equal protection, since it is precisely the same distinction regarding partner that is drawn in state laws prohibiting marriage with someone of the same sex while permitting marriage with someone of the opposite sex. . . .

Today's opinion is the product of a Court, which is the product of a law-profession culture, that has largely signed on to the so-called homosexual agenda, by which I mean the agenda promoted by some homosexual activists directed at eliminating the moral opprobrium that has traditionally attached to homosexual conduct. One of the most revealing statements in today's opinion is the Court's grim warning that the criminalization of homosexual conduct is "an invitation to subject homosexual persons to discrimination both in the public and in the private spheres." It is clear from this that the Court has taken sides in the culture war, departing from its role of assuring, as neutral observer, that the democratic rules of engagement are observed. Many Americans do not want persons who openly engage in homosexual conduct as partners in their business, as scoutmasters for their children, as teachers in their children's schools, or as boarders in their home. They view this as protecting themselves and their families from a lifestyle that they believe to be immoral and destructive. The Court views it as "discrimination" which it is the function of our judgments to deter. So imbued is the Court with the law profession's anti-anti-homosexual culture, that it is seemingly unaware that the attitudes of that culture are not obviously "mainstream"; that in most States what the Court calls "discrimination" against those who engage in homosexual acts is perfectly legal; that proposals to ban such "discrimination" under Title VII have repeatedly been rejected by Congress; that in some cases such "discrimination" is mandated by federal statute (mandating discharge from the armed forces of any service member who engages in or intends to engage in homosexual acts); and that in some cases such "discrimination" is a constitutional right, see *Boy Scouts of America v. Dale*, 530 U.S. 640 (2000).

Let me be clear that I have nothing against homosexuals, or any other group, promoting their agenda through normal democratic means. Social perceptions of sexual and other morality change over time, and every group has the right to persuade its fellow citizens that its view of such matters is the best. That homosexuals have achieved some success in that enterprise is attested to by the fact that Texas is one of the few remaining States that criminalize private, consensual homosexual acts. But persuading one's fellow citizens is one thing, and imposing one's views in absence of democratic majority will is something else. I would no more require a State to criminalize homosexual acts—or, for that matter, display any moral disapprobation of them—than I would forbid it to do so. What Texas has chosen to do is well within the range of traditional democratic action, and its hand should not be stayed through the invention of a brand-new "constitutional right" by a Court that is impatient of democratic change. It is indeed true that "later generations can see that laws once thought necessary and proper in fact serve only to oppress," and when that happens, later generations can repeal those laws. But it is the premise of our system that those judgments are to be made by the people, and not imposed by a governing caste that knows best.

☐ *Justice THOMAS, dissenting.*

I join Justice SCALIA's dissenting opinion. I write separately to note that the law before the Court today "is . . . uncommonly silly." *Griswold v. Connecticut* (1965) (STEWART, J., dissenting). If I were a member of the Texas Legislature, I would vote to repeal it. Punishing someone for expressing his sexual preference through noncommercial consensual conduct with another adult does not appear to be a worthy way to expend valuable law enforcement resources.

Notwithstanding this, I recognize that as a member of this Court I am not empowered to help petitioners and others similarly situated. My duty, rather, is to "decide cases 'agreeably to the Constitution and laws of the United States.'" And, just like Justice STEWART, I "can find [neither in the Bill of Rights nor any other part of the Constitution a] general right of privacy," or as the Court terms it today, the "liberty of the person both in its spatial and more transcendent dimensions."

■ IN COMPARATIVE PERSPECTIVE

Canadian Courts Forbid Discrimination against Homosexuals and Same-Sex Marriages

In *Egan v. Canada*, 2 S.C.R. 513 (1995), the Supreme Court of Canada held, "on the basis of historical, social, political and economic disadvantage suffered by homosexuals" and the emerging consensus among legislatures, as well as previous judicial decisions, that sexual orientation was embraced by the equality guarantee of Section 15(1) of Canada's Charter of Rights and Freedom, which provides: "Every individual is equal before and under the law and has the right to the equal protection and equal benefit of the law without discrimination and, in particular, without discrimination based on race, national or ethnic origin, colour, religion, sex, age or mental or physical disability."

Later decisions of the Canadian Supreme Court expanded protection for gays and lesbians. In *Vriend v. Alberta*, 1 S.C.R. 493 (1998), for instance, the Court held that Alberta's human rights code must give protection to homosexuals in employment in order to comply with the guarantee of Section 15(1). See also *M. v. H.*, 2 S.C.R. 3 (1999).

More recently, a lower court judge declared Quebec's prohibition against same-sex marriages invalid, in *Hendricks v. Quebec*, J.Q. No. 3816 (S.C.) (2002). Likewise, the British Columbia Court of Appeal declared the common law definition of marriage unconstitutional and required the substitution of the words "two persons" for "one man and one woman," in *EGALE Canada Inc. v. Attorney General of Canada*, B.C.J. 994 (2003). And in *Halpern v. Attorney General of Canada*, No. C39172 (June 10, 2003), the Court of Appeal for Ontario held that Section 15(1) bars discrimination against same-sex marriages.

Writing for the Court in *Halpern*, Chief Justice Roy McMurtry rejected the government's position against recognizing same-sex marriages, upon reasoning:

> No one is disputing that marriage is a fundamental societal institution. Similarly, it is accepted that, with limited exceptions, marriage has been understood to be a monogamous opposite-sex union. What needs to be determined, however, is whether there is a valid objective to maintaining marriage as an exclusively heterosexual institution. Stating that marriage is heterosexual because it always has been heterosexual is merely an explanation for the opposite-sex requirement of marriage; it is not an objective that is capable of justifying the infringement of a Charter guarantee.
>
> We now turn to the more specific purposes of marriage advanced by [the government]: (i) uniting the opposite sexes; (ii) encouraging the birth and raising of children of the marriage; and (iii) companionship.

The first purpose, which results in favouring one form of relationship over another, suggests that uniting two persons of the same sex is of lesser importance.... [A] purpose that demeans the dignity of same-sex couples is contrary to the values of a free and democratic society and cannot be considered to be pressing and substantial. A law cannot be justified on the very basis upon which it is being attacked.

The second purpose of marriage, as advanced by [the government], is encouraging the birth and raising of children. Clearly, encouraging procreation and childrearing is a laudable goal that is properly regarded as pressing and substantial. However, the AGC must demonstrate that the objective of maintaining marriage as an exclusively heterosexual institution is pressing and substantial: see *Vriend* [*v. Alberta*].

We fail to see how the encouragement of procreation and childrearing is a pressing and substantial objective of maintaining marriage as an exclusively heterosexual institution. Heterosexual married couples will not stop having or raising children because same-sex couples are permitted to marry. Moreover, an increasing percentage of children are being born to and raised by same-sex couples.

The [government] submits that the union of two persons of the opposite sex is the only union that can "naturally" procreate. In terms of that biological reality, same-sex couples are different from opposite-sex couples. In our view, however, "natural" procreation is not a sufficiently pressing and substantial objective to justify infringing the equality rights of same-sex couples. As previously stated, same-sex couples can have children by other means, such as adoption, surrogacy and donor insemination. A law that aims to encourage only "natural" procreation ignores the fact that same-sex couples are capable of having children.

Similarly, a law that restricts marriage to opposite-sex couples, on the basis that a fundamental purpose of marriage is the raising of children, suggests that same-sex couples are not equally capable of childrearing. The [government] has put forward no evidence to support such a proposition. Neither is the [government] advocating such a view; rather, it takes the position that social science research is not capable of establishing the proposition one way or another. In the absence of cogent evidence, it is our view that the objective is based on a stereotypical assumption that is not acceptable in a free and democratic society that prides itself on promoting equality and respect for all persons.

The third purpose of marriage advanced by the [government] is companionship. We consider companionship to be a laudable goal of marriage. However, encouraging companionship cannot be considered a pressing and substantial objective of the omission of the impugned law. Encouraging companionship between only persons of the opposite sex perpetuates the view that persons in same-sex relationships are not equally capable of providing companionship and forming lasting and loving relationships.

Accordingly, it is our view that the [government] has not demonstrated any pressing and substantial objective for excluding same-sex couples from the institution of marriage. For that reason, we conclude that the violation of the Couples' rights under Section 15(1) of the Charter cannot be saved. . . .

Note: the full text of the opinion in *Halpern v. Attorney General of Canada* is available on the website of the Court of Appeal of Ontario at www.ontariocourts.on.ca/decisions.

12

THE EQUAL PROTECTION OF
THE LAWS

A | *Racial Discrimination
and State Action*

In its 2002–2003 term the Court decided whether a referendum to stay the implementation of an approved plan for low-income housing violated the Fourteenth Amendment, in *City of Cuyahoga Falls v. Buckeye Community Hope Foundation* 123 S.Ct. 1389 (2003). Buckeye Community Hope Foundation purchased property in Cuyahoga Falls and submitted a plan to develop affordable housing to the city's planning commission, which granted approval, as did the city council. Subsequently, members of the public voiced concerns about crime and drugs, safety, and the "different class" of people associated with low-income housing, and submitted a referendum petition to present the issue of the housing development to the voters. The board of elections approved the petition and stayed implementation of the plan. The foundation sued, claiming violations of the Fourteenth Amendment and the Fair Housing Act. A federal district court dismissed the claims, but the Court of Appeals for the Sixth Circuit found that it had erred in dismissing the equal protection claim and concluded that the foundation had presented sufficient evidence to raise the claim that opposition to the low-income housing project reflected racial bias and that the city gave effect to that racial bias in allowing the referendum to stay the previously approved plan. That decision was appealed and the Supreme Court granted *certiorari.*

Writing for the Court, Justice O'Connor held that Buckeye Community Hope Foundation failed to establish a racially discriminatory intent, as required for an Equal Protection violation, in claiming an injury from the referendum petitioning process, instead of the referendum itself, which never went into effect. In other words, the foundation failed to show that the referendum process was motivated by racial animus.

C | *Affirmative Action and Reverse Discrimination*

In two widely watched cases challenging the University of Michigan's affirmative action programs, the Court revisited the issue of whether achieving diverse student bodies is permissible and withstands Fourteenth Amendment challenges, as Justice Powell held in *Regents of the University of California v. Bakke*, 438 U.S. 265 (1978) (excerpted in Vol. 2, Ch. 12). By a six to three vote in *Gratz v. Bollinger* (excerpted below) the justices struck down the college's program based on a point system. But splitting five to four in *Grutter v. Bollinger* (excerpted below), the justices upheld the law school's program for achieving a "critical mass" of students from groups that have historically been discriminated against.

Gratz v. Bollinger
123 S.Ct. 2411 (2003)

The University of Michigan receives over 13,000 applications for admission into its College of Literature, Science, and Arts, and admits approximately 3,950 students each year. In order to achieve a diverse student body, the college gave preference to applicants from "underrepresented minority groups," including African Americans, Hispanics, and Native Americans. In the mid-1990s the college used different admissions criteria and set aside a number of seats in each entering class in order to achieve a numerical target. In 1998–1999, however, the college changed its policy in favor of a point system. Under that system the college used a "selection index" or ranking on a 150-point scale in three categories: test scores, academic record, and other factors. As many as 110 of those points were based on test scores and academic achievements. A maximum of 40 points were assigned for other factors, including 20 points for students from underrepresented minority groups or from socioeconomically disadvantaged families; 16 points for state residents from rural areas; four points for children of alumni. In general, applicants in the range of 100 to 150 points were admitted; those between 95 and 99 were admitted or postponed; 90 to 94 postponed or delayed; 75 to 89 delayed or postponed; and 74 and below were delayed or rejected.

In 1995, Jennifer Gratz applied for admission. Her high school grade point average was 3.8 and her ACT standardized test score was 25. The college initially delayed her admission and then placed her on an extended wait list. Under the college's guidelines at the time all underrepresented minority applicants with Ms. Gratz's credentials were admitted, regardless of whether they were in- or out-of-state residents. Ms. Gratz filed a class action lawsuit challenging the constitutionality of the admissions program. In December 2000, a federal district court held that the college's admissions system in 1995–1998 violated the Fourteenth Amendment, but held that its use of a point system was permissible and advanced a compelling governmental interest in promoting diversity in higher education. Ms. Gratz appealed that decision.

The lower court was reversed by a vote of six to three. Chief Justice Rehnquist delivered the opinion of the Court. Justices O'Connor, Breyer, and Thomas filed concurring opinions. Justices Stevens, Souter, and Ginsburg filed dissenting opinions.

☐ CHIEF JUSTICE REHNQUIST *delivered the opinion of the Court.*

We granted *certiorari* in this case to decide whether "the University of Michigan's use of racial preferences in undergraduate admissions violate[s] the Equal Protection Clause of the Fourteenth Amendment, Title VI of the Civil Rights Act of 1964." Because we find that the manner in which the University considers the race of applicants in its undergraduate admissions guidelines violates these constitutional and statutory provisions, we reverse that portion of the District Court's decision upholding the guidelines. . . .

Beginning with the 1998 academic year, the OUA [Office of Undergraduate Admissions] dispensed with the Guidelines tables and the SCUGA point system in favor of a "selection index," on which an applicant could score a maximum of 150 points. This index was divided linearly into ranges generally calling for admissions dispositions as follows: 100–150 (admit); 95–99 (admit or postpone); 90–94 (postpone or admit); 75–89 (delay or postpone); 74 and below (delay or reject).

Each application received points based on high school grade point average, standardized test scores, academic quality of an applicant's high school, strength or weakness of high school curriculum, in-state residency, alumni relationship, personal essay, and personal achievement or leadership. Of particular significance here, under a "miscellaneous" category, an applicant was entitled to 20 points based upon his or her membership in an underrepresented racial or ethnic minority group. The University explained that the "'development of the selection index for admissions in 1998 changed only the mechanics, not the substance of how race and ethnicity were considered in admissions.'" . . .

During 1999 and 2000, the OUA used the selection index, under which every applicant from an underrepresented racial or ethnic minority group was awarded 20 points. Starting in 1999, however, the University established an Admissions Review Committee (ARC), to provide an additional level of consideration for some applications. Under the new system, counselors may, in their discretion, "flag" an application for the ARC to review after determining that the applicant (1) is academically prepared to succeed at the University, (2) has achieved a minimum selection index score, and (3) possesses a quality or characteristic important to the University's composition of its freshman class, such as high class rank, unique life experiences, challenges, circumstances, interests or talents, socioeconomic disadvantage, and underrepresented race, ethnicity, or geography. After reviewing "flagged" applications, the ARC determines whether to admit, defer, or deny each applicant. . . .

It is by now well established that "all racial classifications reviewable under the Equal Protection Clause must be strictly scrutinized." *Adarand Constructors, Inc. v. Peña*, 515 U.S. 200 (1995). This "'standard of review . . . is not dependent on the race of those burdened or benefited by a particular classification.'" Thus, "any person, of whatever race, has the right to demand that any governmental actor subject to the Constitution justify any racial classification subjecting that person to unequal treatment under the strictest of judicial scrutiny."

To withstand our strict scrutiny analysis, respondents must demonstrate that the University's use of race in its current admission program employs "narrowly tailored measures that further compelling governmental interests." Because "[r]acial classifications are simply too pernicious to permit any but the most exact connection between justification and classification," *Fullilove v. Klutznick*, 448 U.S. 448 (1980), our review of whether such requirements have been met must entail "'a most searching examination.'" We find that the University's policy, which automatically distributes 20 points, or one-fifth of the points needed to guarantee admission, to every single "underrepresented minority" applicant solely because of race, is not narrowly tailored to achieve the interest in educational diversity that respondents claim justifies their program.

In *Bakke*, Justice POWELL reiterated that "[p]referring members of any one group for no reason other than race or ethnic origin is discrimination for its own sake." He then explained, however, that in his view it would be permissible for a university to employ an admissions program in which "race or ethnic background may be deemed a 'plus' in a particular applicant's file." . . .

Justice POWELL's opinion in *Bakke* emphasized the importance of considering each particular applicant as an individual, assessing all of the qualities that individual possesses, and in turn, evaluating that individual's ability to contribute to the unique setting of higher education. The admissions program Justice POWELL described, however, did not contemplate that any single characteristic automatically ensured a specific and identifiable contribution to a university's diversity. Instead, under the approach Justice POWELL described, each characteristic of a particular applicant was to be considered in assessing the applicant's entire application.

The current LSA policy does not provide such individualized consideration. The LSA's policy automatically distributes 20 points to every single applicant from an "underrepresented minority" group, as defined by the University. The only consideration that accompanies this distribution of points is a factual review of an application to determine whether an individual is a member of one of these minority groups. Moreover, unlike Justice POWELL's example, where the race of a "particular black applicant" could be considered without being decisive, the LSA's automatic distribution of 20 points has the effect of making "the factor of race . . . decisive" for virtually every minimally qualified underrepresented minority applicant. . . .

We conclude, therefore, that because the University's use of race in its current freshman admissions policy is not narrowly tailored to achieve respondents' asserted compelling interest in diversity, the admissions policy violates the Equal Protection Clause of the Fourteenth Amendment. We further find that the admissions policy also violates Title VI. Accordingly, we reverse that portion of the District Court's decision granting respondents summary judgment with respect to liability and remand the case for proceedings consistent with this opinion.

□ *Justice O'CONNOR, concurring.*

Unlike the law school admissions policy the Court upholds today in *Grutter v. Bollinger*, the procedures employed by the University of Michigan's (University) Office of Undergraduate Admissions do not provide for a meaningful individualized review of applicants. . . . The selection index thus precludes admissions counselors from conducting the type of individualized consideration the Court's opinion in *Grutter* requires: consideration of each applicant's individualized qualifications, including the contribution each individual's race or ethnic identity will make to the diversity of the student body, taking into account diversity within and among all racial and ethnic groups. . . .

Although the Office of Undergraduate Admissions does assign 20 points to some "soft" variables other than race, the points available for other diversity contributions, such as leadership and service, personal achievement, and geographic diversity, are capped at much lower levels. Even the most outstanding national high school leader could never receive more than five points for his or her accomplishments—a mere quarter of the points automatically assigned to an underrepresented minority solely based on the fact of his or her race. [T]he selection index, by setting up automatic, predetermined point allocations for the soft variables, ensures that the diversity contributions of applicants cannot be individually assessed. This policy stands in sharp contrast to the law school's admissions plan, which enables admissions officers to make nuanced judgments with respect to the contributions each applicant is likely to make to the diversity of the incoming class. . . .

□ *Justice GINSBURG, with whom Justice SOUTER joins, dissenting.*

In the wake "of a system of racial caste only recently ended" large disparities endure. Unemployment, poverty, and access to health care vary disproportionately by race. Neighborhoods and schools remain racially divided. African-American and Hispanic children are all too often educated in poverty-stricken and underperforming institutions. Adult African-Americans and Hispanics generally earn less than whites with equivalent levels of education. Equally credentialed job applicants receive different receptions depending on their race. Irrational prejudice is still encountered in real estate markets and consumer transactions. "Bias both conscious and unconscious, reflecting traditional and unexamined habits of thought, keeps up barriers that must come down if equal opportunity and nondiscrimination are ever genuinely to become this country's law and practice."

The Constitution instructs all who act for the government that they may not "deny to any person . . . the equal protection of the laws." In implementing this equality instruction, as I see it, government decisionmakers may properly distinguish between policies of exclusion and inclusion.

Our jurisprudence ranks race a "suspect" category, "not because [race] is inevitably an impermissible classification, but because it is one which usually, to our national shame, has been drawn for the purpose of maintaining racial inequality." But where race is considered "for the purpose of achieving equality," no automatic proscription is in order. For, "[t]he Constitution is both color blind and color conscious. To avoid conflict with the equal protection clause, a classification that denies a benefit, causes harm, or imposes a burden must not be based on race. In that sense, the Constitution is color blind. But the Constitution is color conscious to prevent discrimination being perpetuated and to undo the effects of past discrimination."

The mere assertion of a laudable governmental purpose, of course, should not immunize a race-conscious measure from careful judicial inspection. Close review is needed "to ferret out classifications in reality malign, but masquerading as benign," and to "ensure that preferences are not so large as to trammel unduly upon the opportunities of others or interfere too harshly with legitimate expectations of persons in once-preferred groups."

Examining in this light the admissions policy employed by the University of Michigan's College of Literature, Science, and the Arts (College), and for the reasons well stated by Justice SOUTER, I see no constitutional infirmity. . . .

☐ *Justice SOUTER, with whom Justice GINSBURG joins as to Part II, dissenting.*

Grutter reaffirms the permissibility of individualized consideration of race to achieve a diversity of students, at least where race is not assigned a preordained value in all cases. On the other hand, Justice POWELL's opinion in *Regents of Univ. of Cal. v. Bakke*, 438 U.S. 265 (1978), rules out a racial quota or set-aside, in which race is the sole fact of eligibility for certain places in a class. Although the freshman admissions system here is subject to argument on the merits, I think it is closer to what *Grutter* approves than to what *Bakke* condemns, and should not be held unconstitutional on the current record.

The record does not describe a system with a quota like the one struck down in *Bakke*, which "insulate[d]" all nonminority candidates from competition from certain seats. The plan here, in contrast, lets all applicants compete for all places and values an applicant's offering for any place not only on grounds of race, but on grades, test scores, strength of high school, quality of course of study, residence, alumni relationships, leadership, personal character, socioeconomic disadvantage, athletic ability, and quality of a personal essay. A nonminority applicant who scores highly in these other categories can readily garner a selection index exceeding that of a minority applicant who gets the 20-point bonus. . . .

The Court nonetheless finds fault with a scheme that "automatically" distributes 20 points to minority applicants because "[t]he only consideration that accompanies this distribution of points is a factual review of an application to determine whether an individual is a member of one of these minority groups." The objection goes to the use of points to quantify and compare characteristics, or to the number of points awarded due to race, but on either reading the objection is mistaken.

The very nature of a college's permissible practice of awarding value to racial diversity means that race must be considered in a way that increases some applicants' chances for admission. Since college admission is not left entirely to inarticulate intuition, it is hard to see what is inappropriate in assigning some stated value to a relevant characteristic, whether it be reasoning ability, writing style, running speed, or minority race. Justice POWELL's plus factors necessarily are assigned some values. The college simply does by a numbered scale what the law school accomplishes in its "holistic review," *Grutter*, the distinction does not imply that applicants to the undergraduate college are denied individualized consideration or a fair chance to compete on the basis of all the various merits their applications may disclose. . . .

Grutter v. Bollinger
123 S.Ct. 2325 (2003)

In 1992 the University of Michigan Law School adopted an admissions policy based on an index score representing a composite of an applicant's Law School Admissions Test (LSAT) score and undergraduate grade point average. The policy also affirmed the law school's "commitment to racial and ethnic diversity with special reference to the inclusion of students from groups which have been historically discriminated against, like African Americans, Hispanics, and Native Americans," who, without some preference, "might not be represented in [the] student body in meaningful numbers." Accordingly, the law school makes "special efforts" to increase the number and achieve a "critical mass" of such students.

Barbara Grutter, an unsuccessful white applicant and a 43-year old business woman, challenged the constitutionality of the law school's admission program for relying on race and ethnicity as "predominant" factors and for favoring minority groups and giving them "a significantly greater chance of admission than students with similar credentials." A federal district court held that the law school's admissions program violated the Fourteenth Amendment, but the Court of Appeals for the Sixth Circuit reversed and concluded that the school's interest in achieving a diverse student body was compelling under *Regents of the University of California v. Bakke*, 438 U.S. 265 (1978). Ms. Grutter appealed that decision.

The appellate court's decision was affirmed by a vote of five to four. Justice O'Connor delivered the opinion of the Court. Justice Ginsburg filed a concurring opinion. Justices Scalia and Thomas filed opinions concurring and dissenting in part. Chief Justice Rehnquist and Justice Kennedy filed dissenting opinions.

☐ *Justice O'CONNOR delivered the opinion of the Court.*

The Law School ranks among the Nation's top law schools. It receives more than 3,500 applications each year for a class of around 350 students. Seeking to "admit a group of students who individually and collectively are among the most capable," the Law School looks for individuals with "substantial promise for success in law school" and "a strong likelihood of succeeding in the practice of law and contributing in diverse ways to the well-being of others." More broadly, the Law School seeks "a mix of students with varying backgrounds and experiences who will respect and learn from each other." In 1992, the dean of the Law School charged a faculty committee with crafting a written admissions policy to implement these goals. In particular, the Law School sought to ensure that its efforts to achieve student body diversity complied with this Court's most recent ruling on the use of race in university admissions. See *Regents of Univ. of Cal. v. Bakke,* 438 U.S. 265 (1978). Upon the unanimous adoption of the committee's report by the Law School faculty, it became the Law School's official admissions policy.

The hallmark of that policy is its focus on academic ability coupled with a flexible assessment of applicants' talents, experiences, and potential "to contribute to the learning of those around them." The policy requires admissions officials to evaluate each applicant based on all the information available in the file, including a personal statement, letters of recommendation, and an essay describing the ways in which the applicant will contribute to the life and diversity of the Law School. In reviewing an applicant's file, admissions officials must consider the applicant's undergraduate grade point average (GPA) and Law School Admissions Test (LSAT) score because they are important (if imperfect) predictors of academic success in law school. The policy stresses that "no applicant should be admitted unless we expect that applicant to do well enough to graduate with no serious academic problems."

The policy makes clear, however, that even the highest possible score does not guarantee admission to the Law School. Nor does a low score automatically disqualify an applicant. Rather, the policy requires admissions officials to look beyond grades and test scores to other criteria that are important to the Law School's educational objectives. So-called "'soft' variables" such as "the enthusiasm of recommenders, the quality of the undergraduate institution, the quality of the applicant's essay, and the areas and difficulty of undergraduate course selection" are all brought to bear in assessing an "applicant's likely contributions to the intellectual and social life of the institution." . . .

We granted *certiorari* to resolve the disagreement among the Courts of Appeals on a question of national importance: Whether diversity is a compelling interest that can justify the narrowly tailored use of race in selecting applicants for admission to public universities.

We last addressed the use of race in public higher education over 25 years ago. In the landmark *Bakke* case, we reviewed a racial set-aside program that reserved 16 out of 100 seats in a medical school class for members of certain minority groups. The decision produced six separate opinions, none of which commanded a majority of the Court. . . .

Since this Court's splintered decision in *Bakke*, Justice POWELL's opinion announcing the judgment of the Court has served as the touchstone for constitutional analysis of race-conscious admissions policies. Public and private universities across the Nation have modeled their own admissions programs on Justice POWELL's views on permissible race-conscious policies. . . .

We have held that all racial classifications imposed by government "must be analyzed by a reviewing court under strict scrutiny." This means that such classifications are constitutional only if they are narrowly tailored to further compelling governmental interests.

Strict scrutiny is not "strict in theory, but fatal in fact." Although all governmental uses of race are subject to strict scrutiny, not all are invalidated by it. As we have explained, "whenever the government treats any person unequally because of his or her race, that person has suffered an injury that falls squarely within the language and spirit of the Constitution's guarantee of equal protection." But that observation "says nothing about the ultimate validity of any particular law; that determination is the job of the court applying strict scrutiny." When race-based action is necessary to further a compelling governmental interest, such action does not violate the constitutional guarantee of equal protection so long as the narrow-tailoring requirement is also satisfied.

Context matters when reviewing race-based governmental action under the Equal Protection Clause. Not every decision influenced by race is equally objectionable and strict scrutiny is designed to provide a framework for carefully examining the importance and the sincerity of the reasons advanced by the governmental decisionmaker for the use of race in that particular context.

With these principles in mind, we turn to the question whether the Law School's use of race is justified by a compelling state interest. . . . The Law School's educational judgment that such diversity is essential to its educational mission is one to which we defer. The Law School's assessment that diversity will, in fact, yield educational benefits is substantiated by respondents and their *amici*. . . .

As part of its goal of "assembling a class that is both exceptionally academically qualified and broadly diverse," the Law School seeks to "enroll a 'critical mass' of minority students." The Law School's interest is not simply "to assure within its student body some specified percentage of a particular group merely because of its race or ethnic origin." That would amount to outright racial balancing, which is patently unconstitutional. . . .

The Law School's claim of a compelling interest is further bolstered by its *amici*, who point to the educational benefits that flow from student body diversity. In addition to the expert studies and reports entered into evidence at trial, numerous studies show that student body diversity promotes learning outcomes, and "better prepares students for an increasingly diverse workforce and society, and better prepares them as professionals."

These benefits are not theoretical but real, as major American businesses have made clear that the skills needed in today's increasingly global marketplace can only be developed through exposure to widely diverse people, cultures, ideas, and viewpoints. . . .

We have repeatedly acknowledged the overriding importance of preparing students for work and citizenship, describing education as pivotal to "sustaining our political and cultural heritage" with a fundamental role in maintaining the fabric of society. *Plyler v. Doe*, 457 U.S. 202 (1982). This Court has long recognized that "education . . . is the very foundation of good citizenship." *Brown v. Board of Education*, 347 U.S. 483 (1954). For this reason, the diffusion of knowledge and opportunity through public institutions of higher education must be accessible to all individuals regardless of race or ethnicity. The United States, as *amicus curiae*, affirms that "[e]nsuring that public institutions are open and available to all segments of American society, including people of all races and ethnicities, represents a paramount government objective."

Moreover, universities, and in particular, law schools, represent the training ground for a large number of our Nation's leaders. Individuals with law degrees occupy roughly half the state governorships, more than half the seats in the United States Senate, and more than a third of the seats in the United States House of Representatives. The pattern is even more striking when it comes to highly selective law schools. A handful of these schools accounts for 25 of the 100 United States Senators, 74 United States Courts of Appeals judges, and nearly 200 of the more than 600 United States District Court judges. . . .

Even in the limited circumstance when drawing racial distinctions is permissible to further a compelling state interest, government is still "constrained in how it may pursue that end: [T]he means chosen to accomplish the [government's] asserted purpose must be specifically and narrowly framed to accomplish that purpose." *Shaw v. Hunt*, 517 U.S. 899 (1996). The purpose of the narrow tailoring requirement is to ensure that "the means chosen 'fit' . . . th[e] compelling goal so closely that there is little or no possibility that the motive for the classification was illegitimate racial prejudice or stereotype."

Since *Bakke*, we have had no occasion to define the contours of the narrow-tailoring inquiry with respect to race-conscious university admissions programs. That inquiry must be calibrated to fit the distinct issues raised by the use of race to achieve student body diversity in public higher education. . . .

To be narrowly tailored, a race-conscious admissions program cannot use a quota system—it cannot "insulat[e] each category of applicants with certain desired qualifications from competition with all other applicants." Instead, a university may consider race or ethnicity only as a "'plus' in a particular applicant's file," without "insulat[ing] the individual from comparison with all other candidates for the available seats." In other words, an admissions program must be "flexible enough to consider all pertinent elements of diversity in light of the particular qualifications of each applicant, and to place them on the same footing for consideration, although not necessarily according them the same weight."

We find that the Law School's admissions program bears the hallmarks of a narrowly tailored plan. . . . We are satisfied that the Law School's admissions program, like the Harvard plan described by Justice POWELL, does not operate as a quota. . . . Justice POWELL's distinction between the medical school's rigid 16-seat quota and Harvard's flexible use of race as a "plus" factor is instructive. Harvard certainly had minimum goals for minority enrollment, even if it had no specific number firmly in mind. . . .

Here, the Law School engages in a highly individualized, holistic review of each applicant's file, giving serious consideration to all the ways an applicant might contribute to a diverse educational environment. The Law School affords this individualized consideration to applicants of all races. . . .

What is more, the Law School actually gives substantial weight to diversity factors besides race. The Law School frequently accepts nonminority applicants with grades and test scores lower than underrepresented minority applicants (and other nonminority applicants) who are rejected. This shows that the Law School seriously weighs many other diversity factors besides race that can make a real and dispositive difference for nonminority applicants as well. By this flexible approach, the Law School sufficiently takes into account, in practice as well as in theory, a wide variety of characteristics besides race and ethnicity that contribute to a diverse student body. . . .

We are mindful, however, that "[a] core purpose of the Fourteenth Amendment was to do away with all governmentally imposed discrimination based on race." *Palmore v. Sidoti*, 466 U.S. 429 (1984). Accordingly, race-conscious admissions policies must be limited in time. This requirement reflects that racial classifications, however compelling their goals, are potentially so dangerous that they may be employed no more broadly than the interest demands. . . .

In the context of higher education, the durational requirement can be met by sunset provisions in race-conscious admissions policies and periodic reviews to determine whether racial preferences are still necessary to achieve student body diversity. Universities in California, Florida, and Washington State, where racial preferences in admissions are prohibited by state law, are currently engaged in experimenting with a wide variety of alternative approaches. Universities in other States can and should draw on the most promising aspects of these race-neutral alternatives as they develop. The requirement that all race-conscious admissions programs have a termination point "assure[s] all citizens that the deviation from the norm of equal treatment of all racial and ethnic groups is a temporary matter, a measure taken in the service of the goal of equality itself." *Richmond v. J. A. Croson Co.* . . .

It has been 25 years since Justice POWELL first approved the use of race to further an interest in student body diversity in the context of public higher education. Since that time, the number of minority applicants with high grades and test scores has indeed increased. We expect that 25 years from now, the use of racial preferences will no longer be necessary to further the interest approved today.

In summary, the Equal Protection Clause does not prohibit the Law School's narrowly tailored use of race in admissions decisions to further a compelling interest in obtaining the educational benefits that flow from a diverse student body. Consequently, petitioner's statutory claims based on Title VI also fail. The judgment of the Court of Appeals for the Sixth Circuit, accordingly, is affirmed.

□ *Justice GINSBURG, with whom Justice BREYER joins, concurring.*

However strong the public's desire for improved education systems may be, it remains the current reality that many minority students encounter markedly inadequate and unequal educational opportunities. Despite these inequalities, some minority students are able to meet the high threshold requirements set for admission to the country's finest undergraduate and graduate educational institutions. As lower school education in minority communities improves, an increase in the number of such students may be anticipated. From today's vantage point, one may hope, but not firmly forecast, that over the next generation's span, progress toward nondiscrimination and genuinely equal opportunity will make it safe to sunset affirmative action.

□ *CHIEF JUSTICE REHNQUIST, with whom Justice SCALIA, Justice KENNEDY, and Justice THOMAS join, dissenting.*

As we have explained many times, "'[a]ny preference based on racial or ethnic criteria must necessarily receive a most searching examination.'" *Adarand.* Our cases establish that, in order to withstand this demanding inquiry, respondents must demonstrate that their methods of using race "'fit'" a compelling state interest "with greater precision than any alternative means." *Bakke.*

In practice, the Law School's program bears little or no relation to its asserted goal of achieving "critical mass." . . . From 1995 through 2000, the Law School admitted between 1,130 and 1,310 students. Of those, between 13 and 19 were Native American, between 91 and 108 were African-Americans, and between 47 and 56 were Hispanic. If the Law School is admitting between 91 and 108 African-Americans in order to achieve "critical mass," thereby preventing African-American students from feeling "isolated or like spokespersons for their race," one would think that a number of the same order of magnitude would be necessary to accomplish the same purpose for Hispanics and Native Americans. Similarly, even if all of the Native American applicants admitted in a given year matriculate, which the record demonstrates is not at all the case, how can this possibly constitute a "critical mass" of Native Americans in a class of over 350 students? In order for this pattern of admission to be consistent with the Law School's explanation of "critical mass," one would have to believe that the objectives of "critical mass" offered by respondents are achieved with only half the number of Hispanics and one-sixth the number of Native Americans as compared to African-Americans. But respondents offer no race-specific reasons for such disparities. Instead, they simply emphasize the importance of achieving "critical mass," without any explanation of why that concept is applied differently among the three underrepresented minority groups.

These different numbers, moreover, come only as a result of substantially different treatment among the three underrepresented minority groups, as is apparent in an example offered by the Law School and highlighted by the Court: The school asserts that it "frequently accepts nonminority applicants with grades and test scores lower than underrepresented minority applicants (and other nonminority applicants) who are rejected." Specifically, the Law School states that "[s]ixty-nine minority applicants were rejected between 1995 and 2000 with at least a 3.5 [Grade Point Average (GPA)] and a [score of] 159 or higher on the [Law School Admissions Test (LSAT)]" while a number of Caucasian and Asian-American applicants with similar or lower scores were admitted.

Review of the record reveals only 67 such individuals. Of these 67 individuals, 56 were Hispanic, while only 6 were African-American, and only 5 were Native American. This discrepancy reflects a consistent practice. For example, in 2000, 12 Hispanics who scored between a 159–160 on the LSAT and earned a GPA of 3.00 or higher applied for admission and only 2 were admitted. Meanwhile, 12 African-Americans in the same range of qualifications applied for admission and all 12 were admitted. Likewise, that same year, 16 Hispanics who scored between a 151–153 on the LSAT and earned a 3.00 or higher applied for admission and only 1 of those applicants was admitted.

Twenty-three similarly qualified African-Americans applied for admission and 14 were admitted. . . .

[T]he correlation between the percentage of the Law School's pool of applicants who are members of the three minority groups and the percentage of the admitted applicants who are members of these same groups is far too precise to be dismissed as merely the result of the school paying "some attention to [the] numbers." [F]rom 1995 through 2000 the percentage of admitted applicants who were members of these minority groups closely tracked the percentage of individuals in the school's applicant pool who were from the same groups. . . . For example, in 1995, when 9.7% of the applicant pool was African-American, 9.4% of the admitted class was African-American. By 2000, only 7.5% of the applicant pool was African-American, and 7.3% of the admitted class was African-American. This correlation is striking. Respondents themselves emphasize that the number of underrepresented minority students admitted to the Law School would be significantly smaller if the race of each applicant were not considered. But, as the examples above illustrate, the measure of the decrease would differ dramatically among the groups. The tight correlation between the percentage of applicants and admittees of a given race, therefore, must result from careful race based planning by the Law School. . . .

I do not believe that the Constitution gives the Law School such free rein in the use of race. The Law School has offered no explanation for its actual admissions practices and, unexplained, we are bound to conclude that the Law School has managed its admissions program, not to achieve a "critical mass," but to extend offers of admission to members of selected minority groups in proportion to their statistical representation in the applicant pool. But this is precisely the type of racial balancing that the Court itself calls "patently unconstitutional." . . .

□ *Justice KENNEDY, dissenting.*

The Court, in a review that is nothing short of perfunctory, accepts the University of Michigan Law School's assurances that its admissions process meets with constitutional requirements. The majority fails to confront the reality of how the Law School's admissions policy is implemented. The dissenting opinion by The CHIEF JUSTICE, which I join in full, demonstrates beyond question why the concept of critical mass is a delusion used by the Law School to mask its attempt to make race an automatic factor in most instances and to achieve numerical goals indistinguishable from quotas. . . . It remains to point out how critical mass becomes inconsistent with individual consideration in some more specific aspects of the admissions process.

About 80 to 85 percent of the places in the entering class are given to applicants in the upper range of Law School Admissions Test scores and grades. An applicant with these credentials likely will be admitted without consideration of race or ethnicity. With respect to the remaining 15 to 20 percent of the seats, race is likely outcome determinative for many members of minority groups. That is where the competition becomes tight and where any given applicant's chance of admission is far smaller if he or she lacks minority status. At this point the numerical concept of critical mass has the real potential to compromise individual review.

The Law School has not demonstrated how individual consideration is, or can be, preserved at this stage of the application process given the instruction to attain what it calls critical mass. In fact the evidence shows otherwise. There was little deviation among admitted minority students during the years from 1995 to 1998. The percentage of enrolled minorities fluctuated only by 0.3%, from 13.5% to 13.8%. The number of minority students to whom offers were extended varied by just a slightly greater magnitude of 2.2%, from the high of 15.6% in 1995 to the low of 13.4% in 1998. . . .

The narrow fluctuation band raises an inference that the Law School subverted individual determination, and strict scrutiny requires the Law School to overcome the inference. Whether the objective of critical mass "is described as a quota or a goal, it is a line drawn on the basis of race and ethnic status," and so risks compromising individual assessment. . . .

To be constitutional, a university's compelling interest in a diverse student body must be achieved by a system where individual assessment is safeguarded through the entire process. There is no constitutional objection to the goal of considering race as one modest factor among many others to achieve diversity, but an educational institution must ensure, through sufficient procedures, that each applicant receives individual consideration and that race does not become a predominant factor in the admissions decisionmaking. . . .

☐ *Justice SCALIA, with whom Justice THOMAS joins, concurring in part and dissenting in part.*

Unlike a clear constitutional holding that racial preferences in state educational institutions are impermissible, or even a clear anticonstitutional holding that racial preferences in state educational institutions are OK, today's *Grutter-Gratz* split double header seems perversely designed to prolong the controversy and the litigation. Some future lawsuits will presumably focus on whether the discriminatory scheme in question contains enough evaluation of the applicant "as an individual," and sufficiently avoids "separate admissions tracks" to fall under *Grutter* rather than *Gratz*. Some will focus on whether a university has gone beyond the bounds of a "'good faith effort'" and has so zealously pursued its "critical mass" as to make it an unconstitutional de facto quota system, rather than merely "'a permissible goal.'" Other lawsuits may focus on whether, in the particular setting at issue, any educational benefits flow from racial diversity. Still other suits may challenge the bona fides of the institution's expressed commitment to the educational benefits of diversity that immunize the discriminatory scheme in *Grutter*. And still other suits may claim that the institution's racial preferences have gone below or above the mystical *Grutter*-approved "critical mass." Finally, litigation can be expected on behalf of minority groups intentionally short changed in the institution's composition of its generic minority "critical mass." I do not look forward to any of these cases. The Constitution proscribes government discrimination on the basis of race, and state-provided education is no exception.

☐ *Justice THOMAS, with whom Justice SCALIA joins as to Parts I–VII, concurring in part and dissenting in part.*

No one would argue that a university could set up a lower general admission standard and then impose heightened requirements only on black applicants. Similarly, a university may not maintain a high admission standard and grant exemptions to favored races. The Law School, of its own choosing, and for its own purposes, maintains an exclusionary admissions system that it knows produces racially disproportionate results. Racial discrimination is not a permissible solution to the self-inflicted wounds of this elitist admissions policy.

The majority upholds the Law School's racial discrimination not by interpreting the people's Constitution, but by responding to a faddish slogan of the cognoscenti. Nevertheless, I concur in part in the Court's opinion. First, I agree with the Court insofar as its decision, which approves of only one racial classification, confirms that further use of race in admissions remains unlawful. Second, I agree with the Court's holding that racial discrimination in higher education admissions will be illegal in 25 years. I respectfully dissent from the remainder of the Court's opinion and the judgment, however, because I believe that the Law School's current use of race violates the Equal Protection Clause and that the Constitution means the same thing today as it will in 300 months. . . .

INDEX OF CASES

Cases printed in boldface are excerpted on the page(s) printed in boldface.

Other Books by David M. O'Brien

Storm Center:
The Supreme Court in American Politics
6th ed.

Constitutional Law and Politics:
Vol. 1. *Struggles for Power and Governmental Accountability*
Vol. 2. *Civil Rights and Civil Liberties*
5th ed.

Abortion and American Politics
(with Barbara H. Craig)

Judicial Roulette

What Process Is Due?
Courts and Science-Policy Disputes

Views from the Bench:
The Judiciary and Constitutional Politics
(with Mark Cannon)

The Politics of Technology Assessment:
Institutions, Processes and Policy Disputes
(with Donald Marchand)

The Public's Right to Know:
The Supreme Court and the First Amendment

Privacy, Law, and Public Policy

The Politics of American Government
3rd ed.
(with Stephen J. Wayne, G. Calvin Mackenzie, and Richard Cole)

To Dream of Dreams:
Religious Freedom and Constitutional Politics in Postwar Japan
(with Yasuo Ohkoshi)

Judges on Judging
2nd ed.
(editor)

The Lanahan Readings on Civil Rights and Civil Liberties
2nd ed.
(editor)

Judicial Independence in the Age of Democracy:
Critical Perspectives from Around the World
(with Peter Russell)

Government by the People
19th ed.
(with James MacGregor Burns, J. W. Peltason, Thomas E. Cronin, and David B. Magleby)